Surviving the Trail

Five Essential Skills to Prepare Every Hiker for Adventure's Most Common Perils

Dr. Rob Scanlon

ESSEX, CONNECTICUT

FALCONGUIDES®

An imprint of The Globe Pequot Publishing Group, Inc.
64 South Main Street
Essex, CT 06426
www.globepequot.com

Falcon and FalconGuides are registered trademarks and Make Adventure Your Story is a trademark of The Globe Pequot Publishing Group, Inc.

British Library Cataloguing in Publication Information available

Library of Congress Cataloging-in-Publication Data available

ISBN 978-1-4930-9012-9 (paper)
ISBN 978-1-4930-9013-6 (electronic)

Contents

Rocky Mountain human remains may be those of hiker missing since 1983

Death of Grand Canyon hiker: Canadian passes away on Bright Angel Trail

Crews rescue exhausted hikers in the Pacific Palisades

The Los Angeles Fire Department rescued the hikers after they became too exhausted hiking in the blistering heat in the Santa Monica Mountains.

JUN 20, 2022

Houston man, 75, found dead in Big Bend National Park

Two hikers rescued unharmed from Ketchikan trail after losing their way in snow

Posted by Eric Stone | Jul 29, 2022

Hiker dies following snowy rescue on Presidential Ridge

Oregon rescuers recover body of Mt. Hood climber who died after falling 200 feet in March

Dangerous conditions prevented crews from recovering body of Pradnya Mohite from Mt. Hood

22-year-old man dies from suspected heat exhaustion while hiking in Badlands

The man had run out of water, the sheriff's office said.

Grand Canyon visitor falls to death, body found 200 feet below park's North Rim

Hikers suffering from hypothermia and dehydration rescued at Haleakalā on Maui

Hiker found dead at White Sands National Park

Hikers had no gear on cold Colorado trail because it's 'so hot in Texas,' officials say

Jackson County officials talk safety after hiker found dead near Lake Jacomo

by: Sean McDowell
Posted: Jul 13, 2022 / 10:08 PM CDT

3 hikers overcome by heat were rescued from Camelback Mountain

Utah woman dead after fall at Grand Canyon, 4th this year

Salt Lake City woman, 34, was on multi-day boating trip along Colorado River

4 hikers rescued from South Mountain, Phoenix Mountain Preserve trails

Haleigh Kochanski Arizona Republic
Published 8:26 p.m. MT April 2, 2022

Three hikers rescued from Mt. Neva

The three were stranded Monday night with no water or shelter

Three Rhode Island hikers rescued on New Hampshire mountain amid wintry conditions

Introduction

The statistics are difficult to believe, but on average more than ten hikers die and at least another two hundred require rescue in North America every week, adding up to an average of five hundred unintentional deaths and more than ten thousand rescues every year. Data reveals these individuals span the full spectrum of trail experience, and many of these outcomes result from just a handful of preventable causes. Every week hundreds fight to survive in avoidable situations while awaiting overwhelmed and understaffed wilderness rescue teams, amounting to a crisis amid North America's second-favorite outdoor activity.

Most cases of unintentional hiker death and rescue stem from underappreciation of risk, lack of knowledge, inadequate outdoor skills, or dismissal of the facts and passive dependence on the odds. The daunting volume of information on mitigating our risk intimidates and otherwise confuses trail-goers as to how best to put it all into practice. Many hikers therefore venture out without a full understanding of the perils, arriving inadequately prepared and possessing a limited skill set, with little ability to sustain themselves when problems arise.

What can the average hiker do to control their risk of peril on the trails and complete the trek unremarkably?

Over the last twenty years, media attention to survival in extreme circumstances has shifted society's attention away from the fundamentals that empower hikers to resist the elements and minimize peril. The most stressful and confusing situation for adventurers comes when they must find ways to stay alive under duress in the wilderness, scrambling for hours or days to subsist in a resource-limited environment while awaiting location and rescue. All of us should acquire basic survival skills in case the need-to-stay-alive scenario strikes us, but these only apply *after* we encounter trouble; they do not help us *avoid* danger in the first place. The best complement to knowing how to survive is the knowledge base, simple pre-hike strategies, and on-trail skills applied to *every* hike to drastically reduce the chances of the stay-alive scenario. These become, in essence, preemptive survival skills. Controlling how the usual outdoor perils affect us proves infinitely more effective for preserving life than coming less prepared and struggling to remember unpracticed skills to escape these pitfalls once we have become ensnared in their grip.

As a physician and hiker for over twenty years, I have observed the news headlines with a unique perspective. Physicians empower patients to become better stewards of their bodies through education, emphasizing how to proactively prevent complications of their diseases. Seeing the common pitfalls of the outdoors as complications of hiking, I envision a parallel methodology for shifting the emphasis to prevention in the backcountry. This book comes from a deep-seated duty to act, and to reduce the rate of preventable loss and jeopardy of life in the wilderness, in much the same way medical practitioners can make a difference with their patients. *Surviving the Trail* outlines the most common perils of the outdoors, explains their impact on us, fosters a preparatory mindset, and offers solid strategies and skills needed to gain an advantage in the wild.

Every time we head into the wilderness we face many unknowns, testing our abilities, knowledge, and readiness for what

Mother Nature will throw at us. How well prepared the wanderer comes to the wilderness dramatically affects the outcome when unforeseen circumstances arise. While we cannot control the elements, preparation allows us to control their effect on us, making it the ultimate survival skill.

The worldwide hiking community amounts to 130 million, with about half in the United States and Canada alone. In the ten years preceding the pandemic, and especially since then, the number of North American hikers has only increased. Many experienced hikers already prepare well and rely on themselves and their skills. But, while the trails welcome all, more arrive each year with more zeal than know-how. Often, beginner to intermediate level hikers are left to figure things out over time through trial and error, stepping onto the trail as victims in waiting. This book was written for every hiker with a desire to be empowered to adjust the learning curve in their favor.

Making the Case for Preparation

Everyday life offers a swift and unkind reminder of our deficiencies in preparation. The void in planning and forethought becomes easily exploited by the whims of everyday living:

- A family embarks on a driving vacation through country roads unaware of a nearly empty fuel tank.
- A student shows up for an exam not having studied.
- The executive team leader expected to make a presentation shows up to work with no material or slide deck ready.

We can all imagine what outcomes and consequences result from these few examples. Each day tests us on whether we have prepared for what will come, with consequences that follow in one form or another. Situations always arise out of our ability to foresee their occurrence, forcing us to react to these stressful circumstances. The choice to prepare or not for the otherwise common, anticipated events of life determines the amount of undesirable consequence and stress we have in our lives. Humans act habitually; how we behave comes mostly from our own history of routines, regardless of whether they serve our best interest. The wrong habits tend to cause repetitive life problems and stressors, while those that align with our goals create the solution.

Change requires acknowledging the preventable everyday hurdles we face and the effort placed into a new approach. When we contemplate everyday living in a more proactive and anticipatory way, we spend much less energy upfront avoiding the penalties of daily life than we do on their solutions. This in turn creates an overall less stressful life than what ignoring readiness produces. How we approach this depends on our personalities and experiences, but failing an important exam, getting fired or losing out on a job promotion due to our own delinquencies serves among life's hardest lessons that most can learn from to correct the course. Even the most proactive among us lapses in this area of life from time to time. We all occasionally veer off course for one reason or another and experience the resulting stress and chaos. Recognizing this as starkly different from how we would rather live our lives serves as a reminder to get back on track. Creating good preparatory habits serves our own best interest to minimize the myriad consequences of unpreparedness.

Our ability to anticipate and our willingness to prepare for the common consequences of outdoor adventure likely mirror our approach to the day-to-day. Spending all weekend tackling the laundry that piled up all week or ordering takeout most weeknights after avoiding food shopping and meal planning beforehand poses no threat to our existence. Spending our downtime summiting a mountain of undone tasks, however, inhibits more pleasurable pursuits, breeds negativity and undue stress in life, and leaves us unrestored for the week ahead. Food must be consumed, and laundry must be done, but how we conquer these tasks and other necessities results in downstream effects, either positively or negatively. We can habitually choose to put off these necessary tasks to find ourselves regularly having to spend our downtime climbing out of a virtual hole. We can alternatively face these everyday responsibilities proactively to avoid last-minute scrambling and have more time left for positive experiences. When taking a less preemptive approach toward adventuring in the outdoors we leave ourselves less prepared for the common perils of adventure and vulnerable to the consequences that follow. When we regularly follow a relaxed approach toward readiness, evade the perils and return home unscathed, it only reinforces that approach to adventure. Nature, however, awaits the opportunity to exploit our vulnerabilities with its wrath.

The outdoors offers no easy remedy to problems that arise out of a lack of preparedness, as opposed to those of everyday living. Until recently those planning to take a long drive or spend a long day outdoors knew the importance of packing food, drinks, and other supplies. Anticipation of basic needs was built into the mindset, as failure to do so would surely leave us in desperate circumstances. Over the last thirty years most residential areas of North America have evolved commercially. Along our daily path countless solutions exist to effortlessly satisfy real-time needs, such as thirst and hunger. Most of us have benefited from this convenience, but as a society our natural instinct to contemplate our needs ahead of time has perhaps waned. The outdoors, as opposed to our daily stomp, proves itself mercilessly unforgiving to those ensnared in situations they have not arrived ready for. People rescued for bringing little to no water, dressing improperly for weather conditions, and becoming lost commonly occupy news headlines, representing some of the preventable issues unprepared hikers face every day. Consequences produced by these few examples while miles from the trailhead often pose a threat to health and life. We often find no water source along the path to offset dehydration, natural shelter from the rain to avert becoming soaked and hypothermic, or a trail marker to help us find our way out in the rugged expanse of nature. When we come emptyhanded to counteract these and other common situations in the wilderness, three outcomes could happen:

- By sheer good fortune we complete the trek without major impact to health and life.
- We slip deeper into the consequences, call for rescue, and wait hours to days for help.
- The effects become untenable, resulting in death.

This stark reality should not scare anyone from getting outdoors and enjoying the wilderness to its fullest extent. It should motivate lesser prepared adventurers to no longer ignore the 800-pound bear on the trail. The skills that follow detail the most common and preventable ways we encounter trouble in nature. They begin with real examples of those who were rescued from or had succumbed to these perils of exploring the wilderness. This serves first as a tribute, so our fallen and rescued trail siblings' circumstances will not be forgotten. Further, this serves to illustrate the realities of adventuring to the unaware as a learning tool and an outcome never to be repeated. How these pitfalls affect us becomes demystified and better understood, which then leads us to the skills and strategies to successfully wield control over the elements.

As they do in everyday life, disastrous situations arise on-trail that adventurers cannot prepare for, but to fall victim to something common that could have easily been prevented on our own proves even worse. Our eyes should open wider to see the undesirable effects of outdoor adventure before we embark on our own journeys to spark a proactive routine to prevent them. This may take away from the excitement and anticipation of the pre-hike planning for some, but reality tends to strike when it's least expected and takes away all pleasures of the pursuit.

Critics of this preparatory approach preach "Let me hike my own hike," in other words saying, "Leave me alone and let me figure it out," or "What are the chances?" Should there be a similar approach to skydiving, scuba diving, swimming, or even driving? What are the chances, right? Without driver education and certification of competency to operate a several thousand–pound object at speed, how many would die trying to figure it out on their own? Without instruction on how scuba gear works and how to react to trouble under water, how many would panic and drown while figuring out a solution on their own?

Many embark on their excursions simply unaware of the pitfalls they commonly face among this information vacuum and unwittingly arriving on the trails as a victim in waiting. To those who wish to figure things out on their own, believing they are the only ones affected by their tribulations, may they have nothing but good fortune. When their luck does run out, however, they place others' lives at risk, specifically those in mountain rescue teams who voluntarily set out to retrieve these victims from the same challenging conditions they've been caught in. For those who wish to know more about self-preservation before venturing outdoors and not have to learn through life-threatening circumstances, the following chapters offer invaluable information.

Just as the aforementioned student holds themself solely accountable for showing up ready for the exam and the executive due to make a presentation to the team holds themself accountable for showing up prepared to deliver it, we all must take on the mindset of self-accountability when we set out for the backcountry. The responsibility for our safe return home lies in our own hands, as calamities on-trail may not afford the time it takes for a rescue team to arrive. This makes ourselves, our knowledge and skills the best defense we have against the common and preventable issues that threaten our safety and existence. Our knowledge, mindset, and preemptive action therefore become the primary source for the solution to these potential pitfalls. While this book provides the information and outlines the skills, the mindset must come from within. It begins with assuming the responsibility of self-reliance to return home safely and not leaving that in the hands of others. Identifying the potential risks inherent to the specific environment we intend to enter (season, atypical weather patterns, terrain, etc.) provides the road map for the preparatory steps we should take. We cannot control the variables, but routinely approaching wilderness adventures in this way empowers us to control how the variables affect us and our safe return home.

The preparation mindset also compels us to prepare our bodies, both physically and nutritionally, to withstand the demands of our intended excursions. If we plan on trekking to a specific vista point or summit, we cannot control what physical challenges we face to get there. Some prove much harder to tackle than others. Arriving well informed about what it takes to arrive at the point of interest and training ourselves ahead of time to that level of challenge provides us with the best chance to complete the journey. Showing up without having done so highlights the difference between demand and ability in real time. Some turn back early in disappointment, while others push forward beyond their abilities and place themselves in a potentially compromised position with possible need for rescue.

Our military forces use the mantra "Train like you fight." Doing so readies our service members for the ever-evolving dynamics of combat and produces the physical and mental stamina to endure them. Translating this to hiking, we often encounter steeper uphills than expected, longer trails than advertised, and endure soul-crushing false summits and other challenges along our way. Training off-trail and eating with nutritional purpose maintains optimal muscle performance and organ function, leaving us with elevated mental and physical readiness for these hurdles.

Another valuable lesson from our military comes from our special operations forces, which boast a high degree of mission success. This happens not by accident, magic, or superhuman talents. These highly motivated individuals approach every operation with the same method:

- Gather intelligence—learn everything about the mission.
- Formulate a plan of action.
- Prepare and train for the specifics of the task at hand.
- Execute the plan with a focus on the main objectives.

Repeating this preemptive approach becomes second nature and assures the maximum advantage for overcoming obstacles, meeting our goals, and achieving success. Many businesses adopt this same methodology, as do all serious outdoor expeditions. The objectives we strive for in hiking and backpacking should rank in the following order of priority:

1. Everyone gets home safely.
2. Mission success in completing the hike, reaching the summit, and so on.

Setting clear objectives, gathering information about the environmental and physical challenges we will meet, preparing our gear and our bodies for these specifics, and executing the plan place us at a distinct advantage to enjoy the experience while resisting the natural forces that oppose our success.

Bottom Line

Preparation for what lies ahead, both on- and off-trail, serves our own best interest in countless ways. Avoiding preemptive action increases stress and invites the complications of life and of hiking in the outdoors, risking professional advancement, relationships, health and safety. Preparedness for everyday living embodies the countermeasure to these complications, reducing adversity through the things we can control and preserving our time and energy for finding solutions to those we cannot. Approaching our hikes with the mindset of returning home intact above all other goals, and identifying the risk factors specific to the circumstances, focuses us on the few actions we need to take to secure our own safety, as we cannot leave that in anyone else's hands and expect optimal outcomes. Habitually preparing ahead of time becomes easier with repetition and empowers us to continue enjoying the outdoors and facing new challenges while thwarting the common pitfalls of adventure for years to come.

Skill 1

Hydration Strategy

Real-Life Scenarios

1. Two hikers in their early 20s set out in Badlands National Park in South Dakota on a trail to celebrate college graduation in July 2022. Temperatures climbed past 100° F that day. The combination of the heat, no available shade, and running out of water along their trek thrust the pair into crisis. Once the hikers were reported as missing, rescuers assembled and reached their location, pronouncing one deceased at the scene and finding the other in critical condition. He was flown by helicopter to a local hospital and treated for severe dehydration.

2. A group of mountain bikers encountered four hikers en route through Southern California in July 2023. Temperatures hit 106° F that day. These hikers had no food or water on them and were suffering from obvious dehydration. Some bikers stayed behind, while the rest biked to where cell service was restored to call for help. The four hikers were airlifted out to safety, while the mountain bikers who stayed behind continued to the trailhead. One of the bikers who had stayed behind, however, collapsed close to the end of their route due to prolonged heat exposure. Emergency crews responded, but despite resuscitation efforts the 24-year-old Good Samaritan did not survive.

3. A 31-year-old man and his two stepsons, 14 and 21 years old, traveled from Florida to Texas to hike in Big Bend National Park in late June 2023. Temperatures reached 119° F that day. No news reports outline how much water they had among them, but the 14-year-old fell ill and passed out on the Marufo Vega Trail, where no shade or environmental water exists. The stepfather hiked back to his car and hurriedly drove off to find help, while the older brother struggled to carry his brother back to the trailhead. In desperation, he left his listless brother and hitchhiked to a nearby ranger station. Rescue personnel reached the young hiker, who was sadly pronounced deceased. Adding to the tragic day, the stepfather's car was found to have crashed over an embankment and he was also declared dead at the scene.

4. An avid 67-year-old hiker, R.R. set out for a short hike in Joshua Tree National Park in July 2020. For this anticipatedly short trek, he brought 2 liters of water with him. Along his route, he fell and landed on his left hip. Too injured to walk back to safety, he quickly ran out of water in the scorching heat and painfully remained in place wondering if this was his last hike. His son called first responders after not hearing back from his father; he was able to tip them off to the location only because this seasoned hiker had known enough to send his son the hike plan before setting out on the trail. Almost 2 days passed before rescuers arrived, finding him severely dehydrated. After treatment he survived.

Dehydration sits at the top of the list of most common potential threats to those who explore the outdoors. Many of us have experienced this to one degree or another at some point in our hiking lives, possibly without even knowing it. Dehydration happens when we lose more fluid from the body than we have taken into it, and only a small percentage of total body water loss places us into a dehydrated state. As the deficit rises, so do the symptoms and severity. The broad range of severity and symptoms makes it difficult to report its true incidence, as most mild and some moderate cases never gain attention. The instances we read about in local and national news headlines depict only severe and tragic circumstances, representing only the tip of the iceberg.

While out on the trail we can often spot others carrying little to no water with them. These hikers may or may not realize the potential perils that a long hike, a hot day, or an unexpected overnight in the wilderness will bring. Reasons for not bringing this basic need vary from a matter of inconvenience, to lack of forethought about the risks, or knowing the risks but thinking "it won't happen to me." Others simply don't realize what could possibly happen out of a lack of information.

In our off-trail lives most of us never face the inaccessibility of food and water, and gaining access to these essentials in the moment we need them remains ridiculously convenient. This has taken some preservation instincts away from us. The natural reflex to think ahead about what we may, and often will, need becomes softened and untrained when living in a highly developed society. We can easily develop a false sense of security about the ubiquity and access to food and water, exposing us to the inherent dangers of the outdoors when we arrive empty-handed. Potential disaster arises when we forego considering downside risks ahead of when we go places where need and supply exist in opposition.

Hydration fulfills a necessary requirement for survival, whether on-trail or in everyday life, as water makes up 60 to 70 percent of the adult human body. Maintaining this amount of water in the body allows the following functions to happen:

- Regulation of body temperature
- Elimination of waste

- Allows blood to remain in a liquid state to flow around the body to deliver oxygen to tissues and to maintain blood pressure
- Provides an essential component of chemical reactions in the body
- Lubricates joints, tendons, and muscles
- Allows proper function of the eyes and brain
- Facilitates elimination of debris and infectious organisms from the respiratory tract

Without proper hydration our organ systems cannot function as intended. With significant fluid deficiency those mechanisms falter, threatening our survival.

We cannot count on the availability of water in the wilderness, especially when we need it most. Water availability across the Earth varies, depending on region and season. Most of the water we do encounter on the planet cannot be consumed, as it comes from oceans and natural waterways, representing unsafe sources from which to drink. The basic infrastructure of developed countries includes delivery of potable water to most communities and individual homes, isolated regional access and contamination issues aside, so populated regions of these nations rarely experience a lack of access. Modern societies also have multiple convenient locations to purchase water and other liquids when we're away from home.

We should consider ourselves fortunate to take water access for granted in society. However, this benefit has softened our natural instinct to assure access to water ahead of when we will actually need it. If we take the relaxed approach of societal access with us to the backcountry, though, we place ourselves in a disadvantaged position. The lack of water infrastructure in the wilderness leaves us at the mercy of the forces that only favor dehydration unless we take control of that variable. Bringing potable water along with us and having a sound plan to convert groundwater to a drinkable state accomplish this. Our tendency to either prepare ahead of time or not for this issue makes the difference between an unremarkable outing and a potentially tragic one.

Even with unrestricted access to fluids, studies suggest that at least 30 percent of adults in the US do not hydrate enough. This raises the point that many of us underappreciate how much fluid we need at baseline, before we have begun to take our body to its physical limits. That understanding and appreciation for our hydration needs begins with knowing how our body works, and more importantly how our body loses fluid.

Mechanisms of Body Water Loss

Body water loss occurs constantly, even when we are at rest, and only increases with activity, sickness, medication, environmental temperature, and other factors. If maintaining a normal level of hydration allows the body to function properly, and we exist in a constant state of water loss, then the need for regular fluid replacement becomes easier to understand. This concept must remain a priority, especially when planning to venture into a place with limited access to water, such as the wilderness, the desert, or above the tree line on a mountain. The following represents the most common ways we lose water from our bodies:

Sweating represents a potentially major source for body water loss, especially when we are physically active. We do release sweat at rest, but to a much smaller degree. How much water we lose through sweat depends on several factors, such as baseline metabolic rate, ambient temperature, and humidity. As exercise intensifies and continues, body heat naturally rises. Too much internal heat can harm us, so our processes for releasing heat need to kick in. The brain recognizes this change in body temperature and the need to shed excess heat to maintain a safe internal temperature. Nerve and chemical impulses dilate the blood vessels of the skin to recruit the two to three million sweat glands on the body's surface into activation. Sweat, composed of water and electrolytes, accumulates on the surface of the skin and, as it evaporates into the surrounding air, releases excess body heat into the environment. Impeding the evaporation in some way slows the efficiency of this system and allows internal heat to rise. Without a system to rid the body of excess heat, internal temperatures can reach dangerous levels.

As we train and exercise over time, sweat glands become easier to recruit and sweat output increases as compared to lesser-trained states. An average-size person in average temperature and humidity can lose up to 750 ml of sweat per hour with moderate exercise. Sweat output exceeds that amount with exercise in hot, dry conditions, and with higher intensity of exercise (such as uphill hiking, trail running, mountaineering up steep icy climbs with spikes and ice axes, etc.). While complex formulas can more precisely calculate sweat production, using the simpler 750 ml per hour rule and modifying for exercise intensity and environmental conditions helps us understand the volume we need to replace over the time course of our hikes.

Elimination of waste represents another significant method of body water loss. Not a fun subject to raise, it remains a necessary function of life. Blood flowing through the microscopic structures of the kidneys becomes filtered, with metabolic byproducts, excess electrolytes, and water taken from it and flushed down the urinary system of the body. We constantly lose body water in the form of urine, which becomes stored in our bladder until the next time we feel the need to empty it. While exercising, we produce metabolic byproducts at a greater rate than at rest, forcing a higher need for elimination. The higher flow of blood that courses through the kidneys during exercise speeds up the process of urine production. Flushing out the body's waste products at this higher rate requires more water to be taken from the bloodstream. Hydrating ourselves replaces the fluid losses and allows us to continue filtering these toxins from our body.

Applying the Science to the Trail

In times of water deficit, the kidneys adjust by producing more concentrated urine in less volume to conserve body water. Dark yellow or amber urine in a lower than normal volume should therefore be an early clue that dehydration is present.

Significant dehydration leads to stoppage of urine production altogether for the same purpose. This condition allows the toxins and electrolytes to accumulate in the body. Though this process may succeed in conserving body water, the accumulation of these byproducts can become fatal.

Maintaining proper hydration allows this system to function properly.

Normal flow of stool through the intestines requires a certain amount of water, with most becoming reabsorbed in the intestines prior to exit. Normally we lose only a minimal volume, amounting to roughly 250 milliliters (or 8 oz) per day. In times of food poisoning or dysentery, however, the volume of diarrhea produced can take liters of water from our body in a short period of time and become a major cause for dehydration. Camping at a 2- or 3-day hiking distance from the nearest exit point and experiencing onset of dysentery with hourly bouts of large volume output can easily lead to crisis. Where can we possibly obtain that much water to replace our losses? These circumstances happen frequently, so before the backpacking trip we should always consider this scenario.

The respiratory system sheds more body water on average than most appreciate. Depending on environmental conditions, however, it can exceed the losses of the other mechanisms. We normally exhale water vapor in our breath without realizing it. In freezing cold weather, however, we can see the innumerable tiny water droplets freezing in the cold air as they leave our mouth.

This visual gives us a sense of water volume that becomes released from our lungs. We lose about 500 milliliters (16 oz) of water per day in our exhaled breath under normal daily circumstances, varying with body size and depth and rate of breathing.

Humidity influences the amount of respiratory water we lose, with dry air favoring up to a threefold increase in loss of water from the respiratory system over that in humid conditions. Humidified air keeps our airways lubricated and functioning properly. As low humidity causes drying of the airways, the body must add water to the airways to compensate.

Exercise also impacts respiratory system water loss, rising up to fourfold during vigorous exercise compared to resting con-

Applying the Science to the Trail

Infants and children are smaller in size but require a higher percentage (about 75%) of body water than teens and adults. Body water loss mechanisms are the same, but they lose a larger percentage of body water than adults do. Therefore, they have a much higher threshold to produce dehydration, especially in hot conditions or in the face of diarrheal illness, than do teens and adults. In turn, they have a much higher need for fluids than their older and larger counterparts. To make matters potentially more dangerous, they may not show obvious signs of increased fluid needs until moderately to severely dehydrated.

The elderly are normal-size individuals with less body water composition (50%) than earlier in life. Therefore, they have little tolerance for water loss before entering the stages of dehydration. Their body water loss mechanisms tend to lose more water than younger adults due to medications (such as diuretics) and chronic illness as well. Coupling this with a higher threshold for thirst, typical impairment of mobility to satisfy their own thirst, and even impaired ability to ask others for fluids, dehydration occurs easily in this population.

ditions. The increased respiratory rate during exercise, needed to eliminate carbon dioxide and satisfy the demand for more oxygen, increases the rate of water elimination over that at rest. Adding these factors together, know that hours of exercise in a low humidity environment can lead to a tremendous amount of water lost from breathing alone, largely going unnoticed and unaccounted for.

SIGNS AND SYMPTOMS OF DEHYDRATION

The signs and symptoms of dehydration vary, based on the amount of water losses. Age also plays a role, especially with those at either end of the spectrum. Older individuals ordinarily have earlier onset of symptoms due to their lower threshold for developing dehydration. Infants and toddlers, on the other hand, cannot express exactly how they feel and appear otherwise well until moderate to severe dehydration sets in. Bringing much older and younger individuals on-trail should come with a healthy awareness of these issues. By becoming familiar with the recognizable signs of dehydration, we can otherwise intervene on our own behalf or that of others.

Mild dehydration has no universal definition but begins at around 2 percent loss of body water weight as compared to baseline measurements. While out in the wilderness we obviously have no way to measure this, but it illustrates the fact that it only takes a small deficit of water to produce mild dehydration. When a 150-pound (68 kg) person loses this much body water weight, it amounts to a loss of 3 pounds (1.4 kg), equaling roughly 1.5 quarts (nearly 1.5 l) of fluid. The individual with mild dehydration appears physically well, but because water comprises 75 percent of the brain, the function of this organ often begins to suffer first. As muscles need water to utilize stored glycogen optimally for sustained exercise, the function of the muscular system also begins to show signs of slowing down.

Symptoms associated with mild dehydration include:

- A decrease in alertness and increase in fatigue, impaired concentration, and reaction time with decreased ability to make judgment decisions involving skill
- A mild headache and slightly dry mouth
- Exercise performance reduction and muscle cramping

Only having one symptom listed above should not lead us to conclude that we have mild dehydration. Recognizing multiple symptoms confirms the suspicion of this issue, and acting quickly diffuses the situation. Adequate rehydration in the field can reverse the symptoms and cognitive impact of mild dehydration in about an hour.

Call for rescue at all degrees of dehydration beyond this point, as reversal in the field proves much more difficult. Calling for help sooner rather than later preserves life, along with continuing rehydration efforts on site until help arrives.

Moderate dehydration arises around the point of 4 percent loss of body water weight, elevating the circumstances to another level of seriousness. Using the same 150-pound (68 kg) person from above, this amounts to a loss of 6 pounds (2.7 kg), equaling a deficit of 3 quarts, or roughly 3 liters of water.

Signs and symptoms will include:

- Urine looks darker in color and lesser in volume than normal
- More serious headache, obvious confusion, lethargy, and individuals may begin to stagger
- Increasingly dry mouth and thirst
- Significant impairment of muscular performance, increased cramping

- Onset of nausea and vomiting, preventing oral rehydration efforts

The appearance of the patient typically changes, exhibited in sunken eyes and a dry mouth and tongue. One age-old method of assessing for dehydration in the practice of medicine involves pinching the skin of the forearm between the thumb and index finger and pulling it up, away from the arm. When the skin stays up for a few seconds after releasing the pinch (instead of snapping back into place, much like dough would behave), then that patient has dehydration.

Severe dehydration occurs when the victim continues further into the depths of body fluid deficit. The above mental and physical symptoms become more intense. Inside the body, electrolytes become increasingly abnormal and cellular function begins to break down. At this point sweating stops, to preserve body water. The decreasing fluid volume in the vessels progressively lowers blood pressure and organ function continues to decline. Further progression leads to widespread muscle spasms, stopping of urine production, onset of heart rhythm abnormalities, coma, and ultimately death.

Though the concept of hydration on the surface may appear simple and intuitive, and perhaps a nonissue to skeptics, Search and Rescue (SAR) operations data suggests otherwise. If this concept were as simple to grasp and the threat well appreciated, then dehydration should be an uncommon event. However, every year thousands of hikers require rescue for this very reason. One report reveals calls for a dehydrated individual out on the trails generates approximately 50 percent of all SAR requests in the St. George, Utah, area between the months of June and August.

Common factors leading to dehydration include hikers who have become lost, who had not carried enough water with them to anticipate unplanned and extended time out in the wilderness, and the heat of the summer. In June 2018 eight dehydrated hikers were rescued in one week in the St. George area. A study that looked back on SAR operations in Yosemite National Park over a 10-year span, amounting to 1,088 calls, reported that most who were rescued expressed the belief that carrying sufficient water would have been a major factor in preventing their need for rescue when asked to reflect on this in hindsight.

The statistics imply a lack of awareness, underestimation of risk in the pre-hike phase, and lack of forethought about the perils we potentially face in the outdoors, such as dehydration. The lack of appreciation of this and other very real threats breeds complacency and an undercurrent for normalizing insufficient preparation for venturing into the wilderness. A better knowledge base, awareness, self-accountability, and some humility lead to better preparation, which can lower the overwhelming number of SAR operations that occur across North America each year.

Experienced hikers who have the knowledge and understanding of the issue, but who defer hydration until after the hike to save on carried weight, openly invite this perilous result. Habitually relying on hydrating after the fact and getting away with it leads to overconfidence in this approach over time. This sacrifice of trading carried weight in the form of water for increased mobility on the trail amounts to a large gamble for a minor advantage, but eventually everyone's good luck runs out.

Rehydration

Rehydration of the dehydrated victim should begin as soon as possible after recognition of the problem. This prevents prolongation of symptoms and progression to moderate and severe degrees of body fluid loss. As with most medical disorders, the earlier the intervention, the better the outcome and the quicker the recovery.

When addressing mild dehydration, we have an alert person able to tolerate ingesting fluids, making reversal of the condition possible. Drinking fluids to replace body losses leads to quick absorption into the bloodstream with resolution of symptoms within a reasonable timeframe. Out in the wilderness we usually have no choice as to what type of fluid we can use for this purpose, so we use what we have available.

The best fluids to use:

- Plain water, filtered or sterilized if collected from backcountry sources
- Mildly sweetened drinks (such as noncarbonated sports drinks)
- Water with electrolyte additives (in the form of tablets or powders)

Types of fluids to avoid:

- Highly sweetened drinks (such as fruit juices)
- Carbonated drinks (can upset the stomach)
- Highly salty liquids (broth and soups also potentially cause upset stomachs)
- Alcoholic drinks (cause more urination and elimination of more body water)

In the case of highly sweetened or salty liquids, pouring a small volume of these into a larger volume of plain water to provide these elements can benefit the rehydration efforts, if available.

Oral Rehydration Solutions

Oral rehydration solutions have been utilized across the world for decades in third world countries to battle dysentery and the associated death from dehydration, especially in children. Premade solutions purposely contains mostly water with some glucose and sodium. It has been known since the 1950s that the intestines have an increased ability to absorb ingested water when accompanied by these two ingredients, over the rate of absorption in their absence. Oral rehydration solutions exploit this feature of the body to the benefit of patients. This mechanism also remains the basis for popular noncarbonated sports drink formulas.

Many recipes exist for making homemade oral rehydration solutions, but most contain:

- Sodium: two pinches of salt (sodium chloride)
- Potassium: one pinch of salt substitute (potassium chloride)
- Chloride: included in the above ingredients
- Bicarbonate: two pinches of baking soda
- Sugar: a fistful of sugar granules or ½ to 1 cup of fruit juice

The above added to 1 liter of clean water mimics the World Health Organization's (WHO) and other organizations' recipes for rehydration solutions. Preparing this during a hike can be accomplished with like ingredients in our pack, powdered sports drink packets and sport electrolyte tablets added to plain water.

Dr. Rob's Notes

For the scientifically curious, water absorbs through a combined glucose-sodium transport mechanism in the intestines. Adding both sugar and salt to the fluid capitalizes on this mechanism in the intestines to increase water absorption into the bloodstream.

Ingesting this combination, instead of water alone, works nearly as well as IV fluid hydration. This has significantly impacted the rate of death caused by dysentery in third world countries, which otherwise lack resources for widespread IV fluid administration. In much the same way, these two elements in the fluid will help improve the efficiency of water absorption into the body of any dehydrated backpacker, even in the absence of dysentery. Fluid also containing chloride and potassium helps replace sweat-related fluid losses.

As differing levels of dehydration exist, varying amounts of fluid are needed for oral rehydration. According to the CDC:

- As a rule of thumb, have the patient drink 100 milliliters (approximately 3 oz or just under ½ cup) of fluid every 5 minutes until they feel and appear better as a rule.
- In diarrheal disease with large volumes of fluid loss, figure out the volume by multiplying the patient's body weight in kilograms (no. of lbs divided by 2.2) by seventy-five, which determines the total volume in milliliters to give orally over 4 hours.

The dehydrated individual complaining of nausea or vomiting has no chance at recovery by oral hydration in the field. This identifies a moderate to severe degree of dehydration. Mental status (level of alertness and responsiveness of the person) will also begin to decline, also impairing the possibility for oral rehydration. This circumstance represents an emergency. These patients will need IV hydration and evaluation as soon as possible in a medical facility, so **calling for rescue should be the top priority when recognizing a moderate to severe level of dehydration.**

A hydration strategy represents the plan devised before and acted upon during a hike. This proactive approach empowers us to prevent dehydration, opposing a passive mindset toward allowing it to happen and scrambling through the situation. Developing a strategy for on-trail hydration, even when flawed, promises a clear advantage over having no plan at all. Many hikers do plan out their hydration needs ahead of their trek, using anything from simple to complex methods. Regardless of approach, it includes forethought taken into action. Many others do not have a process for figuring out their hydration needs, perhaps not knowing where to begin.

How do we get started?

- Decide to take ownership and responsibility over our own fate.
- Include a conscious awareness of hydration needs with every pre-hike plan, regardless of how short and simple the hike may seem. Make hydration just as much of a priority as any other aspect in the planning for the trek.
- Pack the estimated amount of water needed and a purification method regardless of whether the strategy calls for collecting water along the route or not.
- Critique and fine-tune methods for water estimation after each outing. Analyze whether too little or too much water was brought along.
- Learn from what was done right and wrong and correct the strategy going forward.

Routinely considering hydration needs before every hike raises our awareness of its importance and how easily dehydration can occur in the wilderness. Raising the issue ahead of time and acting on it reinforces that we have control over it, should we choose to take this preemptive stance. Getting started begins the process of empowerment and belief that we are the solution to this problem. Every time we adjust and repeat the process of formulating the hydration strategy, we become more in tune with our needs and ultimately better at protecting ourselves. A well-thought-out plan that makes sense minimizes our chance of facing this pitfall. The strategy should consider numerous factors, such as single day versus multiday hikes, trail distance, terrain, season and weather conditions, because our needs often vary with the unique characteristics of each trek. The approach may include carrying all the water we need or carrying some and collecting more from the environment along the route.

Dr. Rob's Tip: Excess Alcohol and the Hydration Strategy

Ingesting excess alcohol the night before a hike sets the stage for dehydration the following morning. Alcohol acts as a diuretic, leading us to release more water than we have taken in. Cancelling or delaying a big hike the morning after excess alcohol intake spares us from the potential for struggling through the difficult trek.

Pre-Hike Hydration Strategy

The hydration strategy begins the night before the hike. Studies confirm we suffer from poor performance during any exercise regimen if we begin in a dehydrated state. The exercise only influences a greater water deficit, which proves difficult to get ahead of.

On the night before a strenuous or hot weather hike:

- Eat well, keep alcohol intake to a minimum, and hydrate reasonably.
- Sleep for 7 to 8 hours.

Prior to the hike:

- Avoid more than 8 ounces of coffee or caffeinated tea, as the caffeine exerts a diuretic effect and releases more fluid from the body.
- Drink 8 to 16 ounces (250 to 500 ml) of water or other caffeine-free liquid to pre-hydrate before the hike begins, depending on anticipated length, difficulty, and environmental conditions of the hike.

Calculating Estimated Fluid Needs

How much water do we need? Most of us realize we need to bring water with us while hiking. The obvious next question asks how much water we need to consume during the hike to offset the risk for dehydration. Every hike differs from the others, so the answer is "it depends"! Slow, easy walks in mild temperatures for short distances pose little potential for dehydration, with most requiring 8 to 12 ounces, or 250 to 350 milliliters per hour or less, depending on pace and individual needs. Hiking to all levels beyond this calls for higher hourly fluid needs.

Numerous factors affect our water requirements, with some impacting us more than others. The following variables have the greatest influence over our hydration requirements and deserve consideration in deriving our hydration strategy. Each of these, and their increasing levels of impact on us, will ultimately determine how much water we will need per hour.

Hiking pace. How quickly or slowly we hike dictates how much work we put into the effort. The harder we exercise, the more we lose body water. With that comes higher hydration needs to keep up. The average hiker moves at 2 miles (3.2 km) per hour. Highly experienced hikers may go faster at 2.5 to 3 miles (4 to 4.8 km) per hour, and trail runners go even faster! Hiking pace naturally varies between flat, uphill, and downhill trekking, but use the average pace, determined from past hikes. Simply counting how many hours it took to cover so much distance provides us with our pace. Smart watches and phone apps can also calculate our speed for us.

Terrain. Flat trails, those with rolling hills or with long, steep, or technical terrain challenge us very differently. The longer and steeper the inclines along the route, the higher the hydration demands will be. Trail difficulty and elevation gain imply more difficult terrain, so a higher rating assigned to a specific trail should clue us in to more challenging terrain.

Temperature. Outside temperature naturally affects how much water we need to replace during exercise. The hotter the temperature, the more we will sweat to shed excess heat from our bodies. The body water losses that follow need real-time replacement. Extreme cold also affects our hydration needs, and to a much greater extent than most appreciate. Other than offsetting respiratory water losses, hydration remains a key factor in maintaining normal organ function and heat production in frigid conditions. Watching the weather forecast tells us what we need to know for the time we plan to spend on-trail.

Humidity. This element varies greatly across seasons and hiking locations. The lower the humidity, the higher the unappreciated body water losses that follow. We may sweat just as much as in higher humidity, but since sweat evaporates almost instantly in low-humidity environments, we often don't recognize it. Respiratory water loss also rises with lowering humidity, largely without our ability to appreciate its extent. The weather forecast also provides this information.

The above factors help us to focus on the most important elements to account for in figuring out how much water we will need per hour. The average hiker rambling on a moderately difficult trail in average conditions requires about 750 milliliters of water per hour. For those wanting a simple approach, starting at this point and adjusting the estimate for the conditions can accommodate most. However, while this method may work, it does not apply to everyone who steps into the wilderness or for every hike. The unique elements of the trek and the individual modify the necessity for hydration, so our hourly requirements fluctuate between outings and hikers. Those seeking a more accurate estimate of our hourly hydration needs to avoid over- or underestimation of carried water weight require a method with additional complexity.

The next question asks how much water we'll need for the entire hike. Anticipated trekking time completes the equation, taking hiking pace and distance into account. These two variables help us to then figure out how many hours the trek will take. Trail apps and maps help provide the total distance of routes we plan to tackle. For example, a planned hiking distance of 8 miles (13 km) by a hiker moving at the average pace of 2 miles (3.2 km) per hour, will take about 4 hours to complete the route. When hiking in a group the hiking pace only goes as fast as the slowest person, making this important in the calculation.

The following table represents the author's personal approach. The lefthand column contains the four major factors determining hydration needs, as listed above. The rows to the right of these major factors identify increasingly severe features of those factors corresponding to increasing hydration needs. The vertical columns represent four categories (1–4), with the increasing numbers representing ever-increasing hydration needs related to those major factors. The bottom of each numbered category provides the estimated hourly volume of hydration needed, corresponding to the hike features in that column.

Few hikes fall entirely within the features of any one numbered category, so we identify which features our anticipated hike will have. If three or more features of the anticipated hike fall under the same numbered category, then use the hourly hydration recommendation at the bottom of the column. If the features span two or more numbered categories, then take the average hourly hydration recommendation between those categories.

After we have estimated our hourly anticipated hydration needs, based on the above factors, we then multiply that by the number of hours we expect to trek, and we have figured out the total amount of water we should consume for that hike.

Example 1: We anticipate hiking a 6-mile loop trail in maximum 80° F temperature, with a 1,100-foot elevation gain and in 30 percent humidity and our average hiking pace is 2 miles per hour.

Three of those four features fall under "Category 2," so we will need to drink about 750 milliliters of water per hour during that

Fluid Needs Chart

	Category 1	Category 2	Category 3	Category 4
Hiking Pace	< 2 mi/h / 3.2 km/h	2.0–2.5 mi/h / 3.2–4 km/h	2.5–3.0 mi/h / 4–5 km/h	> 3 mi/h / >5 km/h
Terrain	Flat to short, rolling hills up to 500 ft / 150 m elevation gain	Higher and longer uphills with switchbacks, 500–1,200 ft / 150–365 m elevation gain	Mountainous, long, and steep inclines, 1,200–2,000 ft / 365–610 m elevation gain	Class 5 terrain, technical climbing, or > 2,000 ft / 610 m elevation gain
Forecasted Temperature (during anticipated hiking time)	Cool to mild: 45–70° F / 18–24° C	Warm to borderline hot: 70–90° F / 24–32° C	Cold or hot: -10–45° F / -23– 7° C or 90– 105° F / 32–40° C	Extreme cold and heat (including alpine desert or Southwest desert conditions): < -10° F /-23° C or > 105° F / 40°C
Humidity	> 60%	40–60%	20–40%	< 20%
Water need:	16 oz / 500 ml per hour	24 oz / 750 ml per hour	32 oz /1 l per hour	40 oz / 1.25 l per hour

hike, as indicated at the bottom of that column. Given the pace and distance, the hike will take 3 hours. Multiply 750-milliliter-per-hour water need by 3 hours and we have figured out that we need to consume about 2,250 milliliters for the whole hike.

Example 2: While visiting the US Southwest, we plan a hike with a 1,850-foot elevation gain. Humidity measures 15 percent in this location. To avoid the peak heat of the day we will start the hike early in the morning, during which time the temp will only reach as high as 74° F. Our hiking pace averages 2.8 miles per hour, and this will be an 8-mile out-and-back hike.

The features of this hike fall under Categories 2, 3, and 4. We then calculate the average of the hydration needs of these three categories (750 ml/h + 1,000 ml/h + 1,250 ml/h ¸÷ 3 = 1,000 ml/hour). Dividing 8 miles distance by the 2.5-mile-per-hour pace, we anticipate hiking for just under 3 hours. For simplicity, we round up to 3 hours. Multiplying 1,000 milliliters per hour by 3 hours derives our need of 3 liters of water for the entire hike.

The above hourly fluid estimates fit most people's needs, falling between small and large body frames. Those falling outside of this range need to modify the calculation. Petite-framed hikers should reduce the hourly volume by 25 percent, while those with extra-large frames should consider increasing the hourly volume by 25 percent.

Beginning with this starting point, our individual metabolic rate, sweat threshold, urine production, and unique medical background dictate how accurate any formula predicts our needs. Becoming self-aware of how any methodology works allows us to adjust the approach for future hikes. Practicing this routinely enables us to fine-tune our strategy and drastically reduce our risk for dehydration.

Under normal conditions we carry plain water. While stressing the importance of hydration, we must also avoid drinking more plain water than circumstances require, as this invites danger just as much as dehydration does. The sweat we produce from hik-

Dr. Rob's Suggestions

- Drink one quarter of the calculated hourly fluid need every 15 minutes while hiking to keep up with anticipated losses. However . . .
- During breaks from hiking to rest, eat, swim in a lake, and so forth, only drink to satisfy thirst during that time. Resume hydrating on a schedule after hiking begins again.
- Outside temperature often evolves during the hike, especially when starting off in the morning. We need less hydration during cooler early morning hiking, as compared to when the temperature maxes out later. We should not feel obligated to take in all the water determined for those cooler hours, especially if not thirsty, as our needs may increase past the estimated hourly average at the peak temperature.

ing eliminates sodium and chloride from the skin, as well as water. Individual variations in sweat production and electrolyte needs do occur, but the more we sweat the more of these electrolytes we lose. A growing number of endurance athletes in recent years have suffered the effects of overhydration, through the diagnosis of exercise induced hyponatremia (EIH).

The endurance athlete (and hiker) has already lost much sodium from the body during their event, along with water, in their sweat. Drinking too much plain water without also replacing salt dilutes the sodium concentration in their blood. A normal sodium concentration keeps water inside of the blood vessels, but a low sodium concentration (hyponatremia) allows water to seep out of the circulation system into the surrounding tissues, including the brain, causing swelling of the organ. Because of little extra room inside the skull, the brain's swelling causes pressure to build up inside, leading to loss of consciousness, seizures, coma, and often death.

Dr. Rob's Suggestions

Very Important for the Day Hiker

- **If** we have no means to collect and purify water from environmental sources we encounter, or
- **If** we come prepared to collect and purify backcountry water but have not encountered any environmental sources for refilling our water supply . . .

Under these circumstances, regardless of how long the hike has been planned for, **when we have consumed half of the water we have taken with us, the hike is over!** Head back to the trailhead with the other half of the water supply. If we consumed half of the water to get to that point from the trailhead, the other half of the water should suffice to get us back. Play it safe and live to hike that trail another day.

When it comes to hydrating, we must listen to our bodies. The best rule of thumb involves drinking to satisfy thirst. While following a hydration plan, if we find we're not thirsty when it comes time to drink, and we otherwise feel well, then we shouldn't force those fluids. When we sweat excessively and otherwise drink a lot of water according to the hydration plan, we should also eat salty snacks to maintain the sodium balance in our body. Alternatives to salty snacks includes drinking sodium-containing fluids, such as sports drinks, electrolyte tablets and powders, broth, and even pickle juice!

Altitude can potentially modify our hydration needs but will not affect most of us. Several sources have published recommendations about hydration needs at elevation, but from a medical standpoint if we hike to above 8,000 feet and return below it in the same 24-hour period no information from the available scientific studies suggests a need to alter the hydration strategy, other than the other conditions in that environment would suggest. However, if we remain at altitude for an extended, but limited, period of time our physiology produces a neutralizing effect on hydration.

One study flew subjects to altitude to simply exist at rest there and found a decline in thirst response and an increased urinary elimination of fluid, producing a fluid deficit up to 3 liters over several days. However, when they began to train and exercise in the same environment, their bodies began to retain sodium and fluid automatically, offsetting the fluid losses they had experienced at first. The cold temperatures, low humidity, and hypoxia drive the physiologic changes at altitude, which still elude a full understanding by scientists who have spent careers studying this phenomenon. Most of us will not spend days on end at considerable altitudes, especially at rest, unless we visit the basecamps of Mt. Everest, K2, or Denali on medical missions or in the quest for a summit. Planning a mountaineering trip at extreme altitude? Other

Hiker's Tip: Preparing for the Unexpected

Unplanned overnights remain a possibility for us all, especially on long hikes while venturing into unfamiliar territory. Getting lost or finding ourselves far from the trailhead after sundown leads to most unintended overnights in the woods.

In the spirit of preparation for the common perils, hikers also need to contemplate taking more water with them than these higher-risk hikes call for. Always having a means in our pack for filtering or purifying backcountry water in these situations enables us to safely take advantage of that resource. Access to these sources is not guaranteed, though, as we may find ourselves nowhere near mountain streams or lakes.

Ahead of these adventures that expose us to the higher possibility of an unplanned extension of our time in the unforgiving wilderness, consider packing an extra liter of water in reserve for this common scenario.

references provide much more specific information applicable to those expeditions.

Container options for carrying water range from hydration bladders for easy access while on the move to water bottles of varying size and construction in anything from Nalgene and other BPA-free plastic to aluminum and steel. These options all have their advantages and disadvantages. Personal preference, weight, season, liquid temperature, ease of access, and pack design dictate which options are best, which may vary through the year.

Carrying versus Collecting

The option for day hikers and their anticipated water needs comes between carrying all of it for the outing versus saving pack weight and planning to collect backcountry water along the way. Multiday backpackers, on the other hand, have no choice in the matter but to consume water from the environment.

Day hikes and multiday backpacking differ from one another in many ways. Multiday backpacking involves a string of day hikes interrupted by sleeping and eating in the woods. Each new day brings another day hike. Considerations for hydration and nutrition, shelter and sleep system all must be worked out ahead of time. We cannot run out to the store quickly to pick up needed supplies on day 3 of 5 out in the middle of nowhere. What we have in the pack and the environment will be all we have access to. The mindset, planning, and strategy differ greatly from one another, making day hiking and multiday backpacking different subject matter altogether.

The day hiker can bring most, if not all, of the water they will need for that journey. Water weighs 2.2 pounds (1 kg) per liter, so carrying multiple liters comes with a weight penalty. Therefore, collecting water from the environment remains an option for day hikes, especially for long treks or for those who want to keep their pack as light as possible, but it is not an option chosen by most. In the above example where we calculated the approximate water needs for the 8-mile hike, those 3.2 liters of water needed for that hike will add 7 pounds (3.2 kg) to the pack weight. Though this is not an excessive burden for the day hiker to carry for 1 day, multiplying that volume and weight by several or more days of backpacking for water alone becomes unrealistic.

The multiday backpacker, therefore, cannot possibly carry the weight of all the water they will need for several days or longer in the wilderness, plus the weight of all their equipment, so the hydration strategy must include collection of water from the environment. The route must intentionally intersect with environmental water sources throughout their time in the backcountry, to ensure a successful trip. Maps may show a stream or creek along the backpacking route, but on the ground we may only see a dry riverbed, as water may only flow on a seasonal basis. These

Dr. Rob's Tip: Know What to Expect Along the Route

The depth of most North American rivers and streams is monitored by the US Geological Survey (waterdata.usgs.gov) and Environment Canada (wateroffice.ec.gc.ca). These websites provide current and near-future water depths of nearly every body of water in the respective countries.

Study the anticipated backpacking route and deliberately direct it to where sources of water appear on the map. After determining the route, search the appropriate website for the data on specific rivers, streams, and creeks from the map. The websites regularly update the data, so we know exactly how much water flow to expect when we hike up to these waterways.

Knowing what to anticipate takes at least some of the unknowns out of the backpacking equation. Assuring a source for this life-sustaining substance allows us to focus on planning for other variables we cannot know about ahead of time.

resources must therefore be confirmed as active ahead of time, or the multiday backpacking trip will not go as planned, resulting in turning around and returning early or the need for rescue when pushing farther from civilization to find alternative sources.

The typical multiday backpacker has spotty access to these environmental sources for water along their route. Consideration of and planning for daily hydration needs follow the same method as for the day hiker, but the backpacker must assure an adequate supply. An integral part of the hydration strategy involves never squandering the opportunity to refill all water containers when encountering these water sources. Backpackers often carry hydration bladders of varying capacity in their pack, weighing next to nothing when empty but capable of storing liters of water for drinking, preparing food, and other water-based comforts and necessities along the way. Best practice includes filling these at every opportunity and filtering or purifying the water later.

The Downside of Collecting Backcountry Water

Be fully aware that all water collected from the environment (rivers, streams, waterfalls, lakes, etc.) has a high potential for causing sickness, manifested as diarrhea, fever, vomiting, and abdominal pain. This happens because environmental water contains the bacteria in waste products from animals and other humans, as well as viruses and protozoa from the same sources, or otherwise present in the environment. While the water may appear clear, this does not equate with safety. Some advocate for its relative safety based on their personal experience, but there are few among us who have become adapted to the contents of environmental water and drink it without significant negative effect. Avoid drinking unfiltered or untreated backcountry water at all costs, unless dehydration is too significant to ignore.

Longer stays in the backcountry associate with a higher risk for diarrheal illness, due to a higher number of exposures to environmental water and increased potential for lapses in water sterility and hygiene. Those who become ill while miles away from society often find themselves too sick to return on foot and require extraction by a rescue team due to dehydration. The illness and body water loss may require subsequent hospitalization, antibiotics, IV fluids, and prolonged recovery before gut function returns to normal. Those who choose or need to collect water from environmental sources must therefore have a plan for how they will convert this water into a safe and ingestible form.

The most common biological hazards contained in water found in the wilderness are listed in the Biological Hazards Chart.

Biological Hazards Chart

Bacteria	Viruses	Parasites/Protozoa
E. coli (including 0157:H7)	Norovirus	Giardia lamblia
Vibrio cholera / other species	Rotavirus	Cryptosporidium
Salmonella typhi	Enterovirus	
Campylobacter	Hepatitis A	
Shigella		

Sterilization, Treatment, and Filtration of Backcountry Water

The three methods of reducing and/or eliminating the pathogens most commonly found in backcountry water sources are sterilization, treatment, and filtration. Each has an advantage and potential disadvantage to usage, and whether it addresses the full spectrum of bacteria, viruses, and parasites, or only part of it.

Boiling. The best method for sterilization, maintaining the boil for 1 minute (or 3 min above a 6,500-ft elevation) kills the full spectrum of organisms as listed in the Biological Hazards Chart. If unable to get the water to boil, maintaining the water at a "hot to touch" level for more than 10 minutes may be just as effective. One drawback: We can only boil a small volume of water at any one time, proving impractical to treat a full day's supply of water. This requires a heat source, from either a campfire or fuel-based camping stove. Campfires take time and skill to craft, not allowing for quick preparation of water. The fuel required to use a camping stove to boil all the drinking water over several days might amount to more than can be reasonably carried. Most use this method only when stopping for a while to prep a meal.

Iodine. Treating water with iodine has been used all over the world for over 70 years. Ordinarily supplied in the very convenient form of tablet or liquid tincture, this treatment effectively eliminates bacteria and viruses. Maximum effect takes about 35 minutes to accomplish. One drawback: Iodine does not effectively kill parasites as listed in the chart and represents an incomplete method of sterilization on its own. Other than altering the color and taste of the water, usage of iodine can rarely activate previously hidden thyroid disease.

Chlorine. Several forms of chlorine exist for this purpose, used commonly by most municipalities for water treatment. Much like iodine, chlorine comes in a small and near-weightless form, taking roughly 30 minutes to work. Unlike iodine, it does not discolor the water or produce a nasty taste. Chlorine kills bacteria, viruses, and Giardia, but it does not reliably eliminate Cryptosporidium, due to its natural chloride resistance. Since it is not a full-spectrum killer, we cannot rely on chlorine alone for complete protection, unless combined with another method.

Filters. A time-honored method for eliminating organisms in backcountry water, these devices force water through openings smaller than the size of bacteria and parasites. These organisms cannot pass through, but viruses can traverse the micro pores of some filters. Viruses have been traditionally thought of as rare in North America, and previously of little concern, but the emergence of viral-induced diarrheal illness has increased recently and in highly traveled places such as the Appalachian Trail. Viruses become even more of a potential threat when we hike abroad.

Neither traditional backcountry water filters nor chemical treatments represent foolproof methods for tackling the spectrum of organisms. The combination of these two does, however, represent a full-range treatment. Dropping a chemical treatment into a bottle containing water freshly filtered from the environment, and waiting the appropriate time afterward, eliminates all the pathogens we need to avoid ingesting.

Certain branded filter/water bottle combinations (termed "water purifier" to differentiate them from traditional-style filters) have come to market and been advertised to offer small enough pore openings to also eliminate viruses as well as bacteria and protozoa. These are worth consideration for a quick and effective method for producing drinkable water without additional chemical treatment. These purifiers can be used to then transfer the water to standard containers during a water stop along the backpacking route. **Check the product labels carefully**!

Rachel Obendorf (@rachelobendorf [Instagram]) hydrating with filtered backcountry water along the trail.
RACHEL AND MICHAEL OBENDORF

Ultraviolet light treatment. UV treatment kills pathogens and has been taken advantage of in numerous settings, even by hospitals to sterilize entire rooms. Handheld devices that emit this spectrum of light have proven effective for sterilizing water too. Placing one end of the device into the water for about 90 seconds kills bacteria, viruses, and parasites and acts as a full-spectrum killer. However, floating impurities and debris in the water can

Several of the numerous options to treat, filter, or purify backcountry water.

Hiker's Tip: Water Filter Care in Cold Conditions

When hiking in freezing conditions, the water left inside of a water filter can freeze between uses and stop the filter from working. Prioritize flushing the water out and packing the filter away, insulated from the freezing air to maintain use out in the field.

Sleep with the filter inside the sleeping bag in freezing cold conditions to prevent it from freezing overnight.

Dr. Rob's Tip: Hand Hygiene

Studies point to improper hand hygiene as an additional high-potential risk factor for diarrheal illness while backpacking. We all need to eliminate our body waste while living in the wilderness for days. This involves a clean-up process. We need those same hands to prepare our food and eat with. We can unwittingly transfer bacteria from our waste, and all we have touched out in the backcountry, to what we ingest along the way.

Backpackers carry a bathroom kit for management of personal waste. Always pack a small bar of soap to thoroughly clean up after bio breaks and before meals to drastically reduce this risk.

shield these pathogens from the UV light exposure, compromising its efficacy. This method does require the patience to hold the device in place for the 90 seconds and does run the risk of battery failure during an extended trip through the outdoors, but this method remains attractive for a quick and effective alternative to the filter-and-chemical-treatment combination to eliminate the infectious threat.

Conservation of Body Water in Hot Conditions

When hiking in hot and low-humidity conditions, part of the hydration strategy should involve ways of reducing core body temperature, excessive sweating, and body water loss. This further decreases the risk for dehydration.

One method involves **beginning the hike as early in the day as possible**. This requires waking up extra early and arriving to the trailhead at or prior to sunrise. Beginning the day's efforts at this time, guided by the light of the sunrise or a headlamp, assures the hike begins in the coolest temperature of the day, and that much of the day's hiking time has been completed before the day's hottest temperature has been reached. Employing this strategy assures reduction in sweating compared to midday hikes in the heat, allowing for reduction in water needs and less water weight carried along the route.

Another body water–conserving strategy involves **usage of shade**. The amount of shade differs in every location and trail, with some offering much more than others do. Look for the shade from a tree, a dip in the trail, or a rock formation. Use these shady spots for a quick break. The much lower temperature in shade compared to that in the direct sun comes from less radiant heat exposure. Shade allows for an effective cooldown while hydrating or taking in a quick snack. These shady breaks slow our sweat production, enabling our hydration efforts to keep up with our needs. The time of day also dictates the presence of shade, with less available between 10 AM and 2 PM when the sun is directly overhead. Earlier in the morning or later in the afternoon the sun lies off to the side, hitting the ground at an angle and producing more potential shade opportunities.

Slowing our hiking pace allows for lower heart rate and muscle activity, leading to decreased heat production and sweating. Hiking too slowly, on the other hand, leaves us exposed to the sun's radiant heat that much longer. Reducing hiking pace by a small amount, either by perception or by 0.5 miles (0.8 km) per hour as monitored by a phone app or smartwatch, can strike the balance to both reduce body heat production and limit heat absorption from the sun.

Bottom Line

Most of us who have ventured into places without access to water have experienced dehydration to one extent or another. Acknowledging our body's constant state of fluid loss should remind us to hydrate reasonably on a regular basis, to maintain adequate body fluid levels for optimal organ function. When we exercise and place ourselves in various types of environmental conditions, our body fluid losses naturally rise. When coupled with an inadequate supply or access to water, we become dehydrated and our body mechanisms begin to fail.

- Recognize the signs and symptoms of dehydration.
- Call 911 for rescue when recognizing moderate to severe dehydration.
- Understand the concepts of rehydration and what types of fluids we can use.

We all know we should bring water with us on a hike. The most obvious question asks how much of it we need to bring with us. This basic skill provides us with the means to avoid this common peril.

- Decide to become empowered and control the risk we face for dehydration.
- Understand that the unique features of the hike dictate how much water we need to offset dehydration.
- Formulating and executing a strategy for hydration, even when flawed, protects us more than having no strategy at all.
- Fine-tuning our strategy over time improves proficiency to maximize our safe return from future hikes.
- As a Plan B on day hikes, plan to collect water from backcountry sources that becomes the primary source for water on multiday backpacking trips. Know the location of water sources ahead of the day hike, and purposely intersect the backpacking route with these sources to assure a plentiful supply.
- Understand the perils of ingesting backcountry water and have a plan to treat, filter, or sterilize it.
- Take advantage of the above techniques to conserve body water along the way.

References

Baker, L. B., and A. E. Jeukendrup. "Optimal Composition of Fluid-Replacement Beverages." *Comprehensive Physiology* 4, no. 2 (2014): 575–620.

Boore, S. M., and E. Bock. "Ten Years of Search and Rescue in Yosemite National Park: Examining the Past for Future Prevention." *Wilderness and Environmental Medicine* 24, no. 1 (2013): 2–7.

Brooks, Carolyn J. "Racial/Ethnic and Socioeconomic Disparities in Hydration Status Among US Adults and the Role of Tap Water and Other Beverage Intake." *American Journal of Public Health* 107, no. 9 (September 2017): 1387–1394.

Ganio, Matthew S., et al. "Mild Dehydration Impairs Cognitive Performance and Mood in Men." *British Journal of Nutrition* 106, no. 10 (2011): 1535–1543.

Hanson, Hilary. "Hiker Dies in Badlands National Park After Running Out of Water." *Huffington Post*, July 23, 2022.

Heckenliable, M. "Eight Rescues in One Week Prompt Search and Rescue Officials to Issue Warning About Dehydration." *St. George News*, June 18, 2018.

Institute of Medicine (US) Committee on Military Nutrition Research. *Nutritional Needs in Cold and in High-Altitude Environments: Applications for Military Personnel in Field Operations*. Edited by Bernadette M. Marriott et al. Washington, DC: National Academies Press, 1996.

Institute of Medicine (US) Committee on Military Nutrition Research. *Water Requirements During Exercise in the Heat*. Edited by C. Gisolfi et al. Washington, DC: National Academies Press, 1993.

Maughan, R. J. "Impact of Mild Dehydration on Wellness and on Exercise Performance." *European Journal of Clinical Nutrition* 57, Suppl. 2 (2003): S19–23.

Media Advisory. "Two Separate Rescues in Boulder County for Dehydrated Hikers." bouldercounty.gov, September 20, 2021.

Pelham, V. "Palm Springs Police Rescue 4 Hikers in Indian Canyons." desertsun.com, March 8, 2015.

Schleh, M. W., and C. L. Dumke. "Comparison of Sports Drink versus Oral Rehydration Solution During Exercise in the Heat." *Wilderness and Environmental Medicine*. 29, no. 2 (2018): 185–193.

Zhang, N., et al. "Effects of Dehydration and Rehydration on Cognitive Performance and Mood Among Male College Students in Cangzhou, China: A Self-Controlled Trial." *International Journal of Environmental Research and Public Health* 16, no. 11(June 2019): 1891.

Skill 2

Weather and Managing Body Temperature

Real-Life Scenarios

1. A family of three and their dog set out for a day hike in the Sierra Nevada mountains in August 2021 and never returned home. All were discovered deceased on-trail near the Merced River, less than 2 miles from their car. This initially sparked nationwide speculation as to what could possibly have happened.

   The investigation that followed concluded that they succumbed to heat injury made possible by several missteps taken by the couple, who had brought their 1-year-old child along for the journey. Among their missteps, they had taken only 2.5 liters of water for the three of them and their dog. They had not accounted for the peak temperature that day of 109° F. The location was picked from a hiking trip one of them had taken there in the past, but they were likely not aware there was no shade along their route due to destruction of the canopy from recent wildfires. They had attempted to text and call around for help, but not to 911, but the lack of cell service left their efforts unanswered.

2. Two hikers from Las Vegas, J.R. and D.R., visited Valley of Fire State Park for a hike on July 23, 2023. They started the 9.3 mile out-and-back trail interacting with another group on the same trail, who pulled ahead of the duo. The temperature reached 118° F that day. The other group ended their route,

realizing the pair they met earlier were nowhere in sight. A search for them began, finding one of the hikers just a quarter mile from the trailhead and the other further down trail. Unfortunately, both were deceased, each with an emptied, limited capacity water container next to them.

3. A mother and son embarked on a hike in Northwest Colorado in early August 2021 north of Sheep Mountain, leaving their family's patriarch behind at home. That night he reported them as missing to authorities when they hadn't returned home as anticipated. Several search parties rambled all night through the cold mountainous terrain looking for them. Shortly after sunrise they were spotted and a rescue team extracted the pair, who had gotten lost and sheltered in place after sunset while only dressed for summer weather. Flown by helicopter to a local hospital, they were treated for hypothermia and released.
4. An experienced solo hiker, X.C., set out to meet the challenge of the 18-mile Presidential Traverse in Mt. Washington State Park, New Hampshire, on June 18, 2022. That evening his wife called emergency services when the weather took a turn for the worse. Among an unseasonable winter-like storm, with high winds, frigid temperatures, and freezing rain, X.C. texted his wife from the trail. Describing his wet clothes and frigid body, he was in desperate need for help. The mountain rescue team responded and fought through the 80 mile per hour winds and precipitation to reach him at around 10:30 that night, finding him unresponsive and hypothermic. Failed attempts to warm him in the field led to transportation to the local hospital, where despite best efforts he was pronounced deceased.
5. In November 2022 a 19-year-old adventurer, E.S., set out on a solo hike in the White Mountains, working toward completing her goal of summiting New Hampshire's forty-eight

> peaks. She unfortunately never returned. Over a dozen search and rescue (SAR) teams searched for 4 days and tragically discovered her lifeless body off-trail. She was found with light clothing layers and simple trail shoes on, not even approaching adequate protection from the single-digit temperatures, snow, and high winds the region experienced during her trek. Investigators concluded she had become lost off-trail, was caught in the frigid temperatures and rapid winds without any significant means to resist them, and unfortunately died from hypothermia. She was just one of the many amazing adventurers succumbing to cold injury every year, their flames extinguished far too early in life, a fate that likely could have been prevented.

Heat and cold injury rank among the top handful of perils hikers face that lead to death or need for rescue. Though occurrence may depend on season and location, the five preceding cases represent situations that trail-goers potentially face every day. The yearly statistics repeat consistently, outlining yet more hikers and outdoor adventurers who have fallen into the temperature trap. All backcountry explorers confront this potential threat, and their readiness remains the solution to the issue. Maximizing our resistance to heat and cold comes through a better understanding of how the weather develops the upper hand.

The first two of the above scenarios illustrates the close association of dehydration with heat injury and water as the major countermeasure. We can easily see that the amount of water brought in the first scenario for the whole family was not adequate for even one of the adults for that day's hike. On that family's ill-fated trek, an adequate water supply would have been the one key factor in resisting heat injury and changing the outcome of that hike to an unremarkable one that none of us would have heard or read about. The two hikers from Las Vegas either had no idea how hot the day would become, or how much water they'd need to have and consume to prevent tragedy. Their limited water supply left them inevitable victims of that day's heat.

Scenarios 3 and 5 illustrate the phenomenon of becoming lost as a significant factor in lengthening the time of exposure to environmental temperatures beyond original expectations. Wearing or packing appropriate clothing to resist the cold and arriving ready for the characteristically erratic weather patterns in mountainous regions also play significant roles in how things unfold for the adventurer.

Our bodies need to stay at or near 98.6° F for all our organ systems to function properly. When conditions influence our body temperature to depart from that point, complex but short-lived mechanisms activate to redirect us back to 98.6° F. Prolonged exposure to the extremes, continuing to divert our body temperature away from normal, ordinarily defeats those temporary body reactions unless we quickly act on our own or others' behalf. Preemptive strategies serve as the countermeasure to heat and cold injury. Knowing how to ready ourselves for the elements begins with appreciating how our bodies gain and lose heat.

To fully understand the transfer of heat to and from our bodies, realize one simple rule:

Heat transfers from where it is, to where it is not.

A Basic Scientific Example of Heat Transfer

If we take a steel rod at a temperature of 98.6° F and hang it out in 50° F air, or drop it in 50° F water, the heat transfers from the steel rod to the colder air or water until that rod cools down to an equilibrium temperature with its surroundings.

If we place that same 98.6° F steel rod into boiling water (212° F), or into an oven (at the same 212° F), the surrounding heat transfers into the steel rod until its temperature increases to 212° F as well.

Our bodies undergo the process of heat transfer when immersed in cold or hot surroundings. Without mechanisms for retention, production, or loss of heat our bodies will reach the temperature that surrounds us. While in the moment of feeling too hot or cold, our instinct drives us to find ways to resolve the problem. That explains why we drink hot liquids or get into a hot shower or tub when we feel cold, subconsciously knowing these interventions transfer heat into our bodies. Conversely, we instinctively know to drink cool liquids or jump into cool water when we feel very hot, to transfer heat out of our bodies. When out in a remote location without the right supplies and ability to take these instinctive actions, we find ourselves at the mercy of the conditions that surround us.

We need to maintain a normal body temperature to sustain optimal function of the cells, organs, and organ systems of the body, which has greater complexity than the steel rod used in the simple example above. Under normal conditions our bodies produce heat and shed heat at an equal rate, to maintain an equilibrium temperature. When heat production rises, such as with exercise or a fever, the body responds with mechanisms for proportional heat loss to restore normal temperature.

We create our own heat from within by two major mechanisms:

1. **Metabolism.** Each of the roughly thirty trillion cells of the body acts as a tiny factory serving a specific function, consuming calories and oxygen to constantly generate heat as a byproduct. The rate of heat production varies from person to person but depends on several factors, including the types of food we eat, our age, frequency of exercise, biologic gender, genetics, muscle to fat ratio, and hormonal function.

2. **Muscle movement.** The more we work our muscles, the more heat becomes produced. Walking across a room does not generate heat above resting levels, but running a mile generates a significant amount of body heat over that of an inactive state.

Mechanisms of Heat Transfer

The mechanisms of heat loss and gain provide essential information for us to understand, so we can effectively prepare in a way that suits the circumstances. Most of us experience these handful of ways our bodies gain or lose heat on a near-daily basis. While more than one may act at once, a better understanding of the individual processes allows us to use them to our advantage.

Convection involves the movement of heat into or out of an object when exposed to moving air or water. The rate of heat transfer depends on temperature difference between the object and the air or water, speed of flow of the air or water, and whether any barrier lies between the object and it.

How does convection affect us while out on-trail?

- While feeling hot on a summer hike, dipping our bare feet or body in the flowing water of a brook or stream along our way allows us to cool down quickly due to enhancing

Examples of Convection

- Staying under the water flow of a hot shower for a long time leaves us feeling hot and needing to cool off after. Our skin temperature warms up first, but the longer that high-temperature water flows across our body, the more it affects our core temperature.
- We are served hot tea or coffee. What do we do? We blow air onto the surface of that liquid to cool it down enough to not burn us when we take a sip. What we just did is utilize convection to accomplish that.
- Convection ovens differ from traditional ovens, as they forcefully circulate hot air around the food placed inside, as opposed to filling the oven with stagnant, hot air. These ovens cook the food much faster than traditional ones.

heat loss from convection. The flowing water cools us faster than still water.

- When hiking in hot weather, a breeze suddenly comes along, blowing against the skin, rendering an immediate but temporarily refreshing sensation. That short-lived relief comes from convection.
- Cold wind can penetrate our clothing and layers during winter hikes, causing us to lose body heat by convection. A windproof shell worn over our layers blocks the wind and minimizes convective heat loss.

Conduction describes the transfer of heat from one solid object, liquid, or gas to another through direct contact. The amount of heat transfer and how quickly it happens depends on the temperature difference between the two objects or substances. Movement of heat by conduction becomes impaired if we place a barrier between them.

Examples of Conduction

- Placing a hot brick on top of a cold brick allows heat to transfer directly from the hot brick to the cold one until the two become lukewarm and of equal temperature.
- Pour 1 cup of boiling hot water into a container with 1 cup of cold water. The heat transfers from the hot water to the cold water until reaching an equilibrium temperature.
- Remember the hot drink example for convection from above? The cup or mug that the hot liquid sits in absorbs heat from the liquid by direct contact, thus cooling the liquid by conduction.
- Place an ice cube on a hot surface. Heat transfers from the surface into the ice cube forcing it to melt into water, which then increases in temperature toward the heat of the surface.

How does conduction affect us while on-trail?

- Sitting on a cold rock during a long hiking break in the winter allows transfer of heat from our body to that rock, only mildly slowed by standard winter hiking pants.
- Backpackers camping out overnight in the winter lose their body heat to the cold ground while in their tent, inside a sleeping bag. Heat easily transfers through these layers compressed by the person's body weight, allowing conduction to take over. Impeding this process takes removing the backpacker from contact with the ground by placing an efficiently insulating sleeping pad under the sleeping bag.
- Drinking ice cold water while hiking out in the summer heat places that cold liquid in direct contact with the mouth, esophagus, stomach, intestines, and the blood flowing through their walls. Heat from the bloodstream and the internal organs transfers to the water inside our gut, decreasing our core body temperature.
- Wet skin conducts heat away from the body at a rate numerous times faster than dry skin, due to water's greater capacity for heat absorption as compared to air. While an advantage in hot weather, wet skin becomes dangerous in cold weather.
- Immersing ourselves or body parts into still, cool water (lake, pool, or pond) allows the water to conduct heat away from our bodies.

Radiation causes transfer of heat or energy from one source to another over distance, using electromagnetic waves through the air or space.

Examples of Radiation

- It feels hotter out in the sunlight as opposed to in the shade, because the sun radiates heat to where it directly shines.
- We warm up while sitting around a campfire as it radiates heat to its surroundings. That heat transfers to us and the air that's around it.
- Going back to the cup of hot liquid from above, placing our hands closely around the noninsulated cup while not touching it, we can feel heat radiating from it to our hands.

How does radiation affect us on-trail?

- Dark colors absorb more radiant energy from the sun than lighter colors do. Wearing light- and dark-colored clothing help us to either resist or enhance transfer of heat to our clothing and body, respectively. Choosing the right colors for the right weather conditions allows us to take advantage of this.
- Finding a shady spot to take a break during a hot weather hike allows us to limit taking on radiant heat from the sun. Without shade, this heat transfers to our body along the way, on top of the heat generated by our physical activity.
- We wear layers under an insulating jacket and wear a cap over our head in cold temperatures. These trap the heat that naturally radiates from our skin and would otherwise be lost to the cold air that surrounds us.
- When our body heat rises, the body responds by dilating blood vessels in the skin so the higher temperature in the bloodstream can radiate at a faster rate from the surface of our body. We can feel this heat coming off our own body, or from another's.

Evaporation facilitates transfer of heat to the surrounding environment by means of liquid turning into a gaseous state.

Examples of Evaporation

- When we boil water at sea level the maximum temperature always peaks at about 212° F and no higher, no matter how much heat we apply to the pot. Water evaporates into steam, releasing heat in the process. Adding more heat makes the water boil that much harder, releasing more heat in the form of steam.
- Placing rubbing alcohol on our skin produces a cooling effect as it evaporates.

How does evaporation affect us on-trail?

- Sweating on a hot weather hike represents our body's major method for releasing heat when necessary to maintain a stable core temperature. Subsequent evaporation of the sweat from the skin dissipates up to 90 percent of our excess heat.
- The respiratory tract heats and humidifies the air we breathe, when necessary, especially in cold and low-humidity conditions. Each exhaled breath of air in cold climates enables warmed water vapor to transfer from the inside of our body to that air by evaporation. Exhaling in frigid temperatures allows us to see our warm, humidified breath leaving our mouths and freezing on contact with the outside air.

The basic understanding of the mechanisms for heat gain and loss enables us to achieve our body heat goals on-trail. The knowledge enlightens us to a strategy for defense against the elements. When exploring in hot conditions, we aim to maximize heat loss and minimize accumulation of heat. When adventuring in cold conditions, our goal is to continue heat production, control heat loss, and optimize accumulation of heat. Incorporating the correct plan allows us to arrive on-trail with an advantage over the conditions. Every location has its unique weather and temperature patterns, both predictable and unpredictable, which vary with each of the four seasons. Prepping for these environmental factors can prevent the outdoor experience from becoming an unpleasant and dangerous one.

When traveling to an unfamiliar location, become acquainted with the forecast, and doing deeper research provides typical and typically unpredictable weather patterns for that area to be prepared for. Planning includes clothing considerations to either enhance or inhibit heat loss in the right conditions, locating shade and water availability ahead of hot weather hikes and pre-planning the sleep/shelter system appropriate for the weather when camping overnight. Routinely considering this in the pre-hike strategy becomes an easy skill to master, sparing most from the real risks of heat and cold injury.

Heat Exhaustion and Heat Stroke

Heat exhaustion and heat stroke represent the same type of heat injury, only differing in severity. Heat injury occurs when the individual accumulates more heat than they can transfer out of their body. Heat exhaustion, which is less severe, reverses with early recognition and quick intervention without long-term effects to the victim. Heat stroke develops when heat exhaustion continues to worsen to a much larger threat to the victim's life, often leaving survivors with permanent medical issues. In the summer of 2003, a heat wave engulfed Europe causing seventy thousand deaths from heat stroke across the continent. In the United States heat stroke causes about six hundred deaths per year and ranks as the third leading cause of death in athletics. The lack of reporting makes the yearly sum of nonfatal heat-related illnesses unquantifiable, but it likely reaches a much higher number. One study illustrated this by examining summertime Emergency Department visits over a 4-year period. Among all patients seen for heat-related illness, about 6 percent of these patients were diagnosed with heat stroke, whereas 75 percent were diagnosed with the less severe diagnosis of heat exhaustion. This suggests that the victims or those around them can recognize the signs and symptoms of heat-related illness before it becomes a life-threatening issue. While many of the cases of heat stroke have arisen beyond the control of the victim, many more have been avoided by recognition of the issue and early intervention.

Good trail etiquette involves greeting others as we pass, to maintain a friendly and inviting atmosphere, but it also allows for a quick check on those we pass along our route. The person in need may be a total stranger, rather than our hiking partner, whose life may depend on others recognizing the early stages of heat injury.

Recognition

A formal medical education isn't necessary to recognize heat exhaustion. Early recognition and intervention reverse the process, prevent progression to heat stroke, and save lives.

Context and circumstances should open our eyes. We can safely assume we will not encounter heat injury while hiking out in cold, snowy, or wintery conditions. It arises in very warm to hot temperatures with exercise at a moderate to higher degree, with inadequate access to fluids and shade. This "perfect storm" of conditions makes news headlines every summer, describing more hikers who have fallen victim to the heat. Knowing these conditions produce heat injury, we should have a heightened awareness of the potential for heat injury before we've stepped outside.

Formal medical definitions of heat illness and heat stroke involve measurements of core body temperature and other formal data. We have nothing available to us to measure this while hiking out in the middle of nowhere, which makes it pointless to review

Call for rescue as early as possible to get the victim to a higher level of care when:

- Simple treatment has not helped.
- Treatment is not available.
- Other barriers to intervention arise.
- The victim's signs and symptoms are already severe.

these measurements here. We must then rely on what we see in ourselves or another. How the victim appears, feels, and behaves provides the only information we have to make judgments while out in the wilderness. While it is not realistic to expect this brief review to produce experts, nonmedically trained individuals can easily remember some of the common signs of heat exhaustion. Recognition leads to intervention and preservation of life. This empowers us with the ability to do more than watch the victim suffer.

The most common signs and symptoms of heat exhaustion:

- **Fatigue and sluggishness.** The inability to keep up the hiking pace, out of character for that person's usual abilities.
- **Lightheadedness.** The ability to stay upright but mildly dizzy.
- **Excessive sweating.** Early on the body breaks into a pouring sweat, out of proportion to the level of activity, to take advantage of evaporative heat loss.
- **Muscle cramps.** Large muscle groups (thighs, calves, etc.) may cramp up from a low hydration state and electrolyte imbalance (sodium, potassium, magnesium, calcium).
- **Mild headache**
- **Nausea**
- **Change in demeanor.** For instance, if an otherwise happy person becomes quiet and irritable, out of context to the circumstances, but able to think clearly.

These symptoms in the setting of exercising in hot weather should trigger the recognition that there's a problem. Intervening as early as possible makes the largest impact on reversing the process and preserving life. If the signs of accumulating body heat go unrecognized, or unaddressed, the person progressively worsens and develops increasingly severe versions of the above symptoms. As the situation advances to heat stroke, life becomes increasingly jeopardized.

The most common signs and symptoms of heat stroke:

- **Weakness.** Increasing physical inability to continue onward
- **Loss of coordination.** Increasing difficulty staying upright on one's feet
- **Decreased sweating.** Sweating stops (to conserve body water)
- **Severe headache**
- **Vomiting**
- **Confusion/disorientation.** Inability to concentrate/think clearly or make sense
- **Loss of consciousness**
- **Seizure**

Something to Consider While Out There

Be the protector on the trail. Eyeball others as you pass them and to determine whether they seem well. If not, then things may not be well. We may encounter someone along the route already in the grip of severe heat injury who may not have had the good fortune of having another recognize this and intervene earlier.

For these and all other victims with heat stroke, call for rescue as soon as possible, followed by what can be done in the field until help arrives.

At this point, there is a high potential for permanent brain damage, as the proteins and cells that maintain brain function become destroyed by the high internal body temperature, along with multiple organ failure (for the same reasons), coma, and death. Call for rescue as soon as interventions for heat exhaustion have clearly not helped matters, and when recognizing severe symptoms.

Prevention

Prevention of heat exhaustion and heat stroke begins with a strategy for hot weather hiking. This involves less complicated and technical aspects than for cold weather hiking. While actively moving we produce body heat. Radiation from the sun and its reflection off the ground and conduction from the hot air in contact with our skin serve to transfer even more heat into our bodies. The longer our exposure to this environment, and the faster our pace, the more heat we accumulate and the closer we get to heat exhaustion and heat stroke.

First principle: Avoid dehydration. Heat exhaustion and heat stroke have a close association with dehydration. While hiking in hot weather, insufficient body water allows retention of heat, with less available for sweat production and risk for heat injury. Adequate hydration maintains the body's ability to produce sweat in hot weather. Drinking plenty of cold water on a hot day helps us reduce our core temperature. The body transfers heat by conduction to cool liquid in the stomach and intestines until it reaches an equilibrium temperature with the body. The colder the liquid, the more heat that transfers from the body. Consider this in the hydration strategy when planning to get outdoors in hot weather.

In general, preventing heat injury takes producing less from within, resisting accumulation of heat, and releasing heat back to the environment that surrounds us.

Producing less heat involves:

- **Slowing down the hiking pace** to the average of 2 to 2.5 miles per hour or below if necessary, rather than a faster pace. While a quicker speed does limit the hike time and potential exposure to the elements, the rise in body temperature that comes with the faster pace may undermine whatever benefit comes from the shorter hike time.
- **Frequent breaks** along the route interrupt the otherwise constant process of heat production. Adding shade and hydration to these breaks increases the benefit.

Resisting accumulation of heat involves:

- **Early morning hikes** to reduce radiant heat from the sun. We cannot control the air temperature that surrounds us, but we can choose to hike during the coolest temperatures of the day. We do this by beginning the hike early and completing (most of) it before the thermometer tops out, especially if it's going to be a scorcher!
- **Wearing light-colored clothing** to resist accumulating radiant heat. Sunlight heats up darker colored objects and clothing much more than it does light-colored ones. Dressing in light-colored clothing, preferably with SPF protection, helps us reflect the light rather than absorb it and turn it into heat. Consider long sleeve and pant options to avoid sunburn, which interferes with the ability to sweat.
- **Using all available shade along the route**. Shade allows us to both escape the sunlight's radiant heat and surround ourselves with relatively cooler air. Morning and late afternoons provide for more chances of shade on the trail, as opposed to the middle of the day. The sun hits the Earth

at an angle during these times, creating numerous shady spots, as opposed to when the sun lies directly overhead.

- **Hydrate regularly** along the way to enhance internal cooling. Conductive heat loss from the body to the cool water in our stomach and intestines boosts our resistance to the hot weather.

Releasing body heat involves:

- **Choosing clothing made from fabric with excellent wicking properties.** Avoiding cotton and wearing thin wool or synthetics allow our sweat to wick away from the skin and dissipate as quickly as it accumulates.
- **Adequate hydration,** to provide the body with liquid needed to continue sweat production.

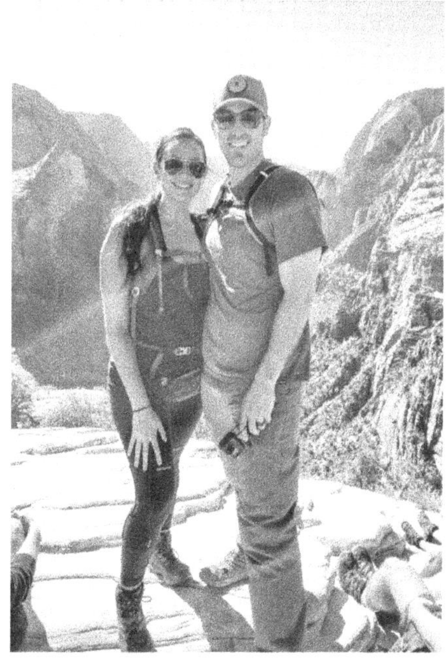

Rachel and Mike Obendorf (@rachelobendorf and @miobe1[Instagram]) dressed for adventure in the heat on Angels Landing.
RACHEL AND MICHAEL OBENDORF

Other preventive measures we can take to mitigate our exposure to the heat and exercise control over how it affects us lie in the pre-hike planning phase. Acknowledging the struggles those with heat injury face, we can channel that to guide us through this process to avoid it altogether. Considering the following strategies can further empower us to control the outcome.

- **Obtain a paper trail map and review the intended route**. Look at satellite images of the trail, looking for favorable features such as trees or adjacent mountains and rock formations (places for shade), brooks or streams (water source and potential natural cooling station). Pick the trails that have these features over those that do not. Search for trail reviews online, which often feature information and insight posted within hours to days of the intended hike.
- **Plan out the timing of the hike**. Know the position of the sun, relative to the trail direction, for that time of day. Will it be in your face, at your back, or off to the side? Ask a friend if you don't know how to assess this. Knowing the sun's position in the sky, and therefore the likeliest places it will cast shade, can prove valuable when needing to know where shady spots exist along the route. When the sun lies directly overhead, it creates the most radiant heat and the least opportunities for shade, so take caution. Tall trees, rock formations, and steep cliffs towering above can still help provide some shade at high noon, typically on the north side of these features in the Northern Hemisphere.
- **Plan and execute the hydration strategy**. Have a method for collecting and decontaminating environmental water should the need arise. **Bring cold water, when available**. When anticipating very hot conditions, consider filling one of the water containers for the day up to the top with ice (when available) and adding water up to the rim before going out. Drink water from other containers first before

they heat up and save the icy container for later. It takes much longer for the hot temps to melt all the ice, so cold water will remain available for later in the hike.

- **Never squander the opportunity to fill an empty water bottle from environmental sources** along the route, again with a method to decontaminate it on hand. Running out of water amounts to potential disaster out in the heat. Favor anticipating the need for water and always having some rather than scrambling to find it when the dire need arises.
- If we have come to a point in a hot weather day hike where half of the water we have brought with us has been consumed, without an environmental source close by from which to collect and replenish our supply, **we *must* turn around and head back**. The hike is over, since the other half of the water will be needed to return to the trailhead.

Treatment

Treatment of heat exhaustion and heat stroke may fall into our hands, as a bystander, or as the victim. Doing something for either ourselves or another person in this situation ends with much better results than having done nothing. We make the greatest positive impact for someone with heat injury by acting early and aggressively. The mechanisms of heat transfer and our own intuition guide us through the treatment, leading to the best possible outcomes. Principles of addressing this problem include minimizing heat production and accumulation, while maximizing release of heat from the body. If the victim has already entered a later stage of heat injury, they need a higher level of care than can be provided on-trail.

If an individual becomes too physically weak to walk, becomes disoriented, confused, or nauseated, or develops vomiting or loss of consciousness among the hot weather, *first* call for help.

Rescue teams typically take hours or longer to assemble and head to the area to locate the victim and intervene. The earlier the call for help, the earlier that person will get to a facility for medical treatment. Activating the Emergency Medical System when the condition is beyond reversibility in the field saves lives. Reaching out may involve a cell phone, satellite phone, satellite messenger, or sending another to the trailhead to find help or a cell signal.

Interventions we can do in the field, either with the intent to reverse early-stage heat injury or to stabilize the victim while waiting on a rescue team, follow the principles of the preventative strategies with the mechanisms for heat transfer in mind. These do not require any medical training.

Early-stage heat exhaustion involves the affected person feeling sluggish, overheated, and not mentally sharp. They likely sweat more than their physical effort would suggest and may complain of a dry mouth. All of the following interventions apply to these individuals who have a high potential for reversibility on the trail:

- **Stop hiking**. Ceasing movement stops the individual from producing more heat.
- **Find shade**. Sit the victim down in a shady spot to avoid their accumulating more sun-related radiant heat.
- **Hydrate** with cool water, plus electrolytes (salt or dissolving electrolyte additive). This takes advantage of conductive heat loss from within and supplies fluid to sweat with.
- **Take off unneeded clothing**, such as a hat, their pack, socks and boots. These items can prevent sweating and evaporative heat loss from the areas they cover.
- **Pour water on the victim's head, chest and back, hands and feet**. Water on the skin conducts heat away from the body, and when this evaporates it further enhances heat loss.

- **Fan air over wet skin** to induce convective heat loss.
- **Place any available ice in the folds** (neck, armpits, groin, behind the knees) to enhance heat loss by conduction. Some first aid kits contain chemical ice packs that activate when the internal ingredients mix together, so search packs for one of these.
- **Immerse bare feet and hands** into a body of water, brook or stream, if nearby, and consider immersing the person up to the waist if needed. The still water of a lake will add conductive heat loss, and the moving water of a brook or stream adds a component of convection to increase the effect.

As a rule of thumb, if the hiker has not improved after 15 to 20 minutes of the above efforts, then call for rescue.

Late-stage heat exhaustion involves a victim who displays worsening physical capability, may not maintain their balance well, complains of nausea and a headache, and exhibits a dulled thought process, has a dry mouth, and sweats more profusely. Most of the above interventions apply here, but remember the following principles:

- **Call for rescue**, if not done already. The low potential for reversibility on the trail makes calling for help the **first** priority.
- **Do not attempt hydration** of a victim who has started vomiting or has become lethargic or unconscious though! If they are only nauseated, try offering small sips at first to test their tolerance.
- **Immersing the person or their body parts may prove unwise**, as they cannot fully assist with mobility, which risks injuring the victim. Use judgment!

Heat stroke follows the previous description and represents a worsening of the spectrum of symptoms and dysfunction of multiple systems of the body. By now, rescue should have been called, and the field treatments should continue as for late-stage heat exhaustion while awaiting a rescue team to arrive.

Hypothermia

Hypothermia develops when a person loses more body heat than they can generate or retain. Hypothermia causes an estimated twenty-five thousand deaths per year in the US. Approximately 7.3 percent of all deaths across thirteen countries, including the US and Canada, have been attributed to cold weather between 1985 and 2012. In fact, cold weather causes twenty times the fatalities that hot weather does. Similar to heat-related illness, the incidence of nonfatal hypothermia likely occurs much more commonly than that which takes lives.

While most heat injury happens during the summer, most hypothermia cases among hikers and backpackers occur between fall and spring. That said, hypothermia can also occur in the summer, particularly at night in the desert and in higher elevations.

A multicountry study examining weather-related deaths over 27 years concluded that most cold weather deaths occurred on mild to moderately cold days, with a small percentage occurring in extreme cold conditions. This suggests milder conditions enable an underestimation of risk, perhaps resulting in suboptimal preparation for the climate. Preventing most cases of hypothermia, then, involves acknowledging the potential effect of even mildly cold days, approaching the weather with extra scrutiny and planning for contingencies.

Any of the mechanisms of heat loss potentially play a role in any one case of hypothermia. Multiple processes of heat loss occur simultaneously in most circumstances.

- Convection (wind penetrating inadequate layers of clothing)
- Conduction (laying on the cold ground with a poorly insulated sleeping pad, heat loss from wet skin through sweating underneath the layers, or accidental or prolonged immersion in cold water)
- Radiation (an inadequate base layer, not trapping radiant heat coming off the skin)
- Evaporation (heat loss through our exhaled breath)

Understanding these mechanisms allows us to better understand the solutions to the problem. Interrupting the mechanisms that enhance body heat loss presents opportunity in the pre-hike strategy, as outlined in the next section. This element of the planning requires forethought though, with the proper motivation. Channeling the instinct to live while planning the adventure minimizes having to exercise the will to live in a desperate survival situation.

Recognizing the signs and symptoms of hypothermia, in ourselves or others, enables us to preserve life in the field. The recognizable early stages of hypothermia should prompt action as soon as possible to stop the progression to increasing severity. The measurement of core body temperature, used by medical professionals to define hypothermia, proves useless to us out in the wilderness. The medically untrained can observe others and easily see when something is clearly wrong. Given the right context and environmental conditions, this tells us the answer.

Recognition

Know that professional medical help does not arrive quickly in the backcountry like it does back home. Therefore, **the earlier we call for help and evacuation, the sooner the victim will be cared for and the higher the chance of their survival and recovery**.

Declining core body temperature leads to a progressive decline in basic body functions. At first, the body will mount its own attempt to generate heat and reverse the process, but sustained conditions that continue to favor body heat loss will outlast these mechanisms. When those attempts can no longer continue, the victim heads quickly toward serious consequences.

Shivering, characterized by multiple large muscle groups violently quivering uncontrollably, becomes triggered with onset of mild hypothermia. This mechanism capitalizes on heat generation through muscle activity.

Mild hypothermia produces finer quivering, less obvious to the casual observer, which may affect the victim's ability to speak smoothly and perform fine motor tasks. At this point quick intervention can reverse the process. When shivering and other interventions successfully raise the victim's body heat back toward normal, the trembling will stop. The victim will both feel and appear better, and coordination normalizes.

Moderate hypothermia demands a greater need for heat generation, as the core temperature of the victim remains unchanged or declines. **At this point, call for rescue**. Signs of advancing hypothermia include:

- More intense and coarse trembling, appearing obvious to the observer and interfering with the victim's coordination for ordinary tasks.
- The victim's thought process becomes slower.
- Fine motor tasks become more difficult, such as picking up small objects, (un)tying shoelaces, and using a fork.
- The victim can stand, but their coordination is affected along with steadiness on their feet.
- Severe hypothermia occurs when the core temperature keeps decreasing despite measures to control or reverse it. Shivering will slow down and stop, but the victim's appearance, movements, demeanor, and thought process continue to decline. The difference between improvement and

decline are unmistakable, regardless of whether shivering has stopped or not. **This point identifies where the potential for reversibility in the field has dwindled, and calling for help must happen if not done already**. As rescue teams typically take hours or longer to arrive, the phone call for rescue during the earlier stage of hypothermia will have proven much timelier.

The severely hypothermic patient's body mechanisms begin to slow down. The following occurs in stages as severity continues to worsen:

- Confusion, poor memory
- Physical incoordination
- Inability to stand or walk
- Slower breathing rate and heart rate

Dr. Rob's Notes

Why does shivering stop with worsening hypothermia?

The widespread violent muscle contractions of shivering require an energy source. Muscle glycogen represents the primary fuel for this body reaction, but the limited glycogen stores become depleted after time, depending on the individual. Circulating blood glucose (sugar) becomes a secondary source for muscle contractions. When the fuel source becomes exhausted, then the shivering mechanism for heat generation slows down and ceases.

Shivering represents a short-lived window of opportunity to generate body heat while capitalizing on the ways we can trap it and stop heat loss.

In the next section you will read about my own experience with hypothermia, and the quick actions I took to regain body heat.

- Drowsiness
- Loss of consciousness
- Loss of respirations and pulse
- Death

In the medical world the saying goes "You are not dead unless you are warm and dead" in the context of resuscitation efforts. The heart may still beat—but with imperceptible blood flow—and still support residual brain function, such that a victim may only appear lifeless. In the hands of rescuers and local medical facilities, rapid infusion of warm IV fluids and other active rewarming attempts focus on reviving these victims. We have all heard of hypothermic victims being successfully resuscitated after hours of hypothermia, so these efforts should continue until the core body temperature has risen to normal. The extreme difficulty of accomplishing this in the field makes early calls for rescue that much more important.

Treatment

Principles of treatment of hypothermia include minimizing heat loss and enhancing heat gain. These strategies embody the practical application of the mechanisms for heat transfer, while enhancing body heat production. It cannot be overstated that an early call for rescue when a victim fails to improve with initial treatment or when already in advanced stages leads to a more successful outcome.

Mild hypothermia. The individual feels cold, with teeth chattering and fine shivering that may not be visible. They can walk and perform fine motor skills (using a fork, picking up a cup, untying their shoes). This stage has a high potential for reversal. Things to consider here:

- **Increase activity**. Walking, jumping jacks, doing push-ups or sit-ups, and other physical activity get the muscles contracting and generating heat.
- **Feed victims.** Calories provide fuel to the individual's cells to maintain metabolism-related heat generation. Focus on carbohydrates, which get absorbed quickly, over fats and protein.
- **Hot drinks,** if available, allow us to take advantage of conductive heat transfer from the liquid through the stomach and intestines to the bloodstream.

Moderate hypothermia. Identified by visible, coarse shivering, decreasing steadiness and coordination on their feet, and disruption of fine motor skills (difficulty with [un]tying shoelaces, picking up small objects, and using utensils), moderate hypothermia represents a worse situation with less potential for reversibility. **Strongly consider calling for rescue here**, after which the following can be done:

- **Do not force victims to walk,** as the incoordination may lead to fall and injury. The increased shivering serves the purpose for heat generation.
- **Handle them gently,** as sudden jolts can trigger abnormal heart rhythms.
- **Lay them down**, preferably with the torso and head up at an angle if possible.
- **Feed them and give them hot drinks**, as described above, when conscious and not nauseated.
- **Replace any wet clothing** (socks, base layer/s, etc.) with dry clothes. Taking water off the skin decreases conductive heat loss from the body's surface.
- **Place a beanie on the victim's head** if not already in place.

- **Add clothing layers** to trap radiant heat from the body.
- Shield **the victim from the wind. Set up a tarp to accomplish this** or even place them in a tent to reduce convection-related heat loss.
- **Start a campfire** and place the individual nearby, allowing the radiant heat to transfer to the victim. We can set up the fire close to the open entryway to the tent, with the rainfly off of the vestibule, if the victim remains inside.

Severe hypothermia develops when the victim's core temperature continues to decline in the face of prolonged exposure to the elements and as the result of multiple mechanisms of heat transfer work against them. At this point shivering has slowed or stopped altogether. The patient cannot walk to generate heat. Their level of consciousness has declined, not permitting eating or drinking. **By this time a call should have been made for rescue**, and what we do in the field only attempts to maintain life while awaiting the arrival of a rescue crew. The following can be done:

- Do not attempt to walk the victim.
- Do not force food or fluids, especially with a lethargic or nauseated patient.
- Follow the other steps as above for moderate hypothermia.
- **Place the victim inside a sleeping bag**, if available, on top of an insulated sleeping pad. Use a tarp or large quilt, if available, to **make a "burrito"** around the hiker and the sleeping bag. This maximizes trapping of radiant heat escaping the body, while eliminating conduction- and convection-related heat loss.
- **Fill a hydration bladder or Nalgene bottle with heated liquid and place underneath the layers of clothing** (but not directly on the skin, to prevent burning) to act like a

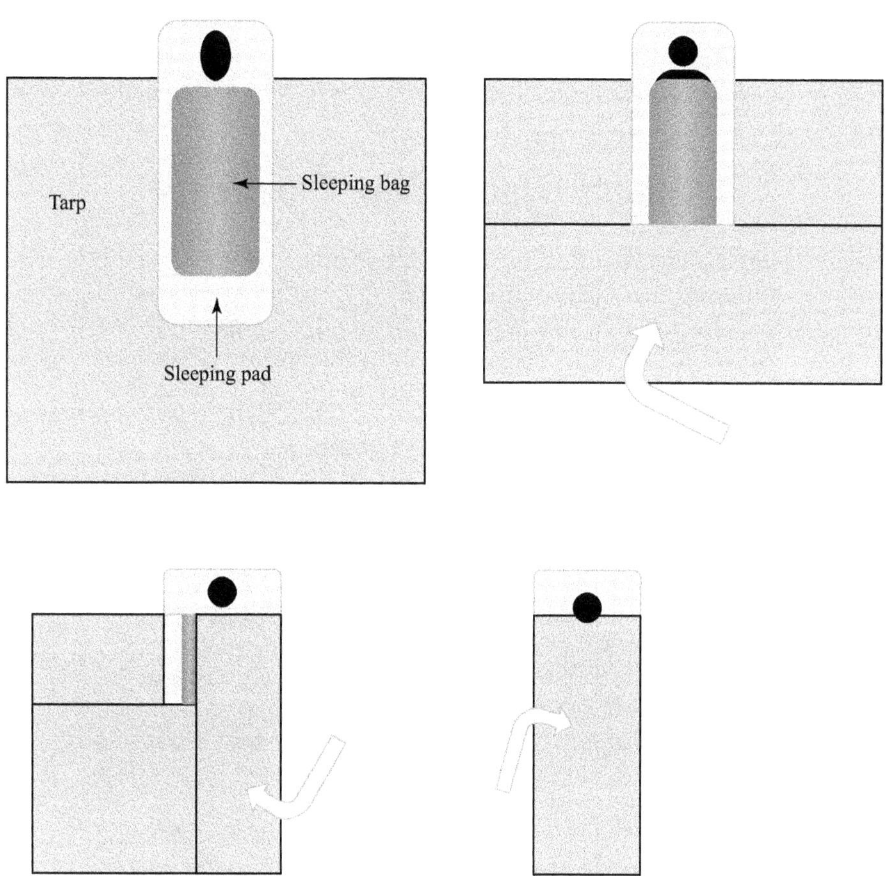

1. With a tarp or emergency blanket laid out, place an insulated sleeping pad on top, if available. The patient is placed in a sleeping bag on top of the mattress, with their head positioned over the top of the tarp.
2. Fold the bottom of the tarp over the victim and sleeping bag.
3. Fold one of the sides over the victim in their sleeping bag.
4. Fold the other side over the victim.

To facilitate transport while keeping the "burrito" intact, a roping method can be used to secure the tarp snugly around the victim.

hot water bottle, transferring heat into the body by conduction.

- Air-activated **hand warmers** can be placed in the armpits or in the groin (for conductive heat transfer to the victim).

Dr. Rob's Hypothermia Experience

Day 6, Lemosho Route, Mt. Kilimanjaro. After a four-limb climb up the steep Barranco Wall, a near 900-foot shelf of ancient volcanic lava flow, we emerged triumphant to the top. After a short celebration and refueling we proceeded on the route toward Barafu Camp, sitting at 15,000 feet. Our optimism for the day ahead came to an early halt when clouds quickly covered the sky, followed by an hours-long storm. The monsoon-like rain overwhelmed my rain gear, such that I could feel the water running down my legs and into my boots.

By the time we arrived at camp I was completely soaked through. The cold temperature and winds at this new altitude only added to the misery, even with the rain having stopped. I headed right to the mess tent and sipped on a cup of hot chocolate. Despite my drink, my teeth began to chatter, and large muscle groups started to twitch all over with increasing frequency and intensity, all within 10 minutes. I knew where this was headed and had to act fast.

I got out of the mess tent and shuffled my trembling legs to get to my tent. These clothes were soaking wet, so first order of business was getting inside and taking my wet clothes off. After the struggle to untie my boot laces, I removed everything. I used a chamois to dry my skin and rifled through my duffel to find a dry set of clothes. Now in a full-body shiver, I donned the new set of clothes and layered up with what I had.

I got into my sleeping bag, downed a carbohydrate-heavy bar, and isometrically contracted large muscle groups of my body until I slowly recovered from what was an early case of moderate hypothermia.

Prevention

Prevention of hypothermia empowers us to take control over the environmental factors that only serve to extract heat from our body. Rather than scrambling under the circumstances to undo hypothermia, avoiding this pitfall in the first place proves to be the better strategy. While on-trail we use the above strategies to optimize heat generation and retention. The process begins with the pre-hike planning and strategy though.

- **Review the trail map ahead of time**. Become familiar with the route, landmarks along the way (lakes and creeks, vista points, etc.), and where other trails break off. Know what to expect ahead of time; bring the map along and refer to it along the way. Avoiding becoming lost minimizes the time spent out in cold conditions and hypothermia risk.
- **Know the weather forecast**, and what trail conditions to expect from the sources listed above. Consider calling the ranger station or referring to recent trail reviews on a trail app for the latest information on trail conditions.
- **Come prepared to dress for the highest *and lowest* temperatures as forecasted**. Be ready to add layers when gaining significant elevation, feeling higher winds, and dropping temperatures.
- **Strongly consider base layers for cold conditions**. How cold? While somewhat subjective, the further it gets below about 40° F the more benefit base layers provide.
- Remember that **multiple layers** insulate better than just one or two. Always pack an extra layer appropriate to the anticipated possibilities, accounting for wind, rain, or snow.
- **Wear dark-colored outer layers** to absorb the radiant heat from the sun and add warmth to the insulating layers. A fleece or wool hat prevents heat loss from the scalp, which

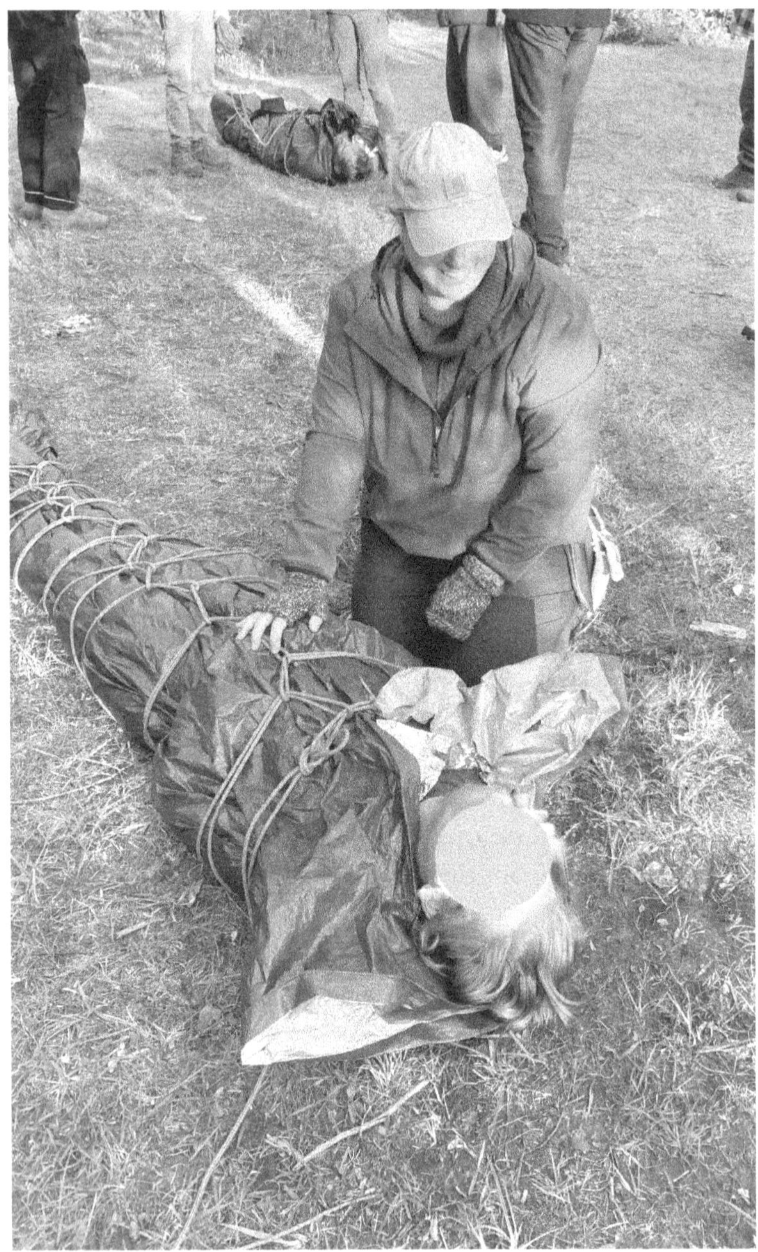

Students of Dr. Teimojin Tan (Instagram—@survival.doctors), a physician and finalist in season 9 of *Alone*, in his wilderness survival course (www .survivenow.online) practicing wrapping one another up in a "burrito." Dr. TEIMOJIN TAN

will otherwise serve as a source for heat loss to the environment. Bring gloves, preferably water- and windproof.

- Figure out the **hydration strategy** ahead of time. Plan to bring heated fluids (herbal tea, soup, hot electrolyte hydration drinks [Yes, some really like them!], etc.), while avoiding too much caffeine. Use insulated steel containers or insulating sleeves for Nalgene-type water bottles. Have a plan and means to heat up fluids along the route, whether by campfire or a fuel stove.
- When hiking in frigid temperatures, **consider wearing sock liners** underneath heavier weight wool socks. Good-fitting and worn in boots with Gore-Tex waterproofing and 400 to 600 grams of insulation, sock liners provide great protection in snowy terrain.

While on-trail:

- **Vary layers and pace** to optimize heat retention and generation, respectively.
- Maintain the generation of body heat through **eating snacks** along the way. Include proteins, as they appear to have more thermogenic effect than carbohydrates or fats do.

Maintaining Body Temperature

Temperature and climate remain in flux, making predictability the exception rather than the rule. This variability holds true throughout most of the landmass of the Earth, whether referring to intraday or seasonal fluctuations in the same region, or those between locations. A simple forecast tells us very little about how the day's weather will unfold in any one locale, especially in mountainous areas, which generate their own atypical and unforecasted weather patterns.

Preserving body temperature remains one of our major goals while venturing outdoors, regardless of the conditions. While mild deviations in weather and temperature pose little threat to our ability to accomplish this, exploring the backcountry in cold or hot temperatures poses a much greater challenge. Fighting the forces trying to alter our body temperature comes through strategy to repel the known elements and to prepare for possible sudden changes in the conditions. We can experience wide fluctuations in climate through any 24-hour period, depending on time of day, location, and altitude. Arriving ready for these changes with the ability to adjust accordingly proves essential for success.

Those native to a hiking location approach their strategy with more confidence than first-time or occasional visitors. Out-of-towners arrive without the awareness of the typically atypical weather patterns and come only prepared for the predicted forecast, only to get caught off-guard when things suddenly change. Locals have no guarantee of success in prepping for the weather, but applying their experience and forethought places them in an advantaged position. Remaining humble about hiking readiness serves us well, however. Regional expertise no longer applies when one travels to another climate, as we now become the out-of-towner, subject to the variables unique to that location. Dressing for the conditions and equipping ourselves for sudden changes in weather becomes a skill to acquire. Each new hike offers varying elements, so the strategy often changes.

The strategy begins **before** the hike. Gain an understanding of the baseline conditions of the area first. Most only look at the weather forecast before traveling, but it often changes as hike time approaches and may not apply to where the hike will actually take place. Forecasts often pertain to the conditions in the nearest city center or local airport and not necessarily those in the hiking areas and surrounding mountains. When hiking at an altitude significantly different from the center of the forecast, expect very different weather than the forecast calls for.

- Research the location and seasonal timing of the outing. Determine the feasibility of the typical conditions based on personal abilities and expectations.
- Look thoroughly into the typical and usual unforecasted weather patterns for that location and season.

Arriving unprepared for typical weather variations can determine the difference between our expectations for the trip and the actual outcome. Not only can this lead to disappointment, such as planning a trip to Colorado in August and arriving with hot weather gear to hike a first 14er, then getting caught in a snowstorm at the summit, but not anticipating the nuances of weather can lead to outcomes that amount to much more than regret. Unwitting adventurers find themselves in such circumstances every week. How do we avoid being one of them? Doing the research ahead of time and packing solid clothing options for protection against all reasonable weather aberrations provides the answer. Taking ownership over our safe return from our adventures involves doing the prep work in advance.

Weather forecast reports represent the cornerstone to our strategy to defy aberrant climate. These can come from numerous sources, including local news reports and internet-based inquiries. Having this knowledge to prepare ourselves and gear ahead of time based on those details places us in an advantaged position over having done so based on expectation and routine.

- Know the forecast for the location nearest to where the hike or backpacking route begins and ends, if far off from one another.
- When anticipating significant elevation gain along the path, also search for the forecast of the highest altitude in the itinerary.

The knowledge we gain from this research provides the basis for our strategy to maintain body temperature through the outing. When we know what to expect, we know what to plan for. Numerous internet-based sources can provide this, but the following sites provide great information:

- The National Oceanic and Atmospheric Administration (**www.noaa.gov**) provides a forecast for nearly every town or zip code in the US, including satellite imagery, plus ocean and coastal conditions.
- **Mountain-forecast.com** provides invaluable data on weather conditions and forecasts for more than eleven thousand mountain summits throughout the world.
- The Weather Network (**www.theweathernetwork.com**) provides detailed forecasts throughout Canada and the US, Europe, as well as Australia and India.

Weather Research Example

We intend to hike the Longs Peak Trail in Colorado, in the Rocky Mountain National Park Wilderness. From the trailhead to the summit, we will ascend from about 9,400 feet to a 14,259-foot elevation. The weather at the trailhead will differ greatly from that we will experience as we approach the summit.

The nearest town on the map, Estes Park, Colorado, sits at 8,000 feet. The modest elevation difference between there and the trailhead makes the forecast for this town close to baseline conditions at the beginning of the hike.

- Search the forecast for Estes Park, Colorado, to get an idea of the conditions we expect early in the hike.
- Separately search the forecast for Longs Peak itself to know what to expect as we approach the summit.

Research these and other reliable sources for weather conditions in the location of interest. Cross-reference multiple sources for this information whenever available, as different weather models may yield varying results. Now that we know what to expect to experience on the ground, we can use this to our advantage to pack and prepare our gear accordingly.

Clothing Choice

Clothing choice, and specifically fabric type, begins our strategy to resist the weather and not become a victim of it. Having become familiar with the mechanisms of heat transfer, we either need to enhance or impede these mechanisms, depending on the conditions on the trail. Using clothing as a tool in this effort significantly impacts how well or how poorly we can preserve our body temperature among the climate that surrounds us. We cannot control the weather, but we can exert some control over how the weather affects us. Overlooking this important aspect of cold weather hiking can lead to disaster, as was the case for two hikers found deceased around Christmas 2024. The 59- and 37-year-olds set out on Christmas Eve Day in the Gifford Pinchot National Forest in a quest to find Sasquatch. A 3-day search through the grueling Washington State winter weather ended in the discovery of their remains, with reports depicting inadequate clothing, layers, and other gear to resist the snow and extreme cold. Wearing the right type of fabric and using the correct clothing strategy while out in the cold backcountry often means the difference between a successful hike and a tragic one.

Cotton remains the top fabric choice for warmth and comfort in our off-trail lives, but it should never be worn while hiking out in the wilderness. This applies to denim, t-shirts, flannels, underwear, and socks. While fine for a casual walk among the trees, trekking in the backcountry otherwise involves sweating and exposure to weather and other sources for moisture, the setting in which cotton becomes our enemy. When wet, this fabric retains moisture that weighs the cloth down to our body, keeping the skin wet and disabling its ability to function normally. Our skin becomes unable to retain heat in the cold weather and less capable of releasing heat in hot weather. When in this situation and having no other choice but to keep hiking, the wet and adherent fabric also causes friction on the skin and chaffing of the mobile areas of the body such as the armpits and groin, inviting skin infections and pain, and limiting hiking in the days that follow. Wet cotton socks cause sores on the ankles, toes, and heels, rendering us unable to walk past a certain point due to the pain and limiting our ability to exit the woods. Cotton offers little insulating defense against windy conditions as well, even when dry. For all the above reasons avoid wearing any cotton until after the hiking/exercising has been completed.

Wool has become known as the best natural fiber for moisture-wicking and insulating fabrics. Wicking of moisture from the body maintains dryness of the skin, allowing excess heat to escape while minimizing penetration of cold air. Its natural odor-resistant properties make it feasible to wear the same articles of clothing multiple days in a row without losing friends. Wool was notorious in the past for a coarse and itchy feel on the skin and was avoided by many. Merino wool, more recently discovered in New Zealand and brought to the rest of the world, has gained popularity with outdoor adventurers over the last twenty years. This version of wool has a smooth, soft, and comfortable feel on the skin, much like cotton. Today this has become the most common type of wool worn during outdoor activities that require the advantage of this fabric. Wool clothing has typically been associated with use in colder climates in the form of base layers and mid-layers, to take advantage of the fabric's insulating properties, but thinner weight Merino wool products offer an advantage in hot weather as well due to its wicking properties and breathability. Wool socks offer the same qualities as the body clothing does, with varying thicknesses and weights appropriate to any hiking climate. Merino wool underwear also offers an inherent advantage over other fabrics due to its unique properties.

Other natural fiber clothing appropriate for outdoor adventure includes silk, which was a preferred base layer and sock fabric back in the days when traditional wool was unbearable to wear. Still available today, silk clothing and socks have become harder to find since the emergence of Merino wool but may offer a viable alternative to those whose skin remains sensitive to all wool products. In recent years Alpaca "wool" has entered the stage, offering soft and comfortable hollow fibers, exerting a greater insulating property than the same weight of lamb's wool. This fabric offers near water resistance, with great wicking and ventilating capabilities. Due to limitation of sourcing and processing, clothing made from this fiber comes at a higher price point. Clothing made from renewable hemp fibers has emerged recently, offering soft, durable options with good wicking and ventilation properties with a linen-like appearance.

Synthetics, such as polyester, nylon, and others (either alone or blended with one another) offer a great alternative to natural fibers for hiking and exercising in general. Their moisture-wicking properties allow for efficient evaporation of water off the skin, and they dry quickly, even after rain or immersion in water. Synthetic material typically stretches as we move, preventing friction in the mobile parts of our body. Synthetics come in all clothing options, from underwear, base layers, and sock liners to fleece mid-layers and outerwear. Mostly used in hotter climates for their excellent ventilating properties, thinner synthetic tops and bottoms have a natural cooling effect. Heavier weight synthetics, on the other hand, prove very effective as base layers, fleece, and other mid-layers, offering great insulating properties for cold climates. Outer "shell" jackets, typically made from synthetic material, repel wind and precipitation, offering further protection from the elements. The natural breathability allows excess moisture and heat to escape, reducing the chances for overheating and sweating underneath it all.

Which fabrics we choose to wear for traversing the trails, between natural and synthetic, may boil down to cost, availability, and other factors. Knowing the fabric types we should consider wearing out there, we can develop a strategy for resisting the weather conditions when applying the right clothing to the appropriate climate.

Clothing cost becomes an important issue when contemplating the best gear and clothing options for our adventures. The big names in hiking, backpacking, and mountaineering offer great products but the high-end gear sits beyond the monetary reach for many would-be hikers. Many Gore-Tex hard shell jackets can run $450 to $600 and upward, for instance. Investing this much in one item to be used just a few times per year gets unreasonable, but when alpine mountaineering most weekends for months out of each year, then the spend proves wise for a much-needed piece of gear. The cost of this clothing may otherwise encourage some to take their chances while dressed in lower-cost cotton clothes on the trails is understandable, but a middle ground exists. Understanding what reasonable protection we need for the potential hazards we face can help to minimize wasting money on unneeded items. We want to utilize our invested dollars in the most useful and cost-effective manner, while procuring the most protective and durable clothing possible. Catching holiday and season-end sales, both online and at name-brand outlet stores, allows us to accumulate good quality gear on the cheap. These season-end sale items may sit idle in the closet until next year approaches, but having them for when the time comes ensures we're just as ready for less money! Most items last for years to come when treated well, so the low rate of replacement helps the wallet too. Reading through real consumer gear reviews helps find a certain item's weak spots, and some reviews may offer better and more affordable alternatives. Rather than go for the top well-known brands, some lesser-known companies make great clothing that performs equally well, from base layers and mid-layers to down-filled jackets, shells, and beyond, at a lower price. Strategizing about what we need for specific activities and climates can help us invest in the right items with the least cost to us.

Clothing Strategy for Cold Weather Hiking

A clothing strategy for cold weather hiking focuses on trapping most of the radiant body heat we emit, while allowing the excess to escape, minimizing convection-related heat loss and capturing radiant heat from the sun. This strategy involves a more complex method than for hot weather hiking, as all the forces of heat transfer work to reduce our body temperature toward that which surrounds us.

Layering represents the key to maintaining warmth in colder climates. Multiple layers of thin and insulating clothing minimize heat loss via radiation by trapping the warm air that emerges from our skin and maintaining it in contact with the body surface. Layering also helps in resisting heat loss through convection by creating a barrier between our skin and the cold wind coming at us. Breathable fabrics allow for release of excess heat while we're on the move, and their moisture-wicking properties remove sweat to keep the skin dry. How we layer affects our success in this effort.

Base layers conform to the body but avoid fitting tightly to the skin. This first line of defense, made of natural or synthetic material, keeps the skin dry and provides a space within the thickness of the fabric where warm air radiating from the skin becomes trapped. Consider both a bottom and top base layer, especially on cold, windy, or snowy days when we choose to venture out in such conditions. As the temperatures drop further and the cold wind whips faster, base layers become increasingly essential for building our resistance to winter weather.

Mid-layers function to maintain the trapping of warm air in the base layer underneath it, as heat otherwise tends to escape.

Generally, "mids" come as tops only, to maintain the temperature in the upper half of the body. This cold weather essential, made from natural or synthetic material and thicker than the base layer, varies between a sweater, a fleece, or a puffy jacket. These come as a pullover or as a quarter- to full-zip top, with or without a hood. Getting this layer right allows trapping of enough heat underneath to maintain body temperature, while still maintaining the capacity for excess heat to dissipate.

On colder outings without high winds, rain, or snow, some may employ a double mid-layer strategy, which can vary between multiple options. Wearing a thick wool or synthetic pullover under a fleece jacket offers great warmth retention and breathability. During outings when we expect a high degree of energy expenditure, we should anticipate an equal amount of heat production. Trapping too much heat causes sweating, becoming the last thing we want. Using mid-layers that unzip at least part of the way enables us to control the amount of heat we trap, or dump to maintain the goal of feeling cool. Personal preference otherwise comes out of trial and error. We get to find out what works for us, as we can stop along the way and adjust to our needs in the moment.

Pants, worn over our bottom base layer, should we choose to wear one, come with several options, depending on the conditions. When we expect dry to at-most light rain or windy conditions, breathable, synthetic pants are best, some of which come with a water-repellant coating. When facing an increasing threat of frigid and windy conditions fleece-lined pants offer an advantage over plain ones, providing a mid-layer concept to the lower body. "Hard shell" pants, made of wind- and storm-repellant material and slipped over plain bottoms, offer the highest level of bottom protection against harsh elements.

Outer layers, generally a puffy jacket worn over our mid-layer, offers further air trapping when needed while offering added protection against light precipitation and wind, neither of which mids can offer. These insulated layers remain an option, depending on the conditions and amount of heat we expect to generate along our way. Many choose to stow a puffy in their pack to wear only for heat retention while idle during snack and meal breaks and place it back in their pack when heading out on foot again. This strategy allows us to take advantage of it when needed.

Shell layers prove useful in colder climates and come as two types. Soft shells, made of synthetic and flexible material with a light fleece lining, prove useful as an outer layer and alternative to a puffy, capable of repelling light precipitation and wind while insulating us from heat loss by way of convection. The outer fabric is stitched and somewhat porous to allow for breathability, allowing excess heat to escape. Soft shells fall short in stormy weather and high winds, both of which tend to penetrate these outer layers. Hard shells, made from multiple thin layers of synthetic material, repel heavy precipitation, block high winds, and resist stormy weather. All have an abrasion-resistant exterior layer (hence the term "hard shell"). More expensive options utilize a Gore-Tex membrane in the middle, while other technologies offer a comparable moisture barrier that "breathes" for a lesser investment. Hard shells offer more weatherproofing and less breathability than soft shells do, so they run the risk of trapping more heat in and promoting sweating during strenuous activity. Better options among hard shells offer zippers in the armpits to shed excess heat while protecting us from the elements. High altitude hiking in colder seasons and climates, known for cold temperatures, high winds, and unforecasted storms, calls for having a hard shell with us for protection from a miserably wet or near-freezing situation.

Regulating Our Own Body Temperature

In both hot and cold temperatures, regulating our own body temperature involves the hiker taking an active role in the process. Doing so represents a practical application of the scientific concepts surrounding body heat gain and loss. This skill allows us

Cold Weather Layering

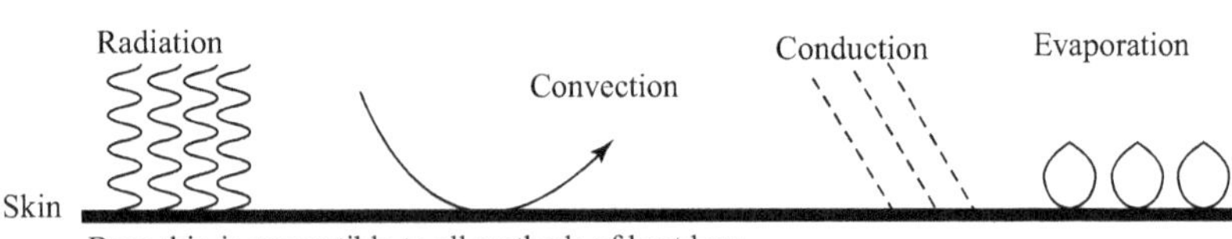

Bare skin is susceptible to all methods of heat loss.

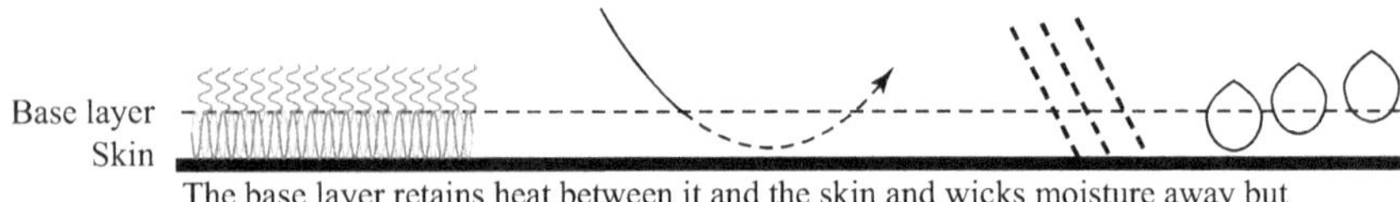

The base layer retains heat between it and the skin and wicks moisture away but offers no protection against Convective and Conductive forces (wind and rain/snow).

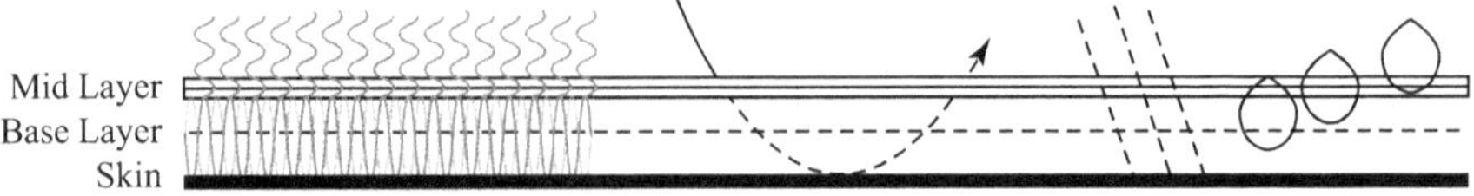

The mid layer adds further heat retention while releasing the excess and further assists with moisture wicking. The mid offers a little help against Convection and no protection against Conduction

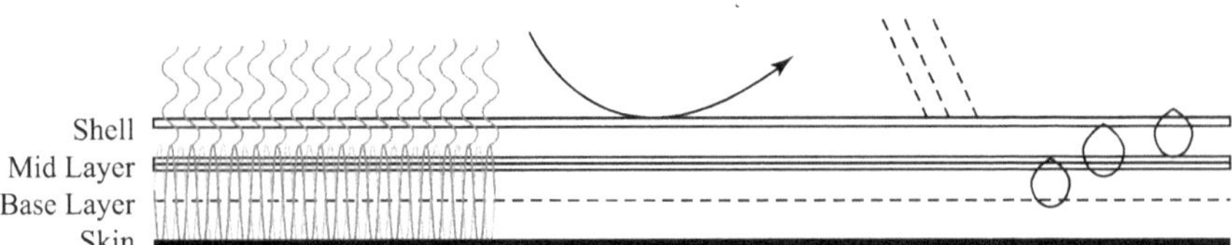

A shell adds protection against Convective and Conductive heat loss,while adding further heat retention. This layer still releases excess heat

Dr. Rob's Layers for His Kilimanjaro Summit

We began the hike from Barafu Camp (15,330 ft elevation) beginning at 11:00 PM in near-freezing temperatures. We ascended for 7 hours, arriving to Uhuru Peak (19,341 ft) at 5:45 AM in -20° C, with high winds. My layering strategy:

- Base: top and bottom, synthetic
- Mid: thick synthetic, hooded top, and fleece-lined pants
- Outer: down, hooded puffy jacket, 850-fill power
- Shell: hooded jacket (worn over the puffy jacket) and pants
- Head: beanie and all three hoods over it
- Hands: double gloves (right glove off in picture so I could access my phone)

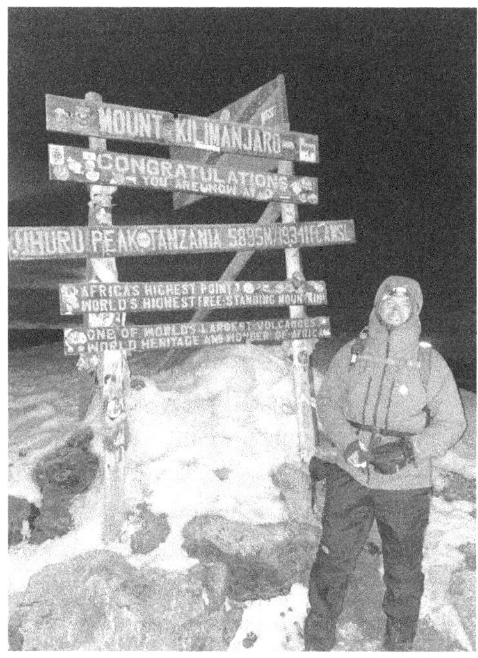

to exert better control over body heat retention and release, based on our needs at the time. Without the proper clothing choices, hydration strategy, and working knowledge of how to regulate our body temperature while out in nature, the elements have the upper hand. Coming prepared places more control in our hands over how the elements affect us. Three practical applications of the scientific concepts enable us to use this skill to our advantage.

Hydration plays a key role in preventing dehydration and in body temperature regulation, regardless of the conditions. Providing the cells with water allows them to function as heat-producing factories and enables the muscles to meet the demands of our outing, as they ramp up the heat production on the move. Furthermore, the temperature of the liquid we drink either adds or subtracts heat from our bodies while in our stomach and intestines. Drinking hot liquids (coffee, tea, soup, etc.) along the route allows the heat to transfer into our bodies by conduction and serves as an additional resisting force against the cold weather. Insulated containers make maintaining the temperature of the liquid easier than noninsulated bottles.

Varying effort helps us regulate our body heat production while on the move. Muscles generate body heat as they contract. More intense and frequent muscle contractions generate a higher level of body heat. We have no control over environmental temperature, but the rate at which we push our bodies represents a modifiable factor for us to control our own body heat production among those conditions. On average, hikers move at a pace of 2 to 2.5 miles per hour (3.2 to 4 km/h), but hiking speed varies between uphills, downhills, and flats, and during season-specific activities such as snowshoeing. Despite this average pace some naturally hike slower than this, while others hike at a naturally faster rate. Tracking our individual average speed during these differing situations provides a personal baseline, which becomes a useful tool for adjusting speed to raise or reduce heat generation per our needs in the moment. Having a smartwatch, app, or other technology to track our pace in real time may be helpful. In general:

- Feeling cold? Increase the hiking pace.
- Feeling like you're overheating? Slow down the hiking pace.

The goal while hiking in cold temperatures is to feel slightly cool. Maintaining this objective helps us avoid heating up to the point where we begin to sweat and create excessive moisture underneath our layers. Though our clothing can wick that moisture away, this decreases the insulative properties of the clothing and eventually exposes us to the effects of the cold air. Sweating and subsequent loss of body heat to the environment poses a significant risk factor for hypothermia. Maintaining vigilance and avoiding feeling overheated enables us to prevent this complication. We cannot measure our core body temperature while out in the backcountry, so remaining mindful of the goal to feel slightly cool represents our best strategy. When we feel like we're heating up beyond that point on the trek, slowing our hiking pace (try reducing it by 0.5 mi/h or 1.5 km/h increments) decreases heat production and returns us toward feeling slightly cool again. If on the other hand we feel cold despite having layered well, increasing the hiking pace (by the same increments) generates more internal heat and elevates us toward how we need to feel. We may find ourselves purposely adjusting our pace up and down through the course of any outing in the cold.

Varying layers during cold weather hiking relies on adding, subtracting, or opening layers to trap more body heat or release it in a controlled fashion to maintain feeling slightly cool among the frigid conditions. Just as varying our hiking pace helps to fine-tune our heat production, varying our layers serves the same purpose. The more the layers trap warmth beneath them, the greater the potential for accumulating heat. We can easily decrease the

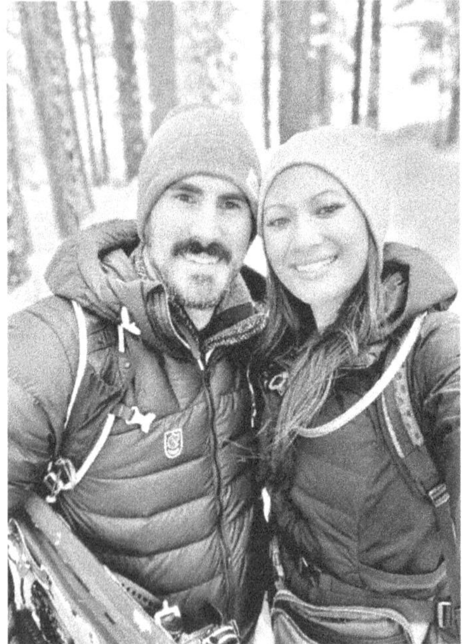

Rachel and Mike Obendorf (@rachelobendorf and @miobe1 [Instagram]) layered up to resist the winter weather while adventuring in the Lake Tahoe area.
RACHEL AND MICHAEL OBENDORF

Dr. Rob's Tip: Fueling Up for Heat Production in Cold Weather

Maintaining the metabolic rate and ability to produce heat requires fuel, primarily in the form of calories. What we eat prior to the hike becomes utilized in 1 to 2 hours, depending on multiple factors, but fueling along the route maintains heat production. Eating snacks along longer routes (more than 4–5 mi) keeps our internal furnace burning in cold weather. Paying attention to ingesting a higher ratio of carbohydrates to protein and fats provides an essential substrate for fueling the metabolism and active muscles. While carbohydrates provide the glycogen that the muscles burn for fuel, proteins exert a heat-generating effect as these more complex molecules require more work by the body to break down into digestible form.

efficiency of the layers by simply opening them up and allowing some heat to escape, and at times when feeling a bit overheated, we may even take a layer away. Adding a layer, on the other hand, helps increase the efficiency of capturing heat and resisting the elements.

Instinct drives us to "bundle up" when feeling cold and to shed layers when we feel warm, so the building blocks for this skill exist in all of us. The layers we have chosen for the outing may or may not work well in reality, so never stick to a plan that isn't working. Paying attention to how we feel and adjusting pace and layers as they suit our needs represents the best plan of action to maintain the goal of feeling slightly cool. Rather than making large changes that lead to a proportionate response and risk overcompensation, consider small and incremental changes. This can make enough of a difference to fine-tune body temperature control. The amount of change usually varies throughout our hike in frigid temperatures, due to required effort and topography. Maintaining flexibility to adjust our layers and pace as those needs evolve can make enough of a difference in many circumstances.

Bottom Line

Those of us who explore the outdoors find ourselves immersed in uncomfortable weather conditions with varying frequency. During these pursuits we knowingly place ourselves in potentially adverse weather conditions. Knowing how the specific settings affect our ability to maintain a normal body temperature allows us to utilize the four mechanisms of heat transfer to counteract these forces and arrive with an advantage over them. Recognizing when the weather has the upper hand on ourselves, or another individual, empowers us to intervene quickly and prevent loss of life. Pre-adventure preparation includes anticipating this possible peril, appropriate to the location and season and using the scientific concepts to our advantage. Doing so places our fate in our own hands rather than leaving our safety to chance. This empowers us to minimize the threat of adverse weather and to return home safely so we can plan the next adventure.

- Know the mechanisms of heat transfer to then apply the weather strategy accordingly.
- Understand the risks of heat illness and its association with dehydration.
- Recognize the symptoms and signs of heat illness and basic strategies to treat it in the field.
- Consider early morning starts for hot weather hikes and wear light-colored clothing to resist accumulating radiant heat from the sun.
- Utilize shade and adjust hiking pace to resist accumulation of heat during hot weather hikes.
- Recognize the signs and stages of hypothermia and the principles of treatment in the field.
- Research the forecast for all elevations along the route and come prepared for both the highest and lowest temperatures.
- Choose the proper clothing for the circumstances.
- Hydration and calories allow for body temperature regulation and fuel the muscles to complete the trek.
- Choose a layering strategy that suits the needs during cold weather hikes and consider wearing darker colored outer layers to absorb radiant heat from the sun.
- Place additional layers, such as a puffy jacket and/or a shell, in the pack for cold weather hikes to have the option to react to the weather and heat-trapping needs at the time.

References

Coris, Eric E., et al. "Heat Illness Symptom Index (HISI): A Novel Instrument for the Assessment of Heat Illness in Athletes." *Southern Medical Journal* 99, no. 4 (April 2006): 340–345.

Dejanović, Božidar, et al. "Multi-System Complications of Accidental Hypothermia: A Case Report." *Medicinski Pregled / Medical Review* 73, no. 11/12 (November 2020): 388–392.

Dow, J., G. G. Giesbrecht, D. F. Danzl, et al. "Wilderness Medical Society Clinical Practice Guidelines for the Out-of-Hospital Evaluation and Treatment of Accidental Hypothermia: 2019 Update." *Wilderness & Environmental Medicine* 30, 4S (2019): S47–S69.

Foggle, John L. "Accidental Hypothermia: 'You're Not Dead Until You're Warm and Dead.'" *Rhode Island Medical Journal* 102, no. 1 (February 2019): 28–32.

Fudge, Jesse, MD. "Exercise in the Cold." *Sports Health* 8, no. 2 (March 2016): 133–139.

Gasparrini, A., et al. "Mortality Risk Attributable to High and Low Ambient Temperature: A Multicountry Observational Study." *Lancet* 386, no. 9991 (July 2015): 369–375.

Gates, Zoe. "Here's How to Avoid Heat Exhaustion on a Hike." *Backpacker*, August 20, 2021.

Hess, Jeremy J., et al. "Summertime Acute Heat Illness in U.S. Emergency Departments from 2006 through 2010: Analysis of a Nationally Representative Sample." *Environmental Health Perspectives* 122, no. 11 (November 2014): 1209–1215.

Kinkade, Scott, and Megan Warhol. "Beat the Heat: Identification and Tx of Heat-Related Illness." *Journal of Family Practice* 67, no. 8 (August 2018): 468–472.

Lipman, Grant S., et al. "Wilderness Medical Society Clinical Practice Guidelines for the Prevention and Treatment of Heat Illness: 2019 Update." *Wilderness and Environmental Medicine* 30, 4S (2019): S33–S46.

Ramer, Holly. "Body of Missing Hiker Found in New Hampshire." Associated Press, November 23, 2022.

Raukar, Neha, et al. "Heat Illness: A Practical Primer." *Rhode Island Medical Journal* 98, no. 7 (July 2015): 28–31.

Reingardiene, Dagmara. "Susalimas" [Hypothermia]. *Medicina* (Kaunas, Lithuania) 39, no. 1 (2003): 90–97.

Rubine, J. M. "Death Toll Exceeded 70,000 in Europe During the Summer of 2003." *Comptes Redus Biologies* 331 (2008): 171–178.

Sharma, Sapna, et al. "Increased Winter Drownings in Ice-Covered Regions with Warmer Winters." *PLoS ONE* 15, no. 11 (November 2020): 1–13.

Zafar, Amina. "Cold Deemed Deadlier than Heat When It Comes to Weather Deaths." CBC News, May 20, 2015.

Skill 3

Crossing Waterways

Real-Life Scenarios

1. Two hikers, S.S. and A.O., encountered the Tule River while in the Sierra Nevadas on April 13, 2017. According to reports, S.S. slipped into the rapidly flowing, chilly water and immediately toppled, careening downstream. Her hiking buddy, A.O., instantly entered the water to save her friend. The body of S.S. was found; the body of A.O. was discovered downstream 10 days after the incident.

2. While hiking in Sequoia National Park on April 22, 2017, K.J. fell into the middle fork of the Kaweah River. The roiling river quickly took the trekker downriver beyond her control. The 21-year-old's body was encountered two miles downstream some days later and extracted by a recovery team.

3. An early summer hike in June 2019 brought an unexpected turn for R.R. as she hiked through Rio Grande National Forest. The 38-year-old rambler reportedly slipped along the bank of the Rio Grande River and became immersed in the swollen and rapidly flowing waterway. Her remains were found miles downstream.

4. Three friends—all experienced backpackers—embarked on a rugged trek leading through the slot canyon of Buckskin Gulch in southern Utah in March 2023. Unseasonal

rainstorms passed through the area during their trip, causing flash flooding in the narrow, sixteen-mile tortuous canyon. A 5-foot-tall wall of water thrust them through the 3-foot-wide slot, slamming and scraping their bodies against the rocky walls for miles. Those at home, concerned about a lack of communication, alerted authorities prompting a helicopter search, which found one of the hikers hypothermic but alive to tell the story. The bodies of the other two were found days later and miles further downstream.

Drowning represents the most common cause of unintentional death in US national parks, at approximately 30 percent of all causes listed. The statistics from the remainder of public outdoor recreation areas of North America remain unclear, due to limited databases, differences in reporting methods, and differing terminology. For example, the word "drowning" has commonly been used to imply a fatal outcome, with "near drowning" emerging as an alternative term to describe recovery of life. To simplify the wording for universal usage, numerous sources propose the definition of drowning as occurring when the victim's airway becomes submerged in water and they require assistance or frank rescue. This simpler definition describes the process rather than the end result.

Using this definition then, "drowning" has only one of three outcomes:

1. Rescue **without** hypoxic (lack of oxygen) brain injury
2. Rescue **with** hypoxic brain injury
3. Death

The circumstances surrounding each occurrence of drowning differ from one another, but these three outcomes essentially imply, in increasing order, how long the victim was submerged and/or how long the victim required resuscitation, and whether those efforts were successful. Regardless of the outcome, both the drowning victim and the rescuer, ordinarily a bystander, both suffer a very traumatic event.

The Threat of Drowning to the Hiker

Drowning in the backcountry most often occurs when encountering streams and rivers traversing the trail and when swimming in lakes along the route. Water volume and rapidity of streams and rivers in most locations depend on environment and season, but these waterways commonly run across or adjacent to mountainous trails. Crossing these bodies of moving water occasionally becomes necessary to reach our destination. Numerous similar crossings exist along well-known paths such as the Pacific Crest Trail (PCT) and are otherwise peppered throughout mountainous regions on the continent. Long, hot days of hiking commonly draw us to dip body parts or our whole self to cool off in these streams that run either perpendicular or parallel to the trail. These circumstances come with multiple potential hazards.

Alpine Lakes

Alpine lakes often become the source for cooling off on long, hot, summer hikes. One relatively universal aspect of these bodies of water is that they are always cold. Most become filled by the runoff of glaciers and summit rains from the peaks above, the force of water often creating currents under the surface, making swimming highly difficult to work against. The body heat lost to the frigid water compounds the peril by decreasing muscular strength to overcome the current. Very strong swimmers are frequently rescued from drowning in these waters, even from less intimidating lakes like Emerald Pool in Yosemite National Park.

Mountain Waterways

Creeks, streams, and rivers fill every spring from the runoff of melting snow in the peaks above, topped by spring rains that follow. Heavier snowfall during winter months brings a larger volume of water into lower elevations when temperatures rise, as opposed to that following milder winters and lighter spring rains. The high season for encountering these river swells typically lasts from spring until midsummer, as most of this frozen reservoir melts and flows downhill during that time. Remember this when planning mountain treks through these seasons! These swollen streams and rivers typically tame toward the end of summer and minimize into fall and winter. This phenomenon does not typically impact arid regions and those surrounded by lowlands to the same extent, but certain waterways such as the Colorado River course far off from their origin, and the flow can reach massive levels. Some research ahead of the hike or backpacking trip helps to maximize awareness.

The excess volume of water in these rivers and streams produces a deeper and swifter-running body of water during the peak season, akin to whitewater rafting conditions. The high volume and force increase the peril for whoever steps in. The hydraulic force of the water can topple trees and move small boulders, so exerting the same effect on a human poses little challenge. During this time, crossing these bodies of water becomes treacherous. Without a human-made or natural bridge traversing the water, we often need to physically get in to make our way to the opposite side, if the stream passes perpendicular to our intended path.

We cannot ordinarily see the bottom and judge the depth through the white, turbulent water from the bank of the stream before stepping in. The depth of these streams and rivers varies along the bottom as a rule, where we may find ourselves ankle-deep for several steps, then experience a sudden increase in depth with the next. Stepping to where the level of the rapidly moving water approaches our knees and deeper both increases our buoyancy and allows hydraulic power to exceed our body weight, easily sweeping an average person off their footing, sending them downstream. The slippery and unstable bed of the stream adds more

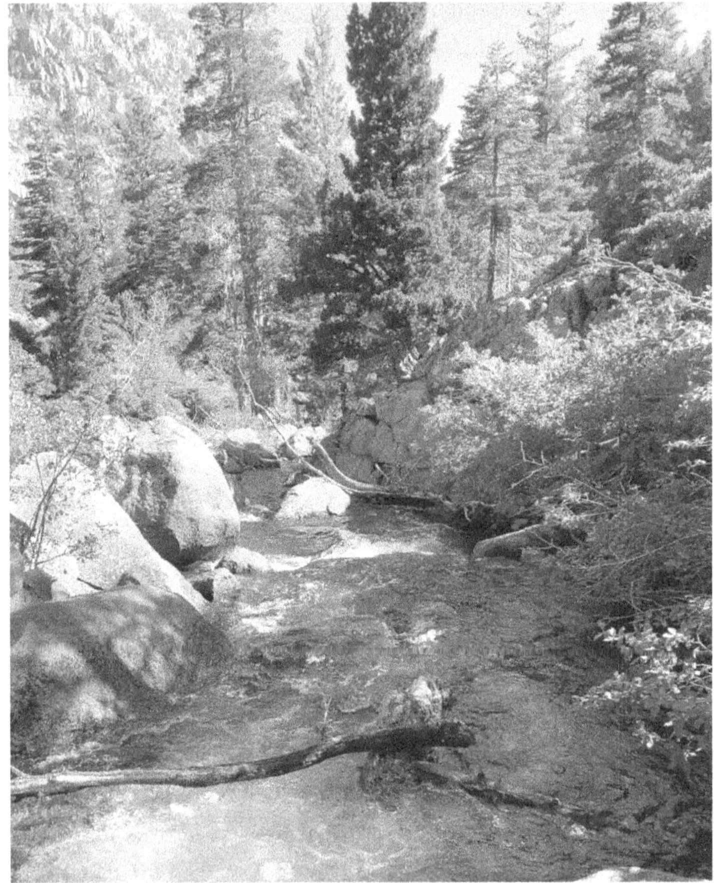

A mountain stream runs fast and deep in the Lake Tahoe area.

likelihood to losing stability and falling into the water already, so it may take much less force to topple us than we might expect.

Everyone who encounters these streams sees the path across in their own unique way. Some attempt hopping between boulders rising above the level of the water in an effort to avoid submerging at all. Others may discover a felled tree across the water and attempt to walk along and over. While this may work out well for most, some may fail in these attempts. These natural bridges may lack stability and traction, leaving the hiker, with an already altered center of gravity and balance from their pack, prone to slipping. Many have fallen off during these attempts due to rolling of the tree or losing their footing on the mossy bark or boulder.

Knowing When and Where to Cross

When we must do so, knowing when and where to cross makes the difference between an unremarkable hike and a tragic one.

Applying Science to the Trail

Submerging our bodies deeper into water increases the amount of water weight that becomes displaced, leading to a rising degree of buoyancy. This causes an escalating degree of weightlessness in the water, increasing the likelihood of floating.

Fluid science suggests the faster the flow of water, the greater the kinetic force it exerts on a submerged object. In the equation that determines the power derived from this kinetic energy ($P=1/2pAv^3$), the speed of running water ("v") is cubed. The area of fluid ("A") takes part in the math as well but only influences power proportional to its rise. Rising water velocity therefore has the greatest influence over the power of the water to move mass and does so in an exponential fashion.

The combination of depth of immersion (degree of buoyancy) and speed of the water are the most significant factors increasing the risk of toppling those who attempt crossing water.

Our best chances for an unremarkable fording involve minimizing our exposure to both factors, but sometimes this cannot be controlled.

Immersing our bodies above the knee in water that flows very slowly poses little risk for our being swept downstream, though we become more buoyant with increasing water depth. Conversely, fast-moving water that measures only a couple of inches deep also poses little risk for our being carried with the current.

Knowing our anticipated route in detail ahead of time prepares us for what we will encounter along the way. Locals to the area know which trails don't require crossing water, and which ones do, and they have the luxury of deciding not to hike on those trails that pose a high risk. The visitor from out of town lacks the deeper knowledge of the area and trails, arriving at a distinct disadvantage. Taking time off from work and spending money on travel and accommodations leaves traveling hikers motivated to proceed with the original plans even under suboptimal conditions to make the most of the time, money, and effort put into the trip. These two factors can exist in conflict.

Essential Pre-Hike Research

Obtain a detailed paper map of the area ahead of time and review the trail and surrounding area from a satellite view online. Studying the trails we intend to explore, their interaction with water, and other potential hazards for that matter provides us the opportunity to make the best pre-trip decision possible in an effort to make the most of the outing and assure an unremarkable trek.

- When a river or stream crosses the trail on the map or satellite images, **search alternative sources** ahead of time for water level reports of rivers and creeks in that region.

Dr. Rob's Suggestion

The **US Geological Survey** (waterdata.usgs.gov) and **Environment Canada** (wateroffice.ec.gc.ca) monitor the depths of most waterways throughout the continent. Check these websites for current and near-future water depths of nearly every creek, stream, and river in their respective countries.

We must know what we are getting into before we step foot on that trail.

- Research trail apps and online forums to determine ahead of time whether bridges, natural or otherwise, exist at these locations.

When: If we discover a deep and rapid river or stream intersecting the desired trail, then strategy will help us succeed.

- **Consider tackling these trails later in the summer and into fall** to experience these paths and cross these rivers/streams with a much lower risk, if possible.
- If we must travel in the spring to early summer, then **consider choosing alternative trails without water crossings to eliminate this potential risk**.
- When forging ahead anyway and deciding to cross based on circumstances in real time, then **leave as early in the morning as possible** to catch the water flow at its lowest and slowest point for the day. Colder temperatures overnight lead to less snow melting from the peaks above and running downhill, so **the flow of the water typically runs slowest and weakest early in the morning**. As temperatures increase after sunrise, flow in these rivers and streams peaks in the late morning into the afternoon, making it the worst time to attempt these crossings. The multiday backpacker should consider plotting out the hike to camp just before encountering the river or creek, such that waking up for an early morning crossing will bring the least depth and rapidity of flow as compared to midday, and the best chance for an unremarkable fording.
- Remember, **the point where the trail meets the river or stream doesn't necessarily identify the best place to cross**, if we decide to forge ahead.

Where: The PCT Association (pcta.org) and other sources provide guidance on fording a river or stream, due to the number of fatal crossing attempts along that trail and others. Online forums and trail app reviews offer more information from other hikers who have trekked the same spots. Invaluable insight can come from this, aiding in our prep for the trip or outing. Consider some basic principles as listed below:

- **Look for dry and more solid-appearing features within the path of the water**, providing a potentially safe crossing. Never trust the stability of a rock or a log, but from the bank of the waterway use a hiking pole, thick stick, or fallen branch to nudge these. If they move, then they are not stable enough to step on.
- **Look for the widest and shallowest area to cross**. Water flow reaches the fastest velocity in the narrowest segments, and slowest in the widest segments of the waterway. This is easily visible from the approaching bank of the stream. The slower water velocity in wider segments exerts much less hydraulic power on those who cross in that spot. If the immediate area does not look wide enough or shallow enough to cross, then **walk up and down the bank to look for an optimal area to cross, or for stable features for footing, such as larger rocks (that can't be moved when nudged) or even a sandbar**. When the water flows slowly, stepping deeper into the water such as knee-level or higher confers less chance of toppling due to the lessened hydraulic force.
- **Straight rivers and streams exhibit the fastest flow and greatest depths in the center**.
- **Curved rivers and streams exhibit their fastest flow and greatest depth on the outside of the curve**.

- If the search for a safe path across comes up empty, then consider turning around and taking an alternate route.

How to Cross a Forceful River or Stream

Getting in and crossing through the water may become necessary at times in our hiking experience. Strategy and technique dramatically increase the chances of an uneventful passage to the opposite bank.

- If anticipating having to traverse the water ahead of time, **consider packing water shoes**. These light and inexpensive foot coverings provide good traction in the water, while keeping our boots and socks dry for the trek on land. We otherwise should keep our boots on rather than going in the water barefoot, as our feet offer little traction along the slimy bed of the creek. Stepping barefooted on sharp rocks makes for sudden unsteadiness and risk for loss of footing as well. Wet boots will eventually dry out.
- **Unbuckle the chest and waist straps of the backpack before stepping in**. In the event of falling into the water, we must ditch the pack. Not having to find and release the buckles while under water allows us to simply slip out of the pack straps. Letting it go downstream leaves us more capable of making our way to the other side and avoid drowning.

The Solo Hiker

When hiking alone, we should have a trekking pole, walking stick, or thick, straight fallen branch with us during crossings. Where we cross should ideally have no visible "strainers" (see next section) or dangerous features immediately downstream from this pathway across, such as a boulder field or a waterfall.

- Through the walk across the bed of this waterway, **the hiker must always face upstream** (facing the direction from where water comes at us).
- **Keep feet at shoulder distance apart, leaning into the oncoming water flow**.
- With the hiking pole or branch in our dominant hand, we **counteract the force coming at us by pushing the end of that pole/stick into the riverbed behind us.** This reinforces us in an upright and forward position against the current coming at us. If we keep the pole/branch in front of us, which some do and advocate, nothing prevents us from falling backward with the water current.
- Placing the bracing pole/branch in a new spot behind us, we then **shuffle slowly across, assuring one stable sidestep at a time** and repeat until we arrive at the opposite side.

Crossing a deep, rapid mountain stream as a solo hiker in Colorado.

Two or More Hikers

Multiple hikers should cross together in a way that minimizes the hydraulic force on the most vulnerable in the group (the smallest, lightest, and least strong). This can be accomplished in two ways:

- The first method resembles that outlined for the solo hiker, but **the group forms a single-file line, running parallel to the flow of water, with the largest/heaviest/strongest hiker in the front** and the others behind in descending order of size.
- The lead hiker leans on their pole/branch in front of them for this method, while **each person in line will support the person in front of them from behind with their outstretched arm on that person's shoulder.** The rear-most individual may brace themself using a pole/branch behind them, such as the solo hiker, if they choose.

A. Cross section of a solo hiker crossing water. Facing and leaning toward the incoming flow of water they sidestep until reaching the opposite side.

B. Cross section of two hikers crossing water, both facing and leaning into the flow of water. In single file, the one behind places their hand on the shoulder of the hiker in front. They both sidestep until reaching the opposite side, using their poles to brace their positioning.

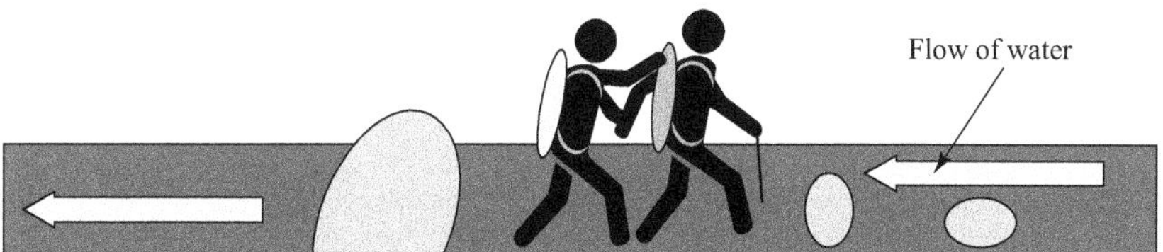

- **Everyone takes a shuffling step to the side together,** working in unison until they have arrived at the opposite bank of the stream. Communication keeps everyone aware of when the next step will come.
- The second method, better for a larger group with a mix of hiker ages, entails **forming an arrowhead**, pointing in the upstream direction (into the flow of the water) with the largest/strongest/heaviest hikers at the tip and on the outside edges of the arrowhead, with the smallest/lightest hikers (children, adolescents, or elderly) inside the arrow.

- **All members of the group lean into the direction of the flow of water** and brace those in front of them if possible. As in the first method, the rear-most individuals may choose to use a pole/branch to brace themselves on the downstream side.
- **Everyone shuffles over in unison**, assuring stable footing and coordinating one step to the side at a time until reaching the opposite bank of the stream.

Falling into the Water

Falling into water that runs deeply and swiftly breeds trouble. Once in the rapids the now anxious and surprised hiker suddenly experiences a water temperature much colder than anticipated, producing a natural gasping reflex regardless of whether their head is above water or not. The entire surface area of the body and attached gear becomes instantly exposed to the hydraulic power of the current. The swollen and rapidly moving water sweeps victims downstream beyond their control, further weighed down by their drenched pack, if it is not ditched. This renders the individual unable to control their direction in the water and unable to stay afloat. The force of the water tosses them into "strainers" strewn beneath the water's surface. These unseen logs, large rocks, and other objects lurking under the surface traumatize random body parts of the individual careening downstream, abruptly tossing them in alternative directions, often causing head trauma with loss of consciousness in the process. These strainers also catch body parts, such as hands and feet, anchoring the victim in place while the force of the water pushes them underneath the surface beyond their ability to break free. Drowning commonly follows this scenario, often with fatal outcomes.

The details and graphic depiction of such events raises awareness of the ugly realities of crossing an otherwise seemingly harmless body of water. These events occur more frequently than expected, including experienced hikers, strong swimmers, and others alike. These circumstances have also been experienced by countless kayakers, tubers, canoers, and rafters either on their own or on a guided tour. In 2020 a total of thirty-four individuals drowned in Colorado's waterways alone from a combination of all these water-related activities.

Drowning tops the list of most frequent causes of fatal injury in Yosemite National Park, largely occurring along the Merced River and in Emerald Pool, which are encountered along the Mist Trail. Physical barriers have been placed between the trail and the Merced River to prevent hikers seeking a quick dip in the water from doing so, specifically due to the alarming number of swimmers who have been swept up by the current and whose lifeless bodies were recovered downstream later. The unsettling number of hikers who continue to sneak past these barriers prompted a research study to uncover behavioral aberrancies that lead these people to voluntarily risk their own lives.

Numerous news stories from the areas surrounding the national parks add to the appreciation for the frequency of these events. They depict such grave outcomes for adventurers on the Yellowstone River along the Montana-Wyoming border as well. One such swimmer, a Chinese national working for the park, was swept downstream in 2015; his skeletal remains were not recovered until February 2018, and it wasn't until a year after that when authorities positively identified him through DNA analysis.

Hiking and backpacking experience does not spare the hiker from the perils of deep, rapidly flowing water. In the summer of 2017 two skilled thru hikers, R.M. and C.W., trail names "Strawberry" and "Tree," drowned in separate spots along the PCT, while another one drowned in Yosemite and another in King's Canyon National Park. Just 3 months earlier the CEO of a very famous hiking apparel company forded a river while hiking in Grand Canyon National Park with his wife and her step-grandson. These latter two individuals sadly lost their footing on the streambed, fell into the water, and were quickly swept downstream. Both unfortunately lost their lives, and the remains of one were sadly never recovered. In another instance, a wintertime hiker encountered a red backpack floating in partially frozen Evolution Lake along the Pacific Crest Trail in King's Canyon National Park. The search and rescue (SAR) team helicopter hovered over to discover a body still attached to the backpack, subsequently extracted and later identified as a well-known and accomplished backpacker. This adventurer may have attempted to cross the lake while frozen, but this remains conjecture only. In yet another example, a several-day SAR operation found a Colorado River guide's body in the water. Initiation of the search came after he didn't return to camp, having left his customers to visit another camp along the river. The guide's boat likely capsized and threw him overboard.

The specific circumstances that surround these and numerous other tragedies in the wilderness vary, but they clearly illustrate that regardless of experience level, we all equally face the dangers of water. Despite our comfort and abilities in controlled circumstances, we need to avoid overconfidence and bypassing precautionary measures for unpredictable conditions. As well-prepared outdoor enthusiasts, whether on land or on the water, we come ready to have fun and a great experience, while remaining aware and respectful of the potential downsides we face.

What to Do Upon Falling into the Water

Slipping and falling into very shallow or deeper/slow-flowing water does not pose a high risk for danger. Doing so in deep and rapidly flowing water otherwise poses the greatest risk of getting swept downstream. This also applies to those who fall out of watercraft (kayak, raft, inner tube, body board, or other) and into rapids. Our survival depends on our ability to think quickly and to act immediately under duress.

In this situation three necessary actions save lives:

1. **Ditch your pack**: Our pack will fill up with water and act as a weight to pull us under the surface of the water. The straps on the pack additionally may catch on underwater branches and other objects, further inhibiting our ability to move as freely as possible. **We therefore must unbuckle the chest and waist straps before we enter the water** to act as quickly as possible. We only need to slip out of the shoulder straps, free ourselves from it, and let it go.
2. **Get into position**: Once free from our pack, we assume the position with our head and chest facing upward and forward, with knees slightly bent, such as in a sit-up position, with our body floating downstream feet first. Our feet and legs will contact objects such as strainers first, which we can then spring away from. This decreases the chance of head trauma and limbs getting caught in strainers.
3. **Get to the side**: While in the above position, we use our arms to paddle and influence our trajectory in the water over to either bank of the river as soon as possible. Despite the warm outside temperatures, the typically frigid water can render us hypothermic in under 10 minutes. The shorter the time we spend in the water, the lesser the chance for hypothermia and significant trauma.

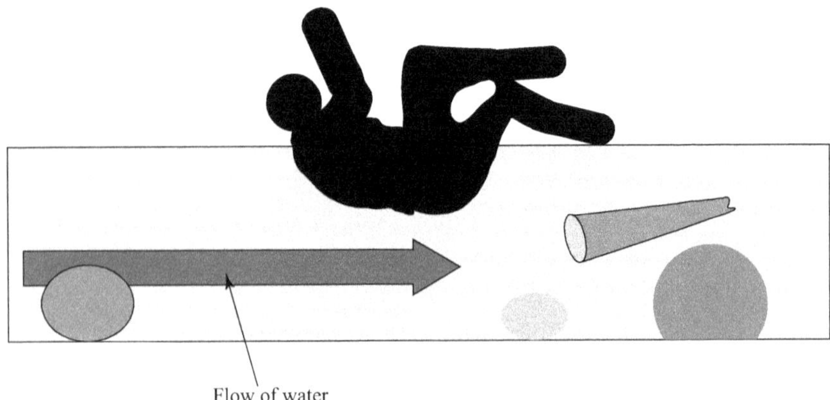

Water Rescue of a Fellow Adventurer

Rescuing a fellow hiker from the water as they flow downstream takes restraint, as the natural instinct to jump in after them will come upon us. **Avoid immediately jumping in**, especially without past specific training and available equipment. We want to prevent turning one potential fatality into multiple fatalities, which has occurred on numerous occasions. In the attempt to extract another from the water in general, the age-old principle of "Reach, Throw, Row, Go" applies.

Reach. We will likely have to run along the bank of the river/creek after the victim in the water, but if we can reach out to them with a trekking pole, long branch, watercraft paddle, or other long, straight object for them to grasp, then they can be pulled over to land without having posed any unnecessary danger to anyone else.

Throw. Circumstances may differ, based on the method of water immersion and immediately available resources. Throwing a (length of climbing or other) rope out to the individual in the water from the bank of the river/creek, or from within a raft/watercraft allows us to rescue the adventurer from the water. Even quickly tying a rope or paracord to a dry bag might suffice to both get to the person out of the water and pull them in, if time allows, while the retained air in the dry bag allows it to act as a small flotation device.

Row. Depending on the circumstances, we may or may not have a watercraft option readily available to reach that victim. If so, and it is safe to utilize for this purpose, then use it. This option applies to open water and not to the scenario when a hiker has fallen into the rapids.

Go. Getting into the water to attempt a rescue comes last, when all other options fail, and should only be attempted by someone with training and very strong swimming capabilities. This still poses significant risk to the well-being of the rescuer who goes after that victim careening downstream in rapidly flowing water.

Resuscitation of the Drowning Victim

Covered in CPR and Basic Life Support (BLS) courses, resuscitation of the drowning victim involves stepping forward in a confusing situation to influence it in a positive direction. Becoming skilled in these important principles of emergency intervention can make us a life-preserving force in another's life. Many of us will unexpectedly encounter others in need in society and while in the wilderness, and under such conditions there is no feeling quite like powerlessness when wanting to intervene but being unable to offer help. The following concepts do not substitute for CPR or BLS certification, which are highly recommended.

Time is life. Upon the discovery of a drowning victim, **act as quickly as possible**. The greater the time that individual remains underneath the water's surface, and therefore not breathing, the closer they approach irreversible hypoxic brain injury and death. Do not hesitate, and act. While initiating any plan of action, direct a bystander, if available, to **call 911**.

Raise the victim's airway above the surface. The first and most important action in the rescue of a drowning individual from any water environment involves raising their airway above the surface of the water as quickly as possible. Whether this took Reaching, Throwing, Rowing, or Going to reach this primary objective, **taking that victim's airway out of the water begins the process of preserving life**. Taking that victim physically out of the water follows as the next priority in the rescue effort, in as little time as possible, to assess that individual for further needs and intervention. If no bystander was present to call 911, then the rescuer must do so.

Airway and breathing first. The drowning victim needs to resume breathing immediately. If conscious and not under significant influence of drugs or alcohol, that individual usually resumes breathing on their own, along with spontaneous coughing (a good sign). These **victims should be transported to a local Emergency Department ASAP** for medical assessment, as some may become worse after initial improvement. For the rescued but unconscious drowning victim, assume they need assistance with respirations until proven otherwise.

Current CPR and BLS courses have begun introducing the concept of "compression only" CPR. While this applies to the individual who is in cardiac arrest on dry land, this form of CPR does not benefit the drowning victim, who needs air in their lungs to restart oxygenating their blood immediately.

- **Assess the airway and breathing** with the chin lift maneuver as taught in BLS classes.
- With the side of our face over the victim's mouth to **listen and feel for air transfer**, watch the chest for respiratory effort (rises and falls). When airflow and chest movement is weak or absent, begin rescue breaths right away, as taught in BLS classes.
- By now someone has called 911 for assistance and immediate transport to a local Emergency Department.
- **Assessment of circulation** and need for chest compressions should immediately follow these initial rescue breaths, as outlined in CPR and BLS courses.

Other Aspects of Care

The rescued drowning victim emerges wet, cold, and prone to lose more heat to the point of hypothermia. Wet clothing in constant contact with the skin pulls heat away from the body, further decreasing body temperature. For conscious rescued victims, **change wet clothing for dry, if available**, and cover them with what is on hand to limit heat loss and begin the natural rewarming process.

For the unconscious victims who require CPR no opportunity to dry or warm that victim will present itself, so continuing efforts to restore breathing and circulation remains the priority. Maintain contact with 911 and/or the rescue team, if possible, to facilitate transfer of that victim to the local hospital.

Bottom Line

Drowning commonly causes death and need for rescue wherever hikers encounter water with certain attributes. Research the hike ahead of time to anticipate the elements that will be encountered. Success in overcoming these hurdles requires strategy and skill.

- Hikers and backpackers who must cross mountain waterways between spring and midsummer need to realize they face a higher potential for peril than in late summer and fall, due to excessive downhill volume of snowmelt and spring rains.

  Knowing what perils we potentially face ahead of our adventures and choosing readiness over chance places us in the position to exert more control over our safe return.
- **Study a detailed map and satellite images** of the intended route for potential hazards, such as rivers and streams that require crossing, to know what to expect ahead of time and provide opportunity to decide on alternative trails.
- **Research water depth** and flow of waterways that intersect the intended route at waterdata.usgs.gov or wateroffice.ec.gc.ca for the US or Canada, respectively.
- **Consider bringing water shoes** when deciding ahead of time to forge ahead with crossing bodies of water.
- **Consider a water crossing as early in the day as possible** to catch the flow at its lowest volume and speed when planning to do so in a high-risk location and time of year.
- **Find the least hazardous way to cross the water**, based on the above guidelines.

- **Use the above guidelines and techniques** to minimize danger when fording deep and rapidly flowing water.
- **If falling into the water should occur, prepare to act quickly** to avoid drowning and head trauma by ditching the pack and assuming a safe position in the water.
- **Enter the water as a last resort to help rescue another** who has fallen into rapidly flowing water. Follow the Reach, Throw, Row, Go principle.
- **Come prepared, having taken a CPR course** to make a positive impact on the life of a drowning victim.

References

Bouchard, Jay. "Deadly Rivers: At Least 10 People Have Drowned in Colorado This Year." *5280*, July 3, 2019.

Girasek, D.C., et. al. "Patterns of Behaviour That Pose Potential Drowning Risk to Hikers at Yosemite National Park." *Journal of Travel Medicine* 23, no. 1 (January 2016).

Hauser, Christine, "Two Hikers Swept to Their Deaths by Floods in a Utah Canyon." *New York Times*, March 16, 2023.

Hill, Pat. "Life and Death on the Yellowstone." montanapioneer.com, July 2008.

"Remains of 2015 Yellowstone River Drowning Victim Found and Identified." nps.gov, August 1, 2019.

"Searchers Recover Body of Man Swept Away in Yellowstone River." *Billings Gazette*, August 13, 2021.

Serna, Joseph. "Rivers Swollen from Melting Sierra Nevada Snowpack Claim Another Life in the Central Valley." *Los Angeles Times*, May 22, 2017.

Statistics on drowning in US National Parks. nps.gov.

Woods, Betsy. "Creek and River Crossings: A Significant Risk for Hikers and Backpackers." *Wilderness Medicine Magazine* 37, no. 2 (May 2020).

Wu Chengcheng, Zang Xiaolu, et al. "Study on Characteristics of Water Flow Under Different Riverbed Structures in River Narrowing Section." MATEC Web of Conferences 246, 02044, 2018.

Skill 4

Awareness of Heights and the Risk of Falling

Real-Life Scenarios

1. Eighteen-year-old T.F., visiting the US from Israel in 2019 prior to his obligatory military service back home, hiked with a group on the Mist Trail in Yosemite National Park. After stopping for lunch at the top of Nevada Fall, he asked a fellow hiker to take a picture of him. He then proceeded to purposely slip partially over the edge of the cliff to mimic a popular social media post at the time. He lost his grip, drawing more of his body past the edge. Despite the hurried attempt by other hikers to assist him back up, he fell over 800 feet into the gorge below.

2. A visitor to the US from Hong Kong in 2019 traveled to Grand Canyon National Park on a group tour seeking first-hand experience of the awe-inspiring views. While taking a selfie and pictures of the gorge below Eagle Point, he lost his footing on the edge of the cliff where he was standing and fell about 1,000 feet into the canyon.

3. A hiker arrived at Taft Point in Yosemite National Park in 2018 to discover an unaccompanied camera on a tripod. A

call to park rangers led to a SAR mission, which discovered the remains of a man (V.V.) and a woman (M.M.) 1,000 feet below that vista point. Review of the photos from the camera revealed the travel blogging couple was posing for pictures on the edge of the cliff.

4. In January 2022 a 21-year-old backpacker photo-documented his trip through the Superstition Mountains east of Phoenix, Arizona. While attempting to take a selfie on a peak along his route, he slipped and fell 700 feet off that point to his death.

Nonfatal falls happen frequently. We commonly trip and stumble over when trekking through the great outdoors through the erratic topography, aboveground roots, and scree of the trail ground. This has and will happen to all of us at some point, and for the most part it cannot be prepared for. The frequency and occurrence also have little to do with experience. A research study was conducted to find commonalities among individuals who fall more frequently than others, which identified several risk factors:

- Older individuals with some level of visual impairment
- Suboptimal fitness
- Mild overweight status

These risk factors do not protect young, fit hikers with good vision from tripping and falling, however. We all accidentally stumble along our route, and minor injuries will happen. Backpackers twist an ankle on the trail and fall, slip on ice and land on a hip, or we may trip on a rock and fall on an outstretched hand, sustaining a wrist fracture. These and other common orthopedic injuries lead to other issues out in the middle of nowhere, but many come from minor falls. No data set outlines the true frequency of these events, as most go unreported, but they happen much more often than we appreciate, deserving mention. Beyond this level lie more notable occurrences, with major falls commonly leading to significant injury and worse.

According to US National Park Service (NPS) data, falling causes approximately 20 percent of all unintentional deaths within the park system, making it one of the most common ways to die in the outdoors. Just as with drowning, the risk of death and injury due to falling depends on the features of the specific environment. While slipping off high cliffs and overlooks ranks among the most common ways to perish in places like Grand Canyon National Park and Yosemite National Park, serious injury and mortality from falling rarely occurs in parks with mostly flat terrain. Where perilous drop-offs exist, adventurers who reach them arrive with an elevated potential for falling, but mitigating that risk lies well within reach.

An alarming number of hikers plummet to their deaths each year in US national parks and other high-mountain hiking areas across North America. While the most accessible data comes from the US national park system (NPS), its roughly eighty-five million acres represents about 25 to 30 percent of the total hikeable landmass in North America. The combined land, totaling over three hundred million acres, also includes National Recreation Areas, US National Forests, US state parks, Parks Canada, and Canadian provincial parks. The numbers as reported by the NPS therefore underestimate the actual figure across the continent.

The data may also underestimate the exact incidence of falls in the NPS itself, as search and rescue (SAR) teams often unintentionally discover remains of hikers previously reported as missing in these locations, well after the fact. Two such examples of this are as follows:

- A SAR team was called to Glen Canyon National Recreational Area in the fall of 2020 to recover a 25-year-old hiker who fell from a cliff. Upon finding his body in the canyon, multiple other victims' remains were discovered in the same location. This unexpected discovery identified those remains among the list of hikers previously reported as lost.

- In September 2021, search for a missing vacationer in the Grand Canyon led to the discovery of another victim of an apparent fall approximately 600 feet below an overlook before finding the original visitor's body elsewhere about 430 feet below the South Rim.

These two exist among many such instances as reported by news outlets in the communities surrounding national parks. An average of twelve deaths per year occur from falling in Grand Canyon National Park alone, but by September of 2021 this park already had a count of eighteen such deaths for that calendar year, with 4 months left to go.

Falling vertically, from a ledge or other high ground, comes with a significant amount of trauma, even when from a height of only 20 feet or less. Falling from this seemingly minor height frequently leads to injuries, including broken ankles, legs, and hips, especially when landing on our feet and legs. Falling from higher elevations often leads to tumbling of the falling victim in the air or toppling over from collision with rock formations along the path down. The variation in trajectory leads to other body parts sustaining significant injury, such as the head and face, arms, spine, and ribcage. In the surgical trauma world, a fall from 20 feet or greater represents the threshold height for diverting a recovered victim to a designated trauma center, due to the presumption of a multitude of associated injuries, including those unapparent on primary assessment.

The fall itself does not produce trauma or death. As with motor vehicle crashes, the momentum of the body suddenly decelerates, abruptly impacting a surface harder than itself. This not only causes bones to compress and bend to the point of fracture, but it also disrupts ligament, tendon, and joint integrity.

Dr. Rob's Notes

Most falls from less than 20 feet typically produce less frequent major trauma and death than falls from heights beyond this, largely producing sprains and fractures of varying location and severity. As the height of the fall increases beyond this point, so does the acceleration of the victim and therefore the significance of the impact.

An average-sized person who falls 60 feet will reach 42 miles per hour upon impact, and from about 90 feet that person will accelerate to about 75 miles per hour when hitting the ground. The height therefore dictates the severity of trauma and potential for mortality.

Analysis of case studies of falls and subsequent outcomes reveals that plummets from about 100 feet or higher are nearly 100 percent fatal, but some case studies do depict rare survival of individuals who have fallen 100 feet or greater.

Beyond orthopedic damage, rapid deceleration leads to sudden, severe, and unnatural movements of internal organs, disrupting their integrity as well. The heart, lungs, liver, spleen, and kidneys can fracture apart, causing internal bleeding from broken blood vessels or stopping blood flow to the organs due to clotting within injured blood vessels. This affects vital organ function, causing medical sickness well beyond the bone and joint impact.

Motor vehicle crashes became much more survivable events when airbags became standard equipment in our cars by providing a softer object for the human body to hit. The technology also allows deceleration to occur over a longer period of time than in their absence. These features have significantly decreased the severity of injuries and death from car crashes.

Using the lessons learned from airbags and how they mitigate deceleration injury helps us to understand that the surface onto which an adventurer falls can determine the difference in survivability and injury pattern they suffer from the same given height. More specifically, landing on soft-packed dirt will result in a different deceleration pattern than landing on a large, flat rock. Landing along a steep slope, rather than on a flat surface, alters the injury pattern and severity, affecting survivability. Injuries will still occur, but landings on softer and sloped surfaces are potentially more survivable than those on solid, flat ones. The vertical distance of the fall, however, may make these factors a moot point. The take-home lesson is to avoid falling altogether!

The Story of Clint McHale

On May 4, 2011, Clint and a friend headed up Echo Canyon to Camelback Mountain, as they had often done before. Along the route they chose to go off-trail in favor of a four-limb climb on the rocks as a more adventurous way up, neither one with the equipment or training to do so. As they neared the top, Clint lost his grip. Though his friend reached for his hand, Clint's body weight pulled him from the rock face, resulting in a 50-foot drop. He sustained significant head and bodily trauma. The rescue took 45 minutes to accomplish, due to the precarious topography. While Clint maintained consciousness until this point, he passed away during the helicopter transport to the hospital.

His younger sister, Chelsey, began an unrelenting campaign via media outreach and directly to local politicians to construct and install a sign as a warning to others as to what they potentially face along this trail, both as a tribute to her brother and to spare countless others from a tragic, preventable outcome. Through her persistence, local officials agreed, leading to installation of the sign on May 8, 2014. This sign has enlightened an untold number of uninformed hikers traversing this trail of the potential perils along the way and will serve as a life-preserving memorial for years to come.

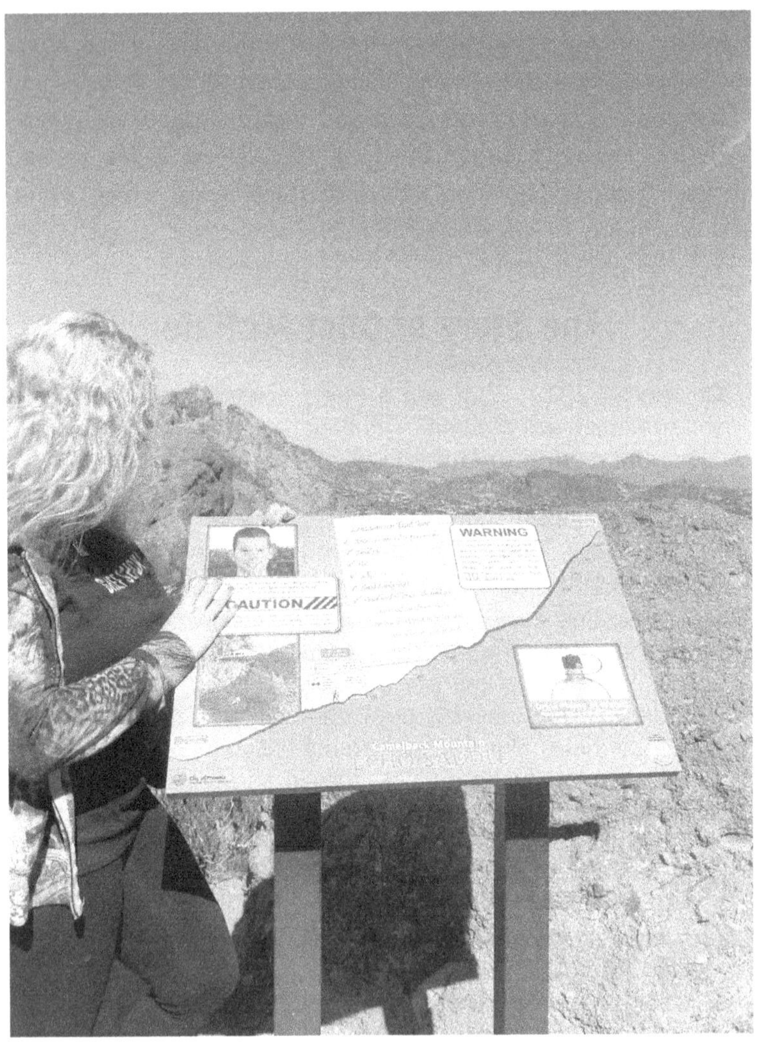

Chelsey McHale visits her brother's sign on Camelback Mountain.
CHELSEY MCHALE

Unsafe Behaviors and Poor Decision-Making

Unsafe behaviors largely occur hand in hand with unintended vertical falls. Many of us amateur explorers seek out the allure of a picturesque canyon overlook. Little else reproduces the awe of these vistas, consuming our visual fields with such earthly majesty. Most of us just stop and soak in the view. Driven by unclear motivations, some behave in ways that defy self-preservation while in these spots, such as attempting their first handstand ever on a cliff's edge. Multiple research articles have examined this phenomenon, using data from the US and around the world to illustrate risk factors and behaviors leading to fatal falls.

One European study identified off-trail hiking accidents as a cause for a much higher percentage of fatalities (15%) than on-trail accidents (4%). Off-trail perils pose naturally greater risk to our safety than those on well-thought-out, previously trafficked, and maintained paths. Trail design comes with hiker safety in mind, purposely diverting us from high-risk perilous features and offering the safest route through the landscape. One natural question asks why hikers go off-trail in the first place. Other than answering when nature calls, many off-trail jaunts intend to capture better views or pictures of a vista. These off-trail outcrops, overlooks, and cliffs may very well offer an amazing view but may exist upon unstable ground, more likely to collapse under the body weight of a hiker than under natural conditions. Locations of designated overlooks do not occur by accident. Rather than having been chosen for offering better views than other spots, they typically offer the best vista in the safest and most stable location in that area. Wandering off-trail to find a better spot from which to take a snapshot brings a higher chance of becoming a regrettable decision than staying on-trail and trusting the trail association's pick for where to take our pictures.

Other Risk Factors

Other high-risk behaviors lead to injury, rescue, and fatality. In just about every location where a railing exists to protect onlookers from the perils beyond that point, we will find people who freely go beyond the barrier and tempt fate. Numerous instances have occurred over the years at Vernal Falls, in Yosemite National Park, where people have snuck past the safety rails, accidentally fallen in the water, been swept over the falls, and plummeted down 318 feet onto the field of large boulders below. In 2011 three park visitors met an early death in this very manner, and all on the same day. This describes just one cluster of human loss on one day in just one location.

Countless instances of falling happen yearly across North America, and the world for that matter. A study conducted by the NPS Office of Risk Management found the majority of those who engage in risky behaviors are:

- Males
- Age 21 or older
- Visiting with or hiking in a group

Risky behaviors in dangerous circumstances lead to tragic outcomes, regardless of our characteristics. Recognizing the perils that surround us should produce a healthy respect for the potential risks. That may not be enough for those who thoughtlessly defy marked trails and safety barriers and tempt fate.

Recent scholarly articles have identified certain personality and psychiatric traits that seem to correlate with the willingness to pursue risky behaviors, especially when they are on display for others to see. These behaviors commonly lead to thoughtless action and subsequent injury. These individuals may act in such a way to seek attention or acceptance from others in the group. Others habitually seek thrilling moments to feed the positive feelings of neurochemical surges from the experience, and yet others have issues with impulse control. The vast majority of us ultimately want to return home safely. In the interest of self-preservation over all other priorities, we must think about the risks before we act foolishly.

Other risk factors for falling include terrain, inexperience, and lack of preparation. One study also identified fall risk as connected to the angle of hiking travel. Most on-trail falls, both fatal and nonfatal, occur while heading downhill from a peak. Uphill scrambling causes less frequent falling, and flat terrain hiking leads to the least number of falls. High-risk terrain offers a greater threat for accidental falls, based on the narrow ridges, loose rock, and high-angle drop-offs, characteristic of Class 3 and 4 terrain. Even the best equipment and training does not guarantee a safe return from high-angle scrambling. Those who come prepared with the appropriate gear and technical know-how maximize their chances of a successful outing. When technical hiking becomes appealing, training and a gradual increase in exposure to this type of terrain, done with experienced climbers, create the safest approach to branching off into this realm.

More unprepared hikers enter technical environments completely unaware of what they potentially face than the number of those who have researched and trained for such conditions. Eager urban dwellers and suburbanites, equipped only with a cell phone to take a picture at the summit, flock to locations remarkable for dangerous terrain and conditions like Mt. Whitney, the highest peak in the lower forty-eight states. Allured by pictures seen on social media and publications, they unwittingly arrive with inappropriate footwear and clothing, no equipment, and an abundance of unearned confidence. Many of these individuals arrive completely unaware of what they must endure to take that picture. Those who dismiss realizing the imbalance between required and available skill and still forge ahead risk endangering themselves and others. Numerous summit hopefuls have reportedly fallen while attempting the steep incline of "The Chute" at Mt. Whitney on the way up to the summit, knocking others off the climb below them like bowling pins, causing multiple victim traumas and fatalities. When rescue personnel respond to calls to treat and extract these victims in such conditions, their safety also is placed at risk. This and numerous other examples demonstrate zealous individuals bypassing the forethought to research and prepare, dress properly, acquire the right gear (such as crampons and an ice axe for winter and spring summit attempts), and train to maintain their safety and that of others in the effort to summit that mountain. The desire to live must outweigh the motivation to pursue the picture.

These and similar technical environments already pose treacherous results for those who have prepared and trained for such risky climbs. In 2017, five hikers fell to their deaths within a six-week span of time in their attempts to climb up to Capitol Peak near Aspen, Colorado. In another circumstance illustrating the dangers of technical terrain, the remains of an experienced 34-year-old hiker/EMT were found in the Trinity Alps in California in August 2019. He had not returned home from a solo trip in these technical mountains, and upon retrieval of his remains the evidence suggested that he had fallen from the steep, technical landscape. Taking on this kind of terrain, laden with loose scree among high angles, and emerging safely comes with a tremendous amount of experience, skill, and equipment.

The Fatal Selfie

An ever-growing phenomenon and source for injury and tragedy in the wild is the fatal selfie. Social media has become a large (and in some cases necessary) part of many of our lives, for better or worse, and allows us to connect with our personal audience from around the world. In recent years, posts based on outdoor landscapes and overlooks have drawn a tremendous amount of attention and desire to visit these depicted places.

Many newcomers bring a lack of preparedness, capability, and an abundance of careless energy to reproduce or outdo previous visitors' efforts. Social media posts from the outdoors have sparked a tremendous interest for newcomers in outdoor spaces, including the national parks. The increase in national park visitors also strongly correlates with the number of social media posts, as identified in one recent article. This increase in visitors has correlated with a higher number of injuries and SAR operations for ill-fated selfies and other causes, such as hiker fatigue, lack of drinking water, and others.

More popular outdoor sites, as driven by interest from social media, seem also to experience more SAR calls and operations than others. For instance, 83 percent of SAR and other emergency medical calls from the national parks within California occur from the four most popular of the nine national parks in that state. Another recent article, monitoring social media posts (specifically tweets) and SAR incidents found a moderate correlation between the two.

The most influential sources for the outdoors on social media platforms lies in the pictures, rather than the written content. Of the innumerable pictures added each day to social media certain ones catch our eyes, with nature snapshots in particular locations garnering much attention. One interesting phenomenon reveals how much more appeal a picture receives with a person in it, especially when facing the lens. A face in the picture represents a natural human cue for nonverbal communication, becoming more instinctively "likable."

Pictures with faces are in fact 38 percent more prone to get likes and more likely to receive comments than those that do not. This positive feedback only drives the selfie phenomenon to continue. These pictures, typically taken with the camera at a high angle and off to the side, force our eyesight to deviate up and away from the ground, naturally weakening our balance. When other factors further strain our equilibrium, falling becomes a greater possibility, even on flat ground.

A recent article outlining behavioral aspects of taking pictures in national parks revealed that cliff edges were the most desired locations to take these snapshots. The article also points out that falling from heights was the most common reported method of injury while taking these selfies. With so many pictures from the same locations appearing like clones of one another, some seek to break up the monotony. What they add may only elevate their proximity to danger. The desire for affirmation through likes motivates many social media hopefuls to engage in riskier behavior than they would under normal circumstances, amounting to an internally driven or perceived peer pressure. This pressure leads to actions that have potentially fatal consequences.

Deaths related to selfies and similar pictures in precarious places and circumstances have been monitored from around the world since early 2008. This research found that one person died during their selfie photo every 13 days, which was consistent through the end of 2020. Since the beginning of 2021, however, the incidence has increased to one death by selfie every 7 days, amounting to a near-doubling of the prior rate of death. The estimated number of lives lost in this manner reached over 380 during this timeframe to mid-2021. The attention this has gained has elevated it to a public health problem, such that the NPS has introduced a campaign of Wednesdays being "Safe Park Selfie Day," to raise awareness and proactivity for self-imposed safety. This unfortunately happens to be the one day of the week that national parks experience the least number of visitors, but this represents a start. The state of Iowa has built and introduced "selfie stations" in their state park system, encouraging selfies being taken from established safe zones. Time will tell whether this effort will make a significant impact on related injury and death, but this novel concept has gained the attention of the NPS. Travel organizations have begun actively raising awareness and encouraging caution in relation to taking photographs while on vacation, stressing a safety mindset.

How We Prepare to Prevent Falling

Preparation to prevent falling begins with acknowledging the risks of an otherwise innocent action and that we don't want to fall. This statement seems overly simplistic, but approaching a cliff without awareness and cautionary instinct explains exactly why most fatal falls have occurred. Falls leading to injury and death have happened beyond the control of the individuals, and they will continue to do so, but most instances have been connected to self-imposed risk. Exercising a healthy degree of respect and caution by maintaining this acknowledgment in the foreground of our thoughts minimizes our chances of repeating most of these preventable tragedies.

How we choose to act in these unique situations varies from person to person. Our differing personalities, desires, expectations, and hopes for the experience we have in these amazing locations may make the difference between who has walked away from the experience and who has succumbed to its perils. What we do in the moment to document and savor the adventures we have in these intrinsically dangerous places may not reflect how we behave in our off-trail lives. Ultimately, we largely control how the dangers affect us and understanding that empowers us. Properly wielding this control minimizes the impact the perils have on us. Passively leaving our safety up to chance and luck, on the other hand, maximizes the potential for the dangers to gain the upper hand. Proactively deciding in the interest of living beyond that experience must be a priority. The decisions we make should then serve this objective. Behaving on-trail with this in mind does not lessen the experience, fun, or degree of amazement and only preserves us for our next mind-blowing trip.

Bottom Line

- **Good judgment.** Judgment calls made with the baseline goal of self-preservation keep us from encroaching on the edge of a cliff but still allow us to enjoy the view from a safe enough distance. Stay on-trail, use park designated overlook points, and stay on the safe side of barriers.

- **Mind the terrain**. Don't attempt to hike in areas with technical terrain without an experienced guide and the proper gear. Pay close attention to the terrain irregularities and scree on the trail to prevent stumbling and injury. Know that the edges of cliffs and trails may be unstable below our feet, crumble under our body weight, and take us downhill or off the edge completely.
- **Know your limitations**. Training to be in our best physical shape keeps us upright and stable on descents and uneven terrain. We all have weakness, at least in some areas, so humbly acknowledge physical limitations before attempting to push those boundaries.
- **Check your wild side**. Those with a wild and spontaneous side must resist crazy behaviors in the places where gravity exists as the enemy of life. Doing so will not prevent an amazing and fun time. Save the antics for soft, level ground far from danger.
- **Selfie safely**. Go ahead and take pictures and post the experiences on social media, knowing the dangers of careless behavior, and do so at a safe distance from the edge of any cliff.

References

Ari Shapiro interview with Kathryn Miles. "Hundreds Have Died in Selfie-Related Deaths Since 2011." npr.org, May 6, 2019.

Flaherty, Gerard, and Paul Joon Koo Choi. "The 'Selfie' Phenomenon: Reducing the Risk of Harm While Using Smartphones During International Travel." *Journal of Travel Medicine* 23, no. 2 (2016): 26.

Fonseca, Felicia. "Human Remains Found During Search at Grand Canyon." *Las Vegas Review Journal*, September 15, 2021.

Granhed, H., et al. "Injuries Sustained by Falls: A Review." *Trauma and Acute Care*, April 3, 2017.

Güell, Oriol. "Rise of Selfie Deaths Leads Experts to Talk About a Public Health Problem." *El País*, October 29, 2021.
Hill, Craig. "Inexperience May Have Played Role in Mount Rainier Accident." *News Tribune*, June 1, 2018.
Howe, Steve. "A Dozen Ways to Die." *Backpacker*, March 12, 2008.
Hutchinson, Alex. "The Science of Why We Fall on Mountain Trails." *Outside*, May 17, 2018.
Knauf, Amanda. "Climbing Accidents Involving Inexperienced Hikers Increase in Norway." Climbing.com, August 15, 2018.
Lu, Z., A. Briggs, et al. "The Associations Between Visitation, Social Media Use and Search and Rescue in U.S. National Parks." *Wilderness and Environmental Medicine* 32, no. 4 (December 2021): 463–467.
McCormick, Erin, et al. "Is Our Life Just Worth a Photo? The Tragic Death of a Couple in Yosemite." *Guardian*, November 3, 2018.
Michelson, Megan. "Mt. Whitney Has Turned into an Overcrowded Catastrophe." outsideonline.com, August 9, 2018.
Miles, Howard. "Danger Lurks in National Parks, but Not Necessarily Where You Expect It." *Washington Post*, February 25, 2021.
NPT Staff. Deaths Rising in National Park System. *National Parks Traveler*, June 22, 2021.
Rappold, R. S. "That Selfie May Be Epic, but Not Worth Your Life." WebMD, May 23, 2019.
Read, Richard. "Inexperience Cited in Death of Three Mount Hood Climbers." *Oregonian*, February 14, 2014.
Rogers, Paul. "'Selfie Epidemic': How Israeli Teenager Fell to His Death in Yosemite." *Los Angeles Daily News*, April 1, 2019.
Smith, Stephen. "Hiker Falls 500 Feet to His Death from Ridge at Sequoia National Park, Woman Falls Trying to Save Him." CBS News, June 2, 2021.
Statistics on Falling in US National Parks. nps.gov.
Teufel, Alex. "Five Most Dangerous Places to Take a Selfie in Zion National Park." myutahparks.com, July 7, 2021.
Veidt, Emma. "Hiker Falls to His Death in the Grand Canyon as a Deadly Year Continues at the Park." *Backpacker*, September 2, 2021.
Weckback, S., et al. "Survival Following a Vertical Free Fall from 300 Feet: The Crucial Role of Body Position to Impact Surface." *Scandinavian Journal of Trauma, Resuscitation and Emergency Medicine*, October 25, 2011.
Whalen, Jenny. "Inexperience, Not Just Rockfall, a Factor in Yosemite Climbing Deaths." *San Francisco Chronicle*, October 11, 2017.

Skill 5

Land Navigation

Real-Life Scenarios

1. L.M., a 34-year-old hiker, planned a 3-hour hike in the Santa Cruz Mountains on June 11, 2024, with minimal supplies. When he didn't show up for a family gathering 5 days later authorities were notified. A Sheriff's Office drone spotted him on day 10 and rescuers rushed to his location. News reports depict alteration of trail landmarks from recent wildfires as the cause for getting lost. He survived on backcountry water alone.

2. Two young hikers embarked on a trek through Little Cottonwood Canyon, outside of Salt Lake City, Utah, in the fall of 2021. The hike lasted longer than anticipated, with at least several miles left to go by nightfall. The pair became lost after sunset, unable to see without any light source in their packs. They had no extra food or layers to shield them from the hunger and cold they would experience during their unanticipated night in the wilderness. A search and rescue (SAR) operation began the following morning, leading to a successful recovery of the hikers in a near-hypothermic state.

3. A young woman, C.P., took a solo hike on the Lost Mine Trail in Big Bend National Park in the fall of 2023. Family and friends had no details other than her trip to the park, but

they notified authorities after days of not hearing from her. Multiple agencies became involved in a search, which found her 7 days after she began the hike. She had become lost on this seemingly innocent 5-mile out-and-back trail, ran out of water, and wandered for 1 week, surviving on rainwater alone. She was extracted by helicopter and treated in a hospital near Midland, Texas.

4. Twenty-five-year-old T.B. became lost in April 2024 while intending to hike up to Thurston Peak in the Uinta-Wasatch-Cache National Forest on a Friday night, camp overnight, and catch the sunrise on Saturday. Along the route he took a wrong turn and eventually realized he was lost. His friends at home called rescue personnel late Saturday, starting an unsuccessful search effort that night, which resumed the next morning. By late afternoon on Sunday T.B. had been found while on his way back to the parking lot.

As hikers we frequently lose our way while out on the trails to one extent or another, due to multiple reasons. This naturally unfamiliar environment with distracting sites, intersecting routes, and false trails favors wrong turns and misjudgments of our direction. Many realize the misstep early enough to find their own way back without incident, so most of these instances go unreported. The lesser number of reported occurrences where the hiker cannot find their way back and a search and rescue (SAR) operation ensues still ranks among the most common ways we encounter trouble in the wilderness. The most accessible data comes from the US National Park Service (NPS). Yosemite National Park, for example, fields 250 SAR calls per year, with approximately 66 percent due to lost hikers. While many SAR calls happen for this reason in the NPS system, the national parks only represent 25 to 30 percent of the total explorable land in North America. Search and rescue data from local and state agencies provide further insight into how much this happens outside of the NPS system. A SAR report published by the state of Oregon looking back at 17 years of information indicated "lost hiker" as representing the most frequent cause for rescue operations, at around 330 per year in that state alone. Two separate articles on this same subject agree that approximately two thousand hikers become lost each year in the US. Another article places the yearly number in Canada at twelve hundred. SAR teams find most of these lost hikers alive, but tragic recoveries happen among the reported outcomes as well.

Studies have identified certain risk factors based on the demographics of lost and subsequently rescued individuals. While these may help us examine our own tendency to become lost, avoiding a false sense of security remains important for outliers. Data from the state of Oregon identifies the following risk factors:

- "Solo" hikers accounted for 79 percent of lost hikers rescued in Oregon.
- Males have a 50 percent higher likelihood of becoming lost and requiring rescue as compared to females.
- Approximately 66 percent of those rescued were over 30 years old.

We can all analyze this information in our own way, but some questions come to mind. Does the solo hiker only have their own navigation skills to fall back upon, whereas two or more have a larger pooled skillset to utilize? Do males take on less intuitively navigable and more unfamiliar hikes than their female counterparts or are females better at navigating than their male counterparts? Do older and more experienced hikers come to the trail overconfident and take on more than their actual skill level can handle? Whatever the answers to these and other questions hold, becoming lost in the backcountry happens all too often.

Knowing the Most Common Reasons We Get Lost

Knowing the most common reasons we get lost affords us the awareness of risk before falling into the circumstances that increase its probability. Working backward from the data and diving deeper into the science answers the question as to how and why some become lost. This gives us the opportunity to prepare for these situations and understand our own personal tendency to go astray from the intended route. We can ultimately use this to prepare for and avoid these tendencies to mitigate our chances of becoming a statistic.

Wandering off the trail ranks as the most common reported cause for lost hikers and is responsible for 40 percent of cases. Many take to the trails without a formal navigation plan, other than relying on a phone app and following the visible foot path from entry to exit. For most hikers who follow this plan, it thankfully happens to work out well. Problems emerge when poorly marked forks in the trails arise, the trail itself becomes obscure, false offshoots of the trail throw us off, or our tech fails. The trail should be the most obviously worn pathway through the wilderness, so following this theoretically should come easy. At times identifying the route in this way gets extremely difficult, requiring more scrutiny in the moment, paying attention, and concentrating more in some locations as compared to others. It takes only one small error in judging the path to divert away from the trail. Without a constant consciousness of location and direction we may find ourselves far from the route before we realize we're lost.

Examine the two trails below. On the left we have the Bluebell-Baird Trail in Boulder, Colorado. Here we have a clear-cut path in the woods, presenting itself as difficult to mistake for anything but the trail. On the right we have a section of the Appalachian Trail in Harriman State Park, NY. This uphill section appears indistinct from the surrounding terrain, requiring a pause and careful look around to avoid hiking off in a very different direction.

The above picture on the right reveals a trail marker on a tree toward the upper part of the hill. The tree off to the left of the frame with a small part of its trunk in the foreground completely obscured the marker on the approach to the hill. This made the trail ahead completely indistinct from the surrounding landscape.

Sustaining our concentration to follow the correct trail for the whole route becomes difficult. Most hikers come with the goal of having a break from directed thoughts and the concentration of off-trail life. The sights and sounds of nature that we have come to enjoy distract us in our escape from our ordinary societal stomp. The solution comes with maintaining a balance between the two.

Bad weather represents the second most common cause for hikers becoming lost in the wilderness, at around 17 percent of instances. The sudden onset of a rainstorm or blinding snowstorm forces the pursuit of natural shelter, often off-trail. The disorienting aspect of unexpected weather patterns often leads hikers away from the intended path. Our readiness for and reaction to these changes in weather differ based on local familiarity, pre-hike preparation, and instinctive responses to the unexpected.

Fresh snowfall can obscure the visible path among the generalized whitening of the environment, making getting lost all too easy. Relying on other environmental cues such as unique trees and large rocks helps to reinforce our position in relation to the trail and to maintain our bearings, while closely observing for the natural depression in the terrain going forward. Flash floods from a driving rain can also produce a disorienting effect. The flow of downhill water often follows the trail, both forcing us to step out of its way to keep our boots dry and covering the natural trail floor. Maintaining composure and patience, while analyzing the topography and flow of water, should aid in identifying the trail and discerning it from the surrounding wilderness. Sheltering in place with a tarp or poncho and waiting for the rain to pass can help us resume our way once the skies have cleared.

Knowing the frequency of this cause for getting lost should foment a greater awareness of what comes from unexpected weather and a greater priority to remain on or close to the trail, with diligent pre-hike monitoring of the forecast.

Falling off the trail, causing hikers to become lost and require rescue, occurs with the same frequency as bad weather. By now we have become familiar with the frequency of falling overall. Hiking along saddles, trails that hug the outer edges of peaks and long switchbacks, and other topographically disadvantageous spots can cause hikers to fall to a lower elevation. Falling off the trail may occur when experiencing a loss of footing, tripping, and stumbling toward the edge, or if the ground supporting the edge destabilizes from natural erosion and brings that individual down with it. Injury may ensue, often limiting the hiker from getting back on-trail. The hiker may not otherwise be able to regain the elevation back to the trail due to several factors, including the terrain. These circumstances can easily occur without the hiker having engaged in any high-risk behavior at the edge. However, being mindful of this circumstance should encourage hikers to trek more mindfully and further from the edge whenever possible.

Separation from the group leads to a lost hiker requiring rescue in just under 10 percent of cases. Just about every group contains hikers of varying abilities. Some may not move as fast or be as nimble as others in the pack and might feel self-conscious about it. Instances occur where they encourage the remainder of the group to forge ahead at their own pace, feeling as if they are slowing everyone else down and reassuring everyone they will catch up later. In other circumstances one among the group may go off-trail clandestinely for a bio break, and the remainder of the group unwittingly continues onward. The one hiker left behind then needs to rely on their own directional skills, rather than the collective abilities of the group, to remain on-trail and navigate through unfamiliar territory. Some arrive with exceptional intuition, instincts, and abilities, while others rely on the safety net of

Dr. Rob's Tip for Group Hikes

A group that hikes together moves only as fast as their slowest member. When some in the group forge ahead of the rest, pursuing a quicker completion of the trek, this sets up the fragmentation of the group, raising the risk for someone to get left behind and lost.

Agree to plan hiking only as fast as it takes to maintain the integrity of the group. This may take longer than some faster hikers in the group want, but this represents the best way to assure that everyone leaves the wilderness safely. How horrible will everyone feel if the friend they took into the wilderness required a search and rescue operation to find? Will it have been worth breaking the group up?

A quick, periodic visual head count, such as at snack and water breaks, keeps everyone together. Assigning all in the group with a "trail buddy" to watch out for one another also helps when one needs to break away for a bio break or when a disorienting weather event happens, to ensure nobody will be left alone or behind.

the group to fill the gaps in their own skillset. When thrust into the situation where now that one individual must solely rely on their own capabilities, getting lost becomes a greater possibility.

Other causes for lost hikers include:

- Longer than expected hikes, especially ones that begin in the afternoon and extend past nightfall
- Failure of electronic equipment after accidental immersion in water, dropping, or dead batteries, without a backup analog method to guide navigation

Determining Our Direction and Finding Our Way

Determining our direction and finding our way comes from learned skill and instinct, which some possess in a greater capacity than others. Neuroscientists and psychologists have long asked the question why some can find their way through complex routes in barely familiar territory, and yet others have difficulty navigating through their own neighborhood. Studies on animal models and in humans over decades have sought to answer this question, but in the last 10 to 15 years the science community has come to a much better understanding of the issue. The bottom line? For those who cannot navigate well, even through familiar surroundings, it's not your fault!

Most of the human studies have focused on navigating through streets and neighborhoods, but this applies to our abilities to navigate through the wilderness as well. The studies identified two major methods we use to find our way around.

Route-landmark navigation represents the first method. We use this while traveling frequently through a familiar route between two known points, such as the home-to-work commute. The route has become so familiar after a while that we do not have to think while traveling on it. The familiar landmarks serve as prompts, telling us when to turn, adjust our speed, and what lies ahead. Within Route Learning, an essential component of this method, requires the absorption of the remarkable sights along the way that become subconscious cues to guide us.

Mental map navigation represents the second method. While also useful for frequently traveled routes, the mental map of the location assists us to conceptualize and understand the route in a map-like manner. Between Route Learning, assisted by this different perception, takes landmarks of different routes to the same destination and mentally integrates them, enabling alternate routes to be processed in the moment.

So why do some have such difficulty finding their way around? Regarding our innate abilities to navigate, three general categories of individuals have been defined:

1. **Integrators**. These individuals possess the ability to utilize both methods of navigation. They can integrate the knowledge and understanding of the terrain and routes to derive multiple alternative navigation solutions from both Within Route Learning and Between Route Learning.
2. **Non-Integrators**. These individuals only have the ability to utilize Route-Landmark Navigation and only become familiar with the terrain and route through repetition and Within Route Learning. They cannot apply Mental Map Navigation therefore having difficulty "seeing" how alternative routes connect. Rather than understanding connections between different paths, they learn alternative routes only through repetition.
3. **Imprecise Navigators**. Those who do not easily learn landmarks and routes despite repetition. They eventually can learn the routes over time. They don't possess the ability to recreate a mental map of the route or integrate landmarks to devise alternate paths. They may feel a sense of apprehension when others raise the subject and experience a certain level of anxiety when it comes to finding their own way or while looking at a map of an area.

The difference between these types of individuals has nothing to do with intellect or motivation to learn. Neurocognitive testing has proven the Integrators as consistently superior in 3-dimensional spatial reconstruction tasks to the other two groups, identifying this ability as something they were born with. The difference in this capability likely produces the disparity in navigation capacity between the groups.

In 2009 researcher Giuseppe Iaria published an article outlining a patient who would fit the above description of an Imprecise Navigator, having "a selective impairment in forming a mental representation of the environment," or mental map, without an accompanying structural abnormality of the brain. His research was among the first to point to low activity in the region of the hippocampus within the brain by functional MRI. He termed this condition "developmental topographic disorientation," or DTD. These individuals have normal intellect but require specific, written, turn-by-turn instructions along a route to get to a destination, even when traveled a multitude of times. They may also have face blindness, or prosopagnosia, where one may not recognize others by face. This may also relate to their inability to memorize visual cues along a route as Integrators do.

In 2014 the Nobel Prize for Physiology or Medicine was awarded to John O'Keefe, PhD, and others. Their work took Iaria's findings further by locating different groups of brain cells in the hippocampus region in rats that orient mammals to location, direction, boundaries, and distance. This groundbreaking information confirmed a functional anatomy model explaining ability versus inability to navigate. In that same year Dr. Iaria published another article on DTD patients and functional MRIs demonstrating out-of-sync function between their hippocampus and other parts of the brain.

This research has led to the understanding that multiple clusters of brain cells function in a network with one another to orient us and provide feedback along our route. This system relays this information from one part of the brain to another, allowing individuals to visualize, understand, and integrate routes to a destination. When that network functions improperly it impairs our ability to find our way. No study has stratified lost hikers among the three navigator types to determine inherent risk for becoming lost, though. The fact that anyone can take a wrong turn away from the trail and head away from their intended route, regardless of navigation ability, means we all remain at risk. Integrators may have an advantage in retracing their steps, using spatial orientation, and recognizing natural features they had passed on the incorrect route to find their way back to the trail. They may also possess a better understanding than others of their general location by simply looking at a map.

Knowing our strengths and weaknesses in navigation affords us the ability to understand ourselves a little better. Using this context to prepare for the possibility of becoming lost elevates us to a greater position than having not realized our shortcomings. Those not born a natural navigator should consider taking steps to increase the probability of a safe return from their journeys in the wilderness. Rather than solo hiking along unfamiliar routes, taking a friend with navigation skills provides a broader safety net of abilities and an opportunity to learn along the way and build their own skillset. When trekking solo, consider taking a familiar route that you've taken multiple times. Otherwise, simple loop hikes or straight out-and-back trails can reduce the chances of wandering off in a wrong direction, as opposed to those with numerous turns and accessory trails that add confusion. Part of the hiking experience includes solitude, independence, and the opportunity for self-reliance, but these should not happen at the expense of the hiker's life. Prioritizing our own safety requires having the humility to place safety in front of other goals. Imprecise Navigators should know they can improve their directional skills in other ways with enough discipline and time. Frequently practicing navigation and orientation exercises can develop new brain connections to elevate us to higher capabilities.

Following a Trail

Following a trail requires the right amount of attention paid to detail, analyzing the flow of the terrain, and mindfully monitoring a number of terrestrial and celestial clues. Repeating this with each outing builds the instinct and skill, while not taking away from the experience. This compares to the defensive driver who maintains vigilance on the road, watching the signs and anticipating other drivers' moves, but who can also admire roadside sights along the way. Attaining a better skill level takes practice. Developing the ability to stay on-trail or find the way back to it may one day save the life of that hiker. We can follow a trail on its path through the unknown through several ways, beginning with the basic physical markings along the route.

Cairns have been used for thousands of years to mark trails and roads throughout the world and are still used to this day. Wanderers once built these stacks of rocks along important routes to guide themselves or others through otherwise ambiguous terrain. Recently increasing vandalism and intentional displacement of

cairns have undermined their reliability. Cairns have also become a source for controversy and scorn within the hiking community. The argument favors leaving the elements of the earth in their original place, rather than using them for direction or trail art.

While most trails in North America have other means for identifying direction, some still rely on these for guidance. Trails throughout Canyonlands National Park, for instance, rely heavily on cairns to guide hikers through the landscape. These stone stacks have been placed by park rangers at intervals to keep trekkers from getting lost, which would happen easily and often in their absence. The picture below comes from Canyonlands National Park. Cairns offer immense navigational assistance among an otherwise confusing landscape.

Trail markers represent the most common, modern method for informing hikers where the trail begins and ends, identifying turns and other intersecting trails. These semi-permanent parts of the trail guide us with simplicity, while remaining difficult to alter. Workers in the National Park System or volunteers from the local trail conference place these at reasonable but arbitrary intervals. Trail markers represent the most important, basic source of information a hiker can utilize to navigate their way. No uniform type or methodology has been established in the United States.

Many hiking trails in the western part of the US utilize signs to guide trekkers, either by a specific trail symbol (for instance on the Pacific Crest Trail) or worded wood or metal signs with arrows. They identify where trails begin and end, and where other trails intersect them. While they clearly guide hikers on the right path, there may not be many signs along the route to assure hikers they have remained on the correct trail. This aspect becomes difficult among desert terrain, being easy to mistake off-trail landscape for the trail itself.

In the eastern US most trails have "blazes" to guide hikers, either represented by a painted shape (rectangle, circle, or triangle) on rocky ground, a tree, or boulder. These may also be represented by a durable reflective material of similar shapes nailed to a tree. The blaze's color specifies different trails. The interval distance between these varies, depending on what the regional trail conference sees as necessary. Worded signs also do exist in spots in the East though. Signs serve as self-explanatory guides, but blazes follow a structured pattern for the hiker to interpret.

A single blaze as indicated in the picture below left indicates we're on the route, with the blaze's color indicating the specific trail that we're following on the map. The single blaze tells the hiker to continue straight, and to make no turns until otherwise specified. This trail marker was found along the southern terminus of the Appalachian Trail, with which the white blaze has been most closely associated. Many trails in the eastern US, other than the AT, use white for a blaze color but only when not in the vicinity of the AT itself.

When the trail takes a turn the pattern changes from one single blaze to two, orienting the hiker in the direction of that trail. The second blaze, oriented above the single blaze and off to either the left or the right side, indicates the direction the trail turns. The picture above right indicates a right turn. The large rocks peeking out of the ground represent the trail floor. Without a worn path in the ground, we have no way to otherwise know how the trail courses through the backcountry. Without this blaze pattern telling us to turn here, getting lost would come easily.

After passing one blaze, and especially after making any turn, automatically start looking for the next blaze! Staying on-trail requires a healthy amount of attention paid to where these trail markers have been placed, and to where they lead us.

Most hiking areas have a labyrinth of multiple intersecting trails covering the region. In places where worded signs have been

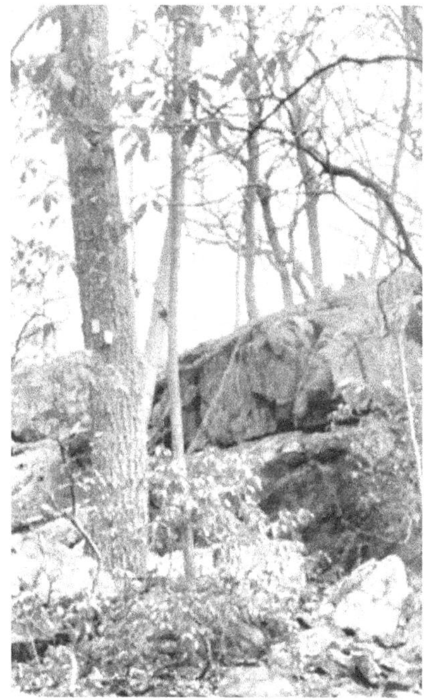

The blaze pattern on the tree at the top of this hill indicates a left turn in the trail once the hiker reaches the top. While looking around and admiring the landscape, vegetation, and local wildlife a hiker can easily miss these turn indicators and find themselves off-trail.

placed, navigating these intersections becomes self-explanatory. When blazes identify the trails, knowing the patterns and symbols becomes very important. Knowing they all have an individual color assigned to them, staying on the same route, or transitioning to another can come just as easily. We may come upon a combination of blazes on the same tree or boulder, ordinarily at points of trail intersection. Each blaze pattern is normally placed such that a hiker coming from one direction can see the option between maintaining on the same path or taking the turn on to the new route.

	You're on trail, stay straight
	Right Turn in the trail
	Left turn in the trail
	Start of the trail
	End of the trail

Canada favors trail signs, with uniformity within provinces and regions. The picture below depicts an example taken from Kalamalka Lake Provincial Park in British Columbia.

Following a trail as marked by either worded signs or blazes represents the most basic of skills to navigate through the area in which we wish to explore. The lack of perspective of how far we have come through the route, and how much further we must go, represents the disadvantage of using this navigation method alone. Additional issues come when painted trail markers have worn to the point of invisibility and nailed-in blazes or signs have been purposely removed as souvenirs or for more nefarious purposes. These circumstances easily misguide hikers off-trail when having no backup source for navigation.

Most of us enter the wilderness seeking to relax and clear our minds from the bustle of everyday living. The natural question asks how that can be achieved when one needs to pay such close attention to detail along the route. We can accomplish both. Following the markers does not require intense concentration, leaving plenty of opportunity to absorb nature's sensory stimulation and to clear our minds while assuring our own safety. The wilderness allows for a peaceful experience, while existing as a brutally unforgiving world when captured in its pitfalls. Knowing we eventually want to leave it to get back home, prioritizing this must come above other goals. When we step 3 feet off-trail in many places we hike, everything looks the same and opens the door to becoming disoriented as to our location. Stopping periodically or when otherwise inspired, while still on the trail, we can look around and admire the surroundings to accomplish the desired relaxation while avoiding becoming lost.

Using a map to guide us proves invaluable for staying on course. It increases our level of information beyond that provided by the rudimentary and occasionally missing or misleading trail markers. Having this additional source for guidance provides awareness of what lies ahead and allows us to focus on specific points along the route. Regularly referencing the trail on a map not only elevates our navigational skill, but also serves as a great way to start becoming comfortable with the use of maps.

Obtaining and reviewing a paper map for the intended hike ahead of time amounts to studying for a test. Familiarizing ourselves with details of the route beforehand places us in a position to lessen the chances of losing our way. Knowing distance between turns in the trail, locations of trail intersections, and notable features along the way gives a framework of expectation to reinforce our location, when acknowledging these during the hike itself. All serious expeditions and our military use this strategy as reconnaissance, or "recon," to embark under circumstances of familiarity rather than with a lack of understanding. This provides an opportunity to plan out the route and timing of the hike, and to manage our own expectations for that outing. Taking the map along with us while out on the trail provides real-time information through the entire hike. The advantage of these paper maps comes with minimal cost, no reliance on battery life, waterproof construction, and ease of use for reference in the field.

The bird's-eye view of a map displays the turns and trail intersections both behind and ahead of our location. Knowing what we have passed already and what lies ahead allows us to hike with anticipation and pinpoint our place on the map as we encounter these features. Anyone can use a map and follow these aspects of the trail without formal map reading skills. The more we use maps, the better we understand them and build upon this skill. Without necessarily paying attention to specific direction, the map provides a turn-by-turn aerial visual of what we see on the ground, much like navigation apps do when we drive.

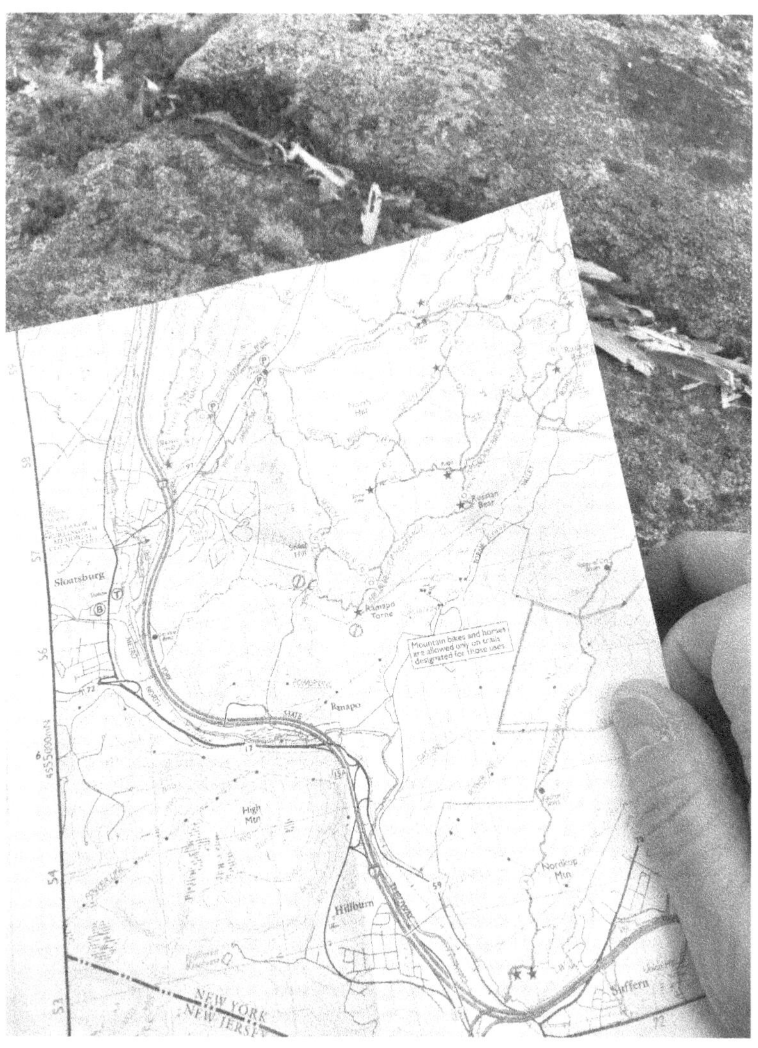

Snowshoeing in Idaho

Anticipating a day snowshoeing in Galena, Idaho, I found a trail map online from Galena Lodge's website and picked out a route I wanted to take. I received a local map of those trails after I arrived at the lodge, representing what I had seen online. I highlighted the route I already picked and studied and referenced it along my way. As I trekked through the curves in the trail, I rotated the map accordingly to see how the trail ahead would appear.

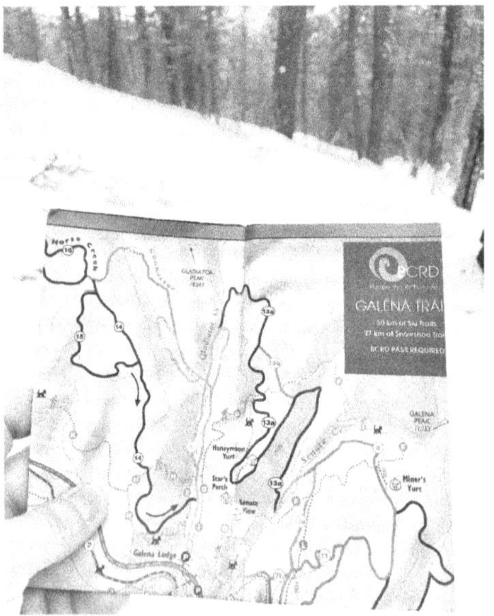

Along the trail I noted where I crossed ski trails, passed yurts and a creek, all as indicated on that map to see exactly where I was in the moment. This provided great feedback that I was making progress and informed me of what lay ahead. I then could anticipate upcoming landmarks, trail features, and turns. The round, yellow trail marker on the tree ahead also reinforced that I was on the right route.

Frequently referencing the map and rotating it according to the curves and turns of the trail makes hiking unfamiliar paths that much easier. As we pass features depicted along the route, it reinforces our location and instills confidence that we remain on the correct path. This simple skill greatly reduces the chances of getting lost. If this were to somehow happen, knowing our last location makes finding our way back to the trail a more realistic possibility.

Electronic navigation, as provided by a trail app or a dedicated GPS-based device, provides great information regarding real-time location and serves as an acceptable alternative to a paper map. The advantage to electronics over paper maps comes with plotting our position on the marked route. Figuring this out on our own then becomes unnecessary. Many hikers utilize these for navigating day hikes consistently without fail. Potential limitations of this tech should be considered in the decision to use this as our sole navigational source.

- The GPS signal may be lost with thick canopy overhead, or deflected in mountainous terrain, making the position marker inaccurate and unreliable.
- The app or device may not have a map overlay on top of the highlighted trail and therefore not display the detail paper maps offer.
- A map overlay may also be outdated, displaying inaccurate route information and possibly extending time spent out on-trail.
- Battery charge dwindles with usage and may deplete before the end of the hike.
- Devices get dropped on rocks, fall out of pockets into streams or ravines, rendering them useless or lost.

When solely counting on these devices for a safe and timely return, there may come a time when they fail to meet that expectation. When planning to use electronic navigation, bring a battery bank and charging cord, download the map rather than rely on cell signal for navigation, and have an analog method as a Plan B.

The Cardinal Directions

The term "cardinal directions" refers to north, south, east, and west. The picture of the globe below shows the North Pole sitting at one point at the top of the Earth, where all the vertical lines on the map grid overlaying the planet converge. The point where the vertical lines all converge at the bottom of the Earth refers to the South Pole. When we say we're heading north it simply refers to traveling in the direction that moves us toward the top of the Earth. When one says that a place lies north of us, it refers to a point between our position and the top of the Earth. The opposite holds true when referring to south. If we head in either of these two directions and keep going, we will come to a point where we can go no further in that direction, as we will have reached either pole.

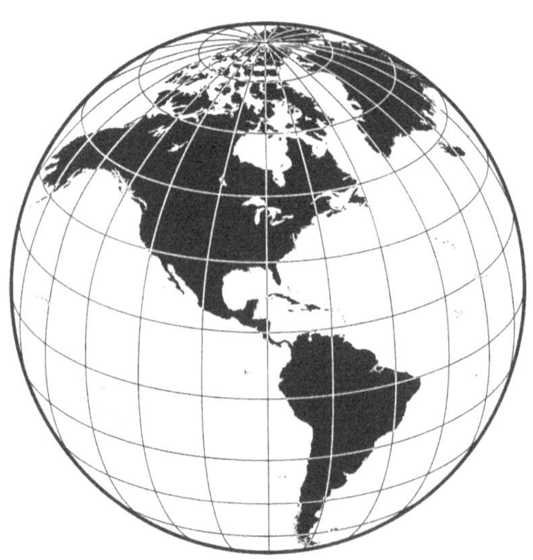

While the vertical "longitude" lines on this grid run between the North and South Poles and end at the top and bottom of the Earth, the horizontal "latitude" lines run parallel to the equator between the poles, encircling the entire globe like rings, without a stopping point. When moving in any direction along a latitude line we either move west or east. If we were to theoretically travel along a specific latitude in the same direction without stopping, we would encircle the entire Earth and return to our original starting point. We can leave New York City on a plane and fly so far west that we would land back in New York City.

The placement of everything and everyone on the planet lies to the north, south, east, or west relative to our position. These cardinal directions lie in a fixed location relative to where we stand or move toward. See the illustration to the left, where the person heads toward the west. We should envision the Earth's compass as lying at our feet, with us positioned at the center, which moves wherever we do. While we and the circle at our feet move together in any direction, the "N" and "S" always point North and South, respectively. The "E" and "W" always point East and West, respectively, regardless of where we move. Where they point stays constant and never changes. Only our position on the Earth changes, relative to those directions. The figure in the illustration below has changed direction of travel, as compared to above, while the compass directions stay in the same position on the circle.

The halfway points between any two cardinal directions, denoted northeast, southeast, southwest, and northwest, provide more specific directional guidance. The figure in the illustration at right appears to be headed southeast.

For those who have difficulty with direction, the first step to a better understanding begins with memorizing how north, south, east, and west relate to one another. Once understood, we can start to figure out our direction of travel once we confirm just one cardinal direction in the 360° that encircle us. When we face north, east will **always** be to our right, west will **always** be to our left, and south will **always** be behind us. Several cues in our surroundings provide clues to indicate at least one of the four cardinal directions, and we can determine our direction of travel from there.

TERRESTRIAL CUES AND CELESTIAL CUES

Terrestrial and celestial cues provide essential information as to our whereabouts, but taking advantage of them requires paying attention to their subtleties. We tend to use landmarks to navigate in our daily lives, whether consciously or subconsciously. When in unfamiliar surroundings, these cues help us collect knowledge about our direction of travel. The presence and prominence of these indicators depend on location, season, and time of day, but consciously seeking them out routinely helps build our skill to understand our position and direction. If we can determine one point of reference for direction, the remaining cardinal directions become easy to determine from our mental compass.

Assessing our position relative to terrestrial landmarks along any route provides invaluable knowledge about our position and direction. Mountains towering above the trail in the western half of the US and Canada serve as great terrestrial cues to help us find our way. Rivers and creeks, lakes, water towers, roadways or a nearby town visible in the distance also serve as indicators of direction. A pre-hike study of the map or satellite image of the area provides the location of these landmarks relative to that of the trail. When spotted along the route in real time, we can then determine our position and direction from that information.

The numerous peaks of the Grand Teton Mountain Range run north-south in direction. This line of mountains sits west and parallel to both US Highway 89 and Teton Park Road, running through that national park. Most of the hiking trails course between the mountains and the roadways. Hikers can use this impossible-to-miss mountainous landmark to their advantage, knowing the north-south orientation of the range, sitting to the west of the trails. When hiking parallel to those mountains off to our left, we're headed north. Knowing this becomes important when planning to return to where we started, as we then need to head south, now with those same mountains off to our right.

Direction of Travel Example

During our morning commute to work we pass a coffee shop on our left as we travel that route. Returning home, along that same road, we pass the same coffee shop on our right-hand side. If we were blindfolded while being driven along that commute, then allowed to see that coffee shop for only a few seconds, we would automatically know whether we were headed to work or home, depending on which side of the road the coffee shop sits. This simplistic example demonstrates that our position relative to that landmark determines our direction of travel.

The Grand Teton Mountain Range sitting west and running parallel to US Highway 89 in the foreground.

When hiking perpendicularly toward those same mountains from the lot, we're heading west. Whether or not we care to know exactly which direction we have gone, we should realize that returning to the parking area requires us to head in a direction with those mountains to our back, heading east.

Unique rock formations can also guide our way along the route, while we note our position relative to them. We can spot these landmarks along the way to reinforce our direction; they remain something to look for on the return from an out-and-back trek.

In most of eastern North America and lesser mountainous regions, hikers have fewer terrestrial cues available to them, especially when a thick tree canopy or dense vegetation reaches above eye level. We may have to rely on a lake or river near the trail, a cell tower, water tower, or a visible community nearby. In these areas of the continent, we may have no visible, land-based cues to help guide us along our way.

Legend tells us that moss only grows on the northern side of trees in the Northern Hemisphere. The sun shines directly over the equator and therefore casts light from the south onto the landmass of the northern half of the Earth. That sunlight hits the southern part of the trees and inhibits growth of moss. It otherwise casts a shadow on the northern side of the tree, allowing moss to grow. This terrestrial cue should be considered unreliable, especially in dense forests, where the plentiful shade allows moss to grow on all sides of the tree. In the case where we observe moss growth on only one side of multiple trees along the trail in the Northern Hemisphere, that likely identifies the north side of those trees. The Southern Hemisphere displays the opposite.

The position of the sun represents the most useful celestial cue we can use while in the outdoors. The Earth rotates in the direction such that the eastern portion of every continent experiences sunlight before the western parts do, except when near the North and South Poles. As most of us will never get that close to either pole, that exception remains moot. For those who have difficulty with the concept: The sun **always** rises in the east and remains in the eastern sky until midday.

- When seeing the sun in the sky before the middle of the day, it's always in the east.
- While in the eastern sky, from sunrise until around 10:30 AM the sun shines on objects and casts their shadow on the opposite side, toward the west.
- Drawing a line between the morning sun's position in the east and the shadow's direction toward the west identifies the east-west directions, making determination of north and south very easy!

The sun **always** sets in the west and remains in the western sky from midday until sunset.

- When seeing the sun in the sky after the middle of the day, it's always in the west.
- While in the western sky, from around 1:30 PM until sunset, the sun shines on objects and casts their shadow on the opposite side, toward the east.
- Drawing a line between the afternoon sun's position in the west and the shadow's direction toward the east again identifies the east-west directions, making determination of north and south very easy!

Just to Be Exact . . .

The exact position of sunrise and sunset does differ between winter and summer. This method may not precisely spot due east and west, but without another way to tell direction this method helps us figure out our general direction and gets us to where we need to go.

As the sun approaches and departs midday positions, the above becomes less accurate, as the high angle of the sun casts its transitioning shadow in a more north-south direction.

At midday the sun sits overhead as it passes from the eastern sky to the western sky, making it difficult, but not impossible, to determine direction.

- At midday the sun sits overhead but rotates over the equator, shining light on the Northern Hemisphere from a southern position.
- Place a straight object, such as a stick, branch, or trekking pole, upright into the ground and watch where the sun casts its shadow. As the sun shines from a slightly southern position, the shadow will appear on the northern side of the object.
- Watch the migration of the shadow and mark the end of it every 5 minutes with small sticks or rocks. The point at which the shadow extends the *shortest* distance from the base of the stick identifies north. Leading up to and following that point we will see relatively longer shadows, pointing at an angle away from north.

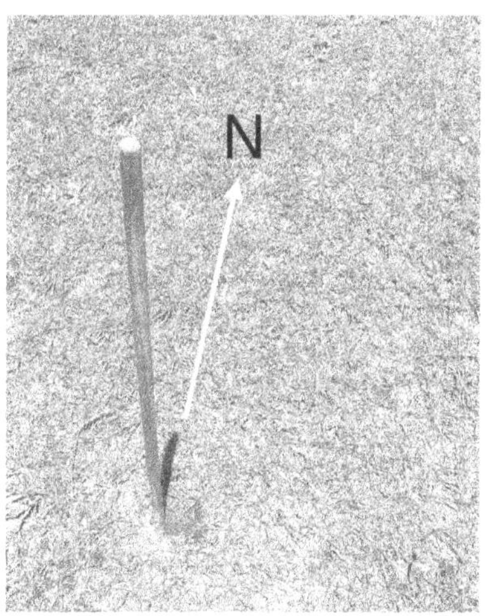

The sun shines from a slightly southern position, casting a shadow that points north. When the sun is directly overhead, the shadow shrinks to the shortest distance from the base of the stick as compared to when the sun is not directly overhead.

Identifying the position of the sun regularly during our work commute while walking outside our home or along the sidewalk in a city helps us become better at using this celestial cue to help us find our way. Is it morning, midday, or afternoon? Where have the shadows of objects been cast? Direction of travel then becomes easy. The following picture was taken at 10:00 AM while walking along the sidewalk in San Francisco. The time of day and the parking meter's shadow cast onto the sidewalk represents all the information we need to determine what direction we're walking. The sun, shining from the eastern sky, casts the shadows onto the sidewalk toward the west, making north our direction of travel.

The morning sun, shining from the east, casts the shadows of the meter and the lamppost onto the sidewalk in the opposite direction, being the west. Walking forward from here, north is the direction of travel.

Paying attention to the sun's position in the sky while driving and other daily activities helps us determine direction of travel. Routinely practicing this builds improved instinctive abilities to follow the cues of this celestial body.

A clear night sky offers several celestial clues to help guide our way, having aided in human navigation dating back almost 1,000 years. The most prominent of these, the moon, rises in the east and sets in the west like the sun. Seasonal differences do dictate where in the eastern and western sky the moon appears, however. Differing phases of the moon also determine the reliability of this cue. According to *The Old Farmer's Almanac*, a full moon serves as a consistent marker for east and west in its rise and fall overnight, respectively. The position of the moon around late March and late September, at the time of the vernal and fall equinoxes, closely approximates due east in its rise and due west in its fall as well. During these times and phases the moon can be used reliably.

Some stars and constellations serve as useful celestial cues for nighttime navigation on a clear night. The most famous celestial body, the North Star (aka Polaris), sits above the North Pole to guide us in its direction. It sits at the end of the handle on the Little Dipper (aka Ursa Minor) and can also be found by drawing a straight line off of the end of the Big Dipper (aka Ursa Major), as depicted in the picture below. When finding the North Star, know that north sits on the horizon below it. If only able to see the Big

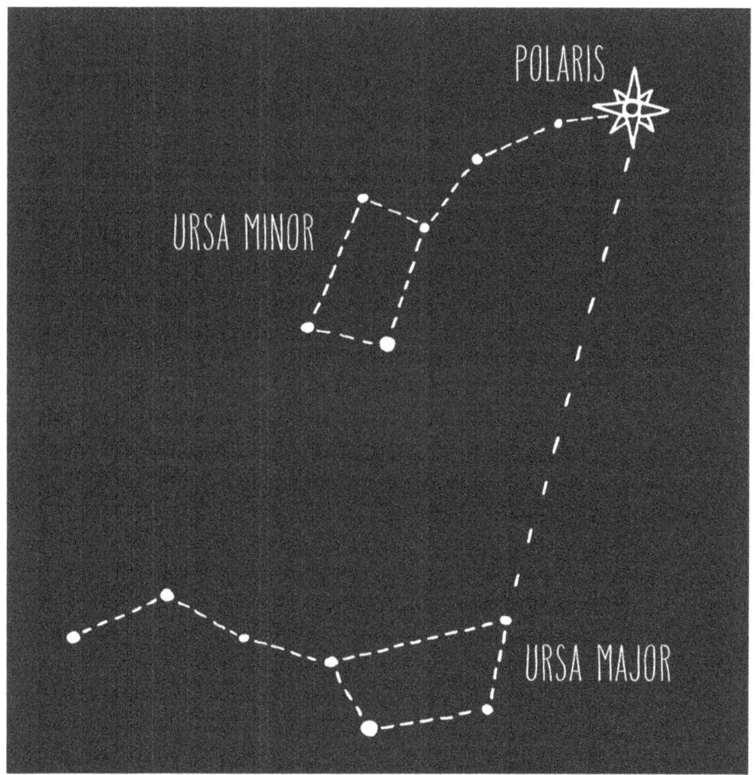

Dipper, drawing a mental line from the end of the bowl section of this constellation will tell us which direction identifies north.

Determining the other cardinal directions can be derived from the line between us and the point that determines north. Once we know where north is, we can identify the other three cardinal directions.

Venus, our nearest neighboring planet, is one of the brightest celestial bodies in the night sky, other than the moon. Its orbit around the sun takes about 225 Earth days, and in relation to our visibility it follows the sun. The timing, placement, and visibility of Venus varies throughout the year. Sometimes it can be seen as a bright body in the lower eastern sky just before sunrise and can be viewed as the brightest body in the lower western sky after sunset. When it otherwise lies in front of or behind the sun it is difficult to see from Earth. Venus can be very useful to confirm direction, when visible, but due to its variability in placement it is a good strategy to research its current status before embarking on the hike, just in the off chance that celestial cues will be needed for nighttime navigation.

Sirius, one of the brightest celestial bodies of the nighttime canopy, is part of the constellation Canis Major. From the northern hemisphere this binary star remains visible in the lower southern sky for about 7 to 8 months out of the year, appearing in the fall and shining until spring. Its light confirms south when we need to know where we are going at night.

Orion, the hunter from Greek mythology, stands as the most recognizable constellation in the night sky. Seen throughout most of the year on a clear night, it shines most clearly in the winter months. Below Orion's Belt, the easiest part of this constellation to spot, lies the lesser-known Orion's Sword. The line of three stars that comprise this part of the constellation points perpendicularly away from the belt and to the south.

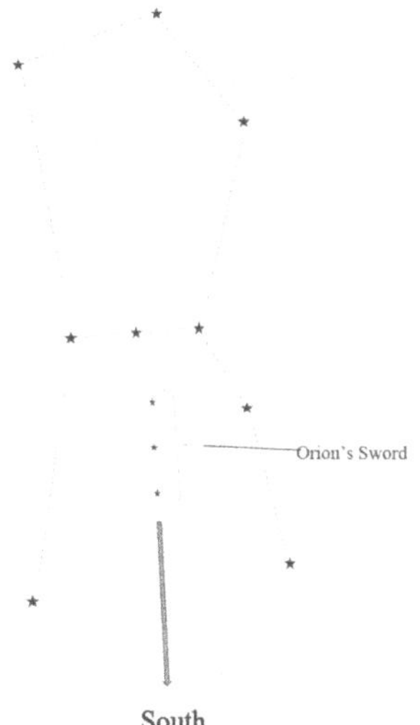

When having to navigate at night in the Southern Hemisphere another constellation, called the Southern Cross, can help us find south. This requires more skill and imagination than with Orion. See the picture below.

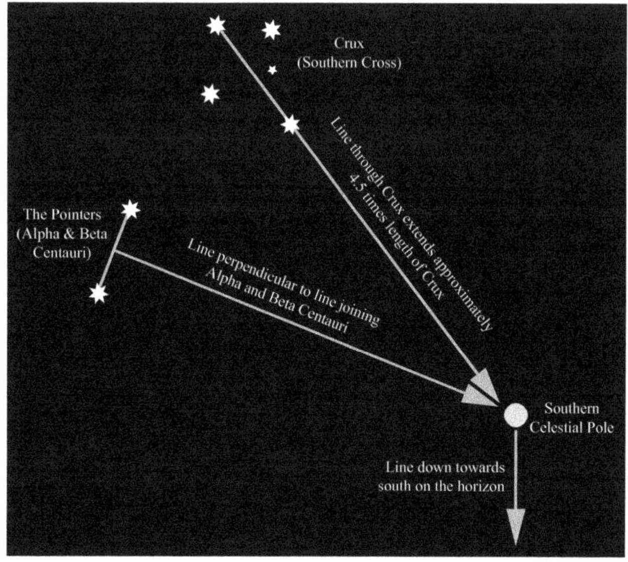

We first draw an imaginary line through the long axis of the cross-like constellation. We then draw another line perpendicular to a nearby constellation, a pair of stars called the Pointers, in the same direction as the line drawn from the Southern Cross. These two lines intersect directly above the South Pole. Mariners and other explorers in the Southern Hemisphere have used this combination of constellations to navigate for hundreds of years.

Becoming lost happens more frequently than we appreciate and occurs for various reasons that may be out of our control. Finding our way to safety or back to where we went off track takes instinct and skill. Terrestrial and celestial cues provide valuable information to help accomplish this, but location, weather, and other factors make these cues too unreliable to count on every time we need them. Learning the skill of simple land navigation elevates our self-reliance, maximizing our ability to control the outcome.

Understanding the Basics of Maps

Using a paper map and analog compass to guide our way through the wilderness has become a lost art and underappreciated skill in our electronic and digital world. Though many still use these, they continue to dwindle in number as time passes. The convenience and relative ease of electronic means for navigation attracts many adventurers to it. The advantage of analog versions comes with lack of dependence on battery life, and cell or satellite signal. They do not break when dropped and continue to work when immersed in water. These mishaps do and will happen to our equipment. Count on it! We need to contemplate our backup option if we experience a hard failure of a primary electronic navigation method. What will we do then? How will we proceed?

Entire books have been written on this one subject, such as the near-300-page US Army Field Manual 3-25.26, *Map Reading and Land Navigation*, and its updated versions. This and other authoritative resources for land navigation, as well as innumerable online videos, cover a body of information that cannot be decanted down into one chapter. This primer lays out the handful of basic map and compass skills that enable us to find our direction, our location, and our way back home. After learning these skills they should be practiced routinely on every hike, as they become forgotten over time. This will amount to a review for those who use these tools already. This should otherwise serve as a springboard for new information for those who do not and will hopefully fill in gaps of knowledge for hikers who have begun to learn but have not yet reached a level of confidence.

Understanding map basics represents the initial step toward land navigation. These 2-dimensional representations of our 3-dimensional planet use artistic and technical aspects to depict the features on the ground, such as rivers, streams, and other bodies of water and trails, powerlines, roads, and railways. Contour lines follow the curves of the Earth along given altitudes, including peaks, plateaus, and valleys. A grid pattern of longitude and latitude lines overlays the map to reinforce north-south and east-west lines. A legend explains the numerous symbols, including a distance ruler with an explanation of the scale of the map. This indicates how much distance on the map represents the amount of distance on the ground.

Beginners can easily become overwhelmed by the dizzying array of information on a map and may not even understand which way to hold it. If we can read the largest words that are upright on the map, then we're holding it correctly. The top of the map orients toward the north and the bottom orients toward the south. Maps view the Earth from the vantage point of hovering above and looking down upon it. This bird's-eye view allows us to appreciate all the ground features on this 2-D paper representation. Viewing maps while horizontal offers the best perspective and applicability to our surroundings. National Geographic trail maps are used and featured in this section.

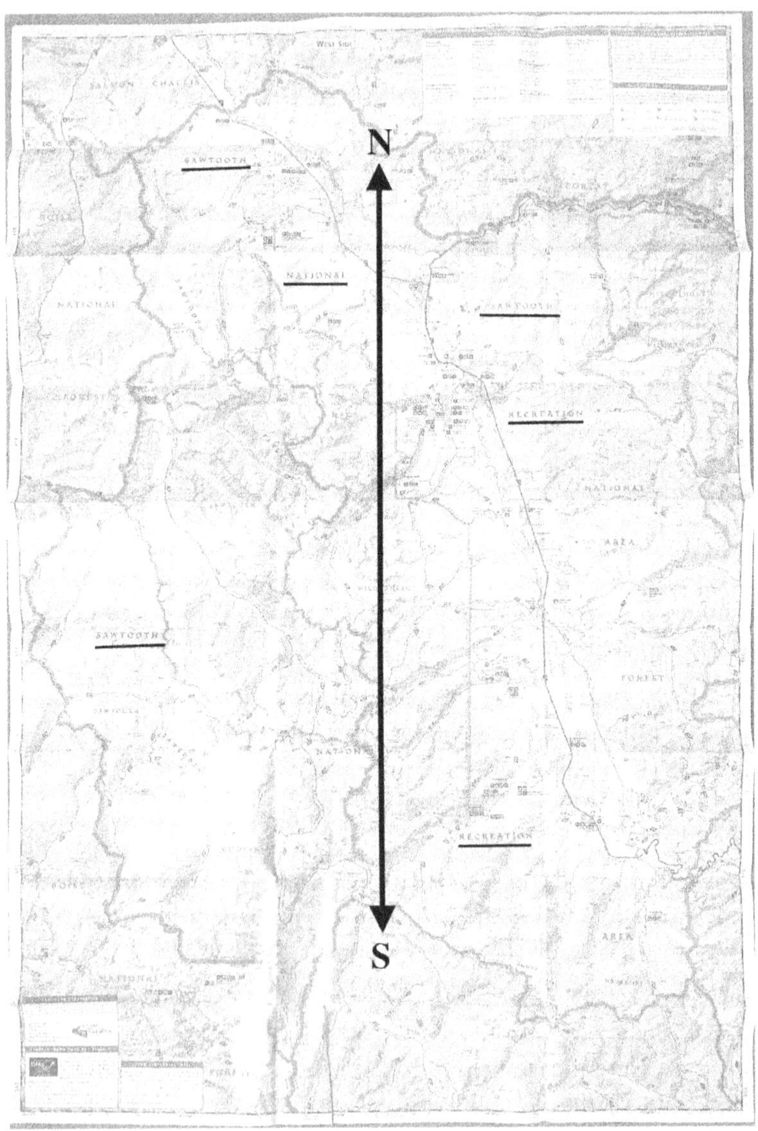

Several of the largest words on the map have been underlined, to reinforce that if these words can be read, then the map is being viewed correctly. When one specific point on the map lies above another, that specific point is oriented to the north of the other.

TRAILS ILLUSTRATED MAP, SAWTOOTH NATIONAL RECREATION AREA / #870

An orienting compass, usually printed toward a corner of the map, further assures us of the cardinal directions. The star at the top of the compass represents True North, or the direction that points to the North Pole. The inner concentric circle also depicts an offset from True North, with its arrow pointing to Magnetic North. The difference between these two will be explained in the coming sections.

COPYRIGHT NATIONAL GEOGRAPHIC PARTNERS, LLC
TRAILS ILLUSTRATED MAP, SAWTOOTH NATIONAL RECREATION AREA / #870

The legend provides us with all the information we need to interpret the various lines and symbols throughout the map and what they represent. It also provides data on distance relative to the grid lines and contour lines depicting the topography. The scale depends on how much area needs to be covered on the map, therefore being unique to each one. The scale of this map, 1:75,000, means one unit of measure on the map (cm or in) represents seventy-five thousand of those same units on the ground. The bottom of the legend explains this.

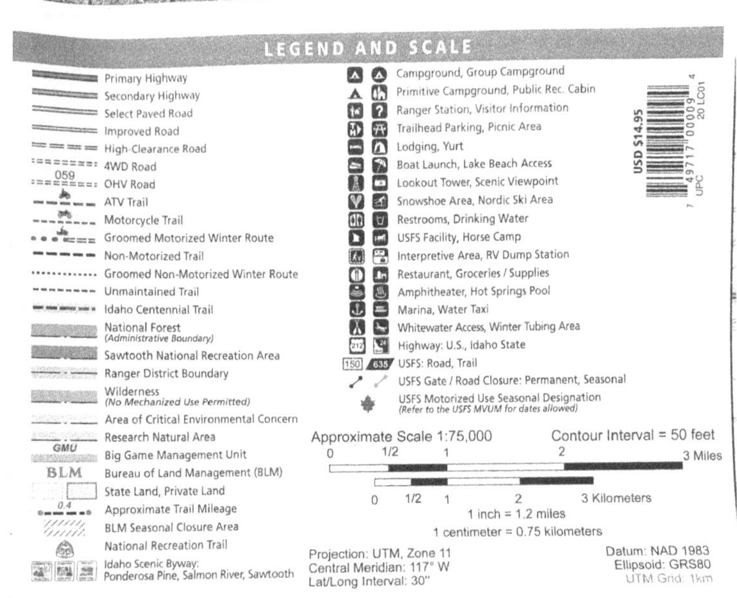

COPYRIGHT NATIONAL GEOGRAPHIC PARTNERS, LLC.
TRAILS ILLUSTRATED MAP, SAWTOOTH NATIONAL RECREATION AREA / #870

The legend also defines the "Contour Interval." Each contour line follows the curves of the Earth at a specific altitude. Numerous contour lines run parallel to one another to represent how those curves appear through changes in altitude. The legend defines the altitude difference between the lines, or contour interval, as 50 feet on this specific map. Looking down on the Earth, as maps do, the visible space between these lines varies, based on how steep or how flat the terrain flows in that location. The closer these lines run to one another, the more rapid the elevation changes over a short horizontal distance, representing a steep incline or decline. A wider space between these lines represents gradual to little change in elevation over a given horizontal distance. The shape of these lines differs with how the curves of the Earth flow through the given altitude. In the case of high-elevation mountains, the lines form concentric circular shapes, contoured to the terrain, becoming smaller toward the summit, until a tiny circle or ellipse outlines the very top.

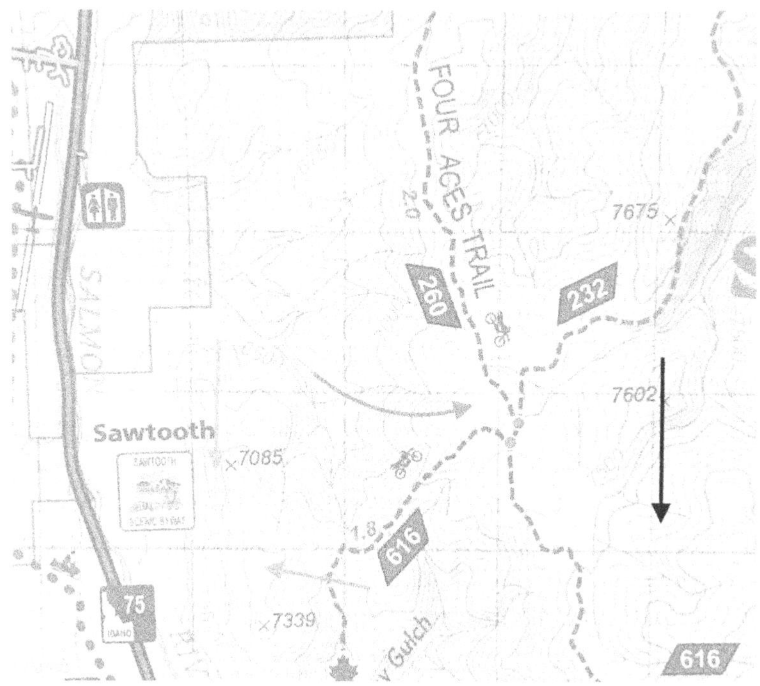

COPYRIGHT NATIONAL GEOGRAPHIC PARTNERS, LLC
TRAILS ILLUSTRATED MAP, SAWTOOTH NATIONAL RECREATION AREA / #870

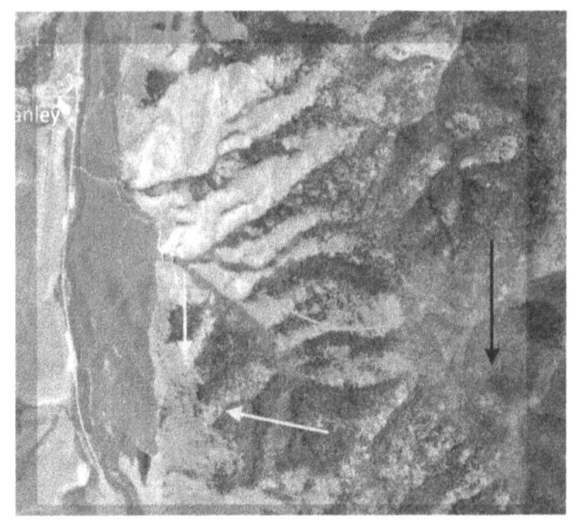

The picture on the preceding page depicts contour lines very close to one another (gray arrow perpendicular to the word "Sawtooth"). This represents a steep ascent or descent, as considerable change in elevation occurs over a short horizontal distance. The contour lines on the right side of the picture (darkest arrow) lie further apart from one another, representing less steep terrain. The curved arrow points to an area void of contour lines, representing a plateau where elevation does not change. Finally, the left-pointing arrow indicates a small circle representing the peak of a mountain. Another peak on the same mountain lies just south of this point, identified by an even smaller circle and an "x" with its elevation marked at 7,339 feet.

Comparing the map view to a satellite view from Google Maps (above), with the arrows in the same locations on each, we can begin to appreciate how the map represents reality. This enables us to identify these and other terrain features by following their patterns.

Some contour lines appear dark, while others appear lighter. The map above shows the darker lines as five lines away from one another. With a contour interval of 50 feet, the elevation difference between dark lines amounts to 250 feet. This allows for quicker calculation of elevation change. Along these darker lines we find the elevation, which remains the same along that line throughout the map. We can use these elevation markers to determine the estimated elevation of a specific feature, and to estimate the anticipated elevation change along our route. Using the same example

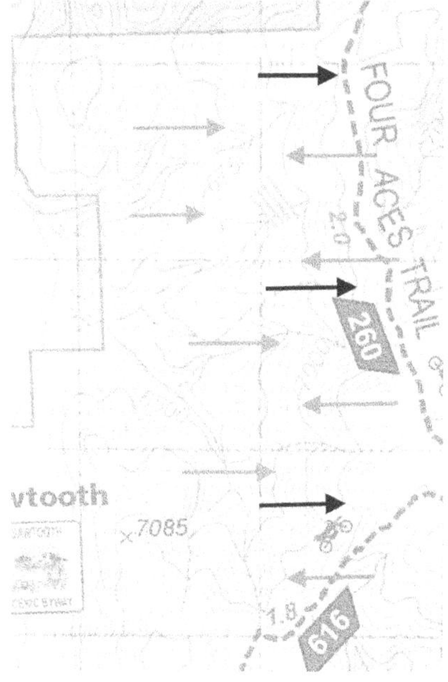

COPYRIGHT NATIONAL GEOGRAPHIC PARTNERS, LLC
TRAILS ILLUSTRATED MAP, SAWTOOTH NATIONAL RECREATION AREA / #870

from the map above, the picture below looks at the Four Aces Trail again. The dotted line depicts the trail, with "2.0" indicating the distance (in miles) of that trail segment. To determine the elevation of that part of the trail we search for the elevation marker closest to the area of interest.

Off to the left (west) of the word "Four" lies a dark contour line marked at "6750" feet elevation. Arrows identify that line as it courses through the terrain. Four hash marks point to light contour lines to its right, each representing 50 feet in elevation change. Two dark lines sit between the 6750 line and the trail, therefore defining another 500 feet elevation difference from there. How do we know if the trail sits above or below the 6750 line? Moving from that line toward the trail, the next dark contour line, identified by slightly darker gray arrows, has been labeled with an elevation of "7000" along its path. This indicates that elevation increases as we get closer to the trail. The next dark line uphill from there has been marked by black arrows and it lies next to the trail, with the elevation number falling outside of the frame of this picture. However, this dark line sits another 250 feet above the last one, so we can deduce that this section of the trail runs at an elevation of approximately 7,250 feet. Notice the trail courses through a narrow plateau, represented by the wider distance

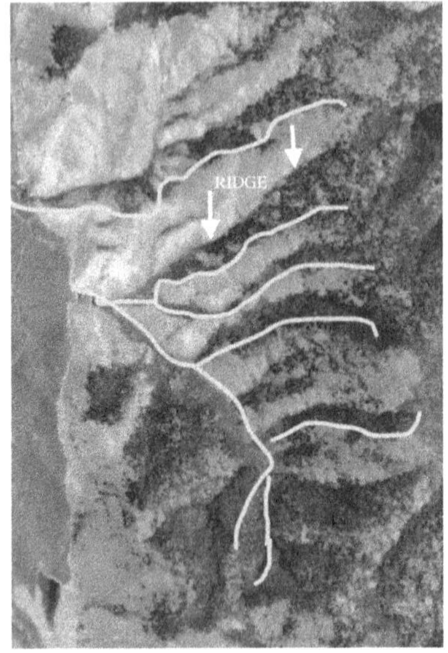

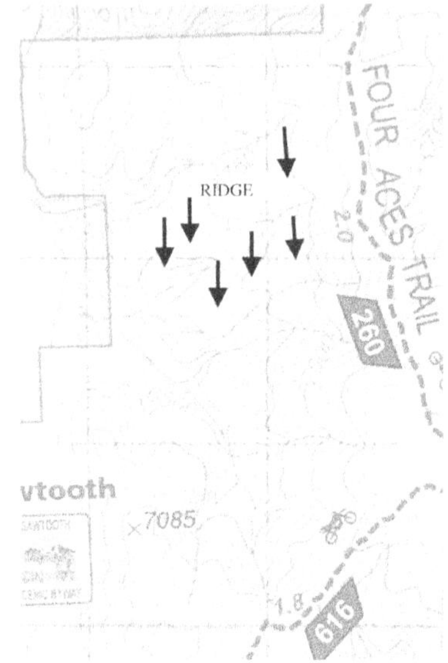

COPYRIGHT NATIONAL GEOGRAPHIC PARTNERS, LLC
TRAILS ILLUSTRATED MAP, SAWTOOTH NATIONAL RECREATION AREA / #870

between contour lines, and runs along the top ridge of the long peaks in this area.

We can easily spot numerous ridges and valleys when viewing mountains on the satellite view on the next page, as they ascend from the base of the mountain to the top ridge, where the Four Aces Trail runs. Identifying these ridges and valleys on the map involves following the pattern of the contour lines along these features. The tortuous contour lines run near parallel to one another and course along these ridges and valleys. Looking at the Four Aces Trail again, and the contour lines between it and the base of the mountain, we can see a series of convexities and concavities along the mountainside. The direction of the contour lines indicates ridges versus valleys. We can easily spot valleys on the map, with thin gray lines along them, representing the small streams that receive snowmelt and rainwater runoff from the ridges above and bring that water downhill toward the Snake River below.

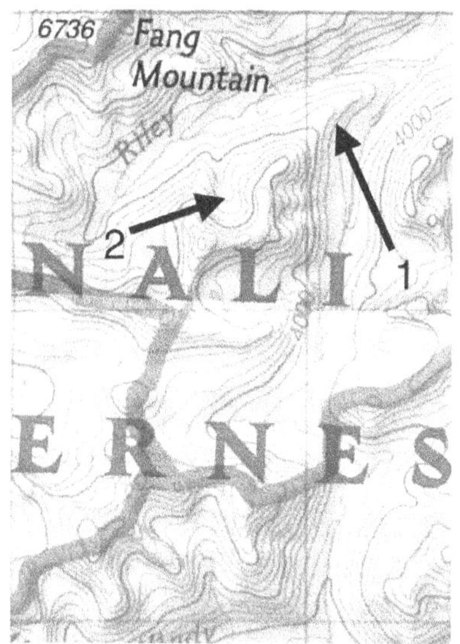

COPYRIGHT NATIONAL GEOGRAPHIC PARTNERS, LLC
TRAILS ILLUSTRATED MAP, DENALI NATIONAL PARK AND PRESERVE / #222

The images above compare a satellite view from Google Maps, focusing on the western part of the same terrain as viewed above, with the same area on the map. Light gray lines have been drawn over the satellite view of valleys to mimic the location and course of these streams, matching the map's representation of their locations between the ridges.

Examine the long uphill ridges rising from the base on the left toward the trail on the satellite view in the pictures above. One of these ridges has been labeled with white arrows. Two adjacent ridges have been identified by black arrows on the map for comparison, represented by a series of convexities in the parallel contour lines. We know the Four Aces Trail runs along the peak in this area. The parallel *convexities* of ridges point **away** from the peak of the mountain. Parallel *concavities* of valleys, on the other hand, point **toward** the peak of the mountain. Seeing the numerous convexities and concavities in parallel on the map, we can then understand their representation compared to the satellite view.

Still having a tough time seeing it? Another example, in the picture above, shows a portion of a map of a small area in eastern Denali National Park. The cartographer masterfully shaded the ridges and valleys, such that they appear more obvious to the eye. An arrow (1) identifies one ridge on this close-up of the map. Notice how the ridge's convex contour lines point **away** from the mountain peak above it. The other arrow (2) identifies a valley and its concave contour lines, pointing **toward** the peak of the mountain.

We can see many other ridges, valleys, peaks, and plateaus in this picture and how they have been represented on paper. When able to identify these features on the map, we can then use them in a simple method to find our near exact location on the map, to then figure out which direction we need to travel toward safety. How do we do that? This requires a compass to accomplish, so keep reading!

Knowing True North versus Magnetic North

Knowing True North versus Magnetic North opens the door to using a compass with a map. This crucial first step allows us to accurately direct ourselves from one specific point to another.

The longitudinal (vertical) lines on a map all converge at the same point at the top of the Earth, called the North Pole. The longitude and latitude lines, and the North and South Poles, were only created out of the need for a symmetrical grid over the Earth for consistent navigation and location of objects (ships, planes, etc.) and features on the planet. The direction that points to the North Pole refers to "True North." This spot, created by humans for travel, location, and uniformity, does not actually fall in the location of the northern magnetic pole of the Earth. Compasses remain ignorant of what the map identifies as north. Its magnetic needle only knows to point toward the location of the northern magnetic pole of the Earth. Compasses therefore point to "Magnetic North."

Since True North and Magnetic North sit in different locations, by necessity we must have a method to translate these to one another. Understanding their difference requires the conception of their physical relationship to one another. Magnetic North rests between the North Pole and North America. Since they sit in two separate locations, but still close to one another, how we "see" the difference between the two depends upon our location on the Earth. Using a simple example to visualize Magnetic North's relation to True North, imagine two trees growing 10 feet

from one another, with one tree labeled "A" and the other labeled "B." If we were to walk in a wide circle around these two trees, metaphorically representing circumferential travel around the Earth, their relationship to one another in our visual field would depend on our location in that circle. At two points opposite of one another in that circle, the two trees lie precisely in line with one another.

If we move to the right or to the left of these two in-line points, tree A and tree B appear either to the right or to the left of one another in our visual field. Which of them sits off to one specific side of the other and how far apart they appear in our visual field depends entirely on where we stand in that circle. The same holds true for where Magnetic North lies in relation to True North. The pictures that follow illustrate this point. Here we have the same two trees, but where they sit in our visual field all depends on our position relative to theirs.

We can stand in one spot where the two trees align with one another. The picture on the left depicts how these two appear in relation to one another if we step to the left of that line, while the picture on the right shows the relationship of the trees in our visual field when we step to the right of that line. If tree A represents True North and tree B represents Magnetic North, then we can appreciate how our location on the Earth dictates their relationship to one another.

The following simple illustration further illustrates the point made by these two trees. This bird's-eye view, looking down at the trees, again shows that their relationship to one another in our visual field depends entirely on where we stand in the circle that surrounds them. The bottom center person (position 1) looks at the two trees and sees them perfectly in alignment with one another, with 0° of difference between their positions. However, if that person moves to the right in the circle (position 2) tree B

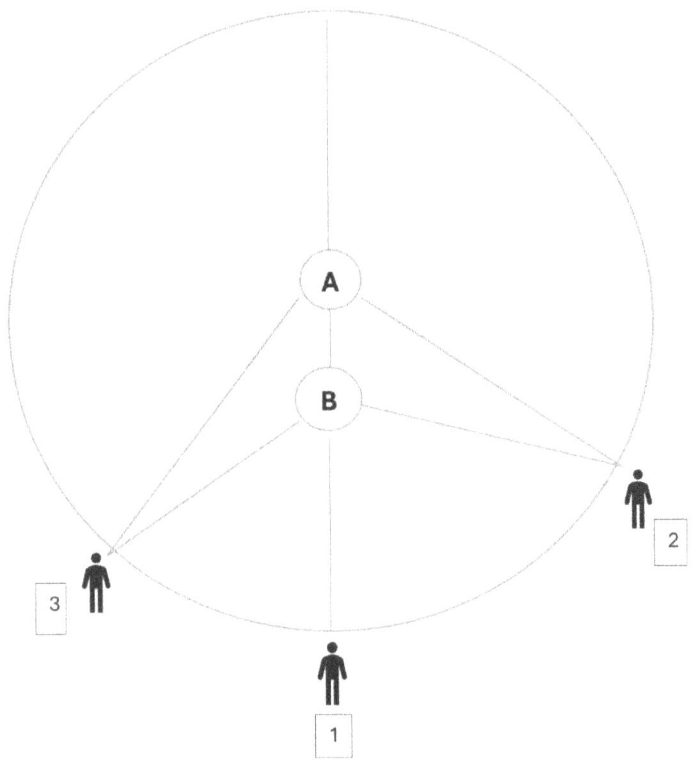

appears to the left of tree A, with an angle corresponding to their relationship to one another in that position.

Should that person move to the other side of the circle to position 3 they now observe tree B lying to the right of tree A in their visual field, with a specific angle corresponding to their relationship to one another in that position. Think of A and B as True North (TN) and Magnetic North (MN), respectively. If position 2 represents a position in the eastern part of North America, and position 3 is a position in the west, then we can see how the relationship of TN and MN change, depending on where we are. While our map refers to A, our compass points to B.

Two lines exist on the Earth, along which Magnetic North and True North align with one another, much like in position 1 from the example above, and follow the same linear direction. One of these lines runs through North America, which curves due to the spherical shape of the planet. At any point along this north-south running line our compass and map refer to the same point as "north." Changing our physical location to the east of that line (position 2, corresponding to any location in the eastern half of North America) shows Magnetic North lying off to the left (or west) of True North. Conversely, if we change our location to the west of that line, also representing any location in the western half of North America, then Magnetic North lies off to the right (or east) of True North (see position 3 in the preceding illustration).

Declination

Declination defines the difference, in degrees of a circle, between how Magnetic North and True North relate to one another. Refer back to position 1 in the two-tree illustration. The trees perfectly align with one another, corresponding to a declination of 0°. The further we move to either side of that 0° line in North America, the greater the declination that exists between the two. In position 2, east of that 0° line, the declination between the two will indi-

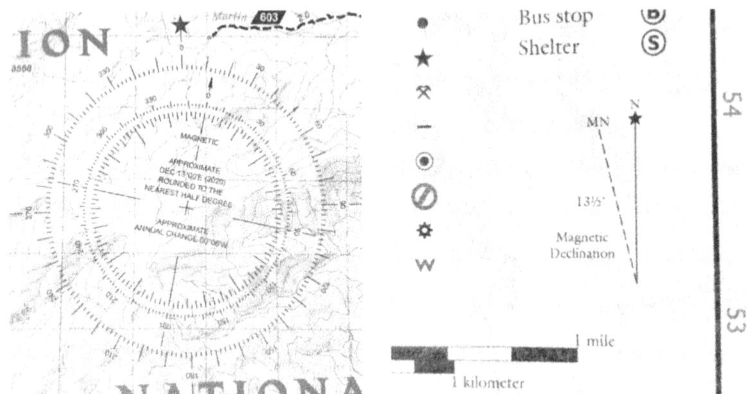

TRAILS ILLUSTRATED MAP, SAWTOOTH
NATIONAL RECREATION AREA / #870

cate Magnetic North (tree B) at an angle off to the left of True North (tree A). In position 3, west of the 0° line, the declination between the two will indicate Magnetic North at an angle off to the right of True North.

The above left picture, taken from a map of the Sawtooth National Recreation Area in Idaho, represents what the magnetic declination would look like in position 3 of the two-tree illustration above. This spot sits west of the 0° line running through North America and indicates the declination of Magnetic North as 13° to the right (east) of True North (star at the top).

The above right picture, taken from the map legend of Harriman State Park in New York (produced by the New York-New Jersey Trail Conference), more simply illustrates the magnetic declination in that location. Similar to position 2 in the two-tree illustration above, New York sits well east of the 0° line running through North America and indicates the declination of Magnetic North as 13.5° to the left (west) of True North.

The North American 0° line runs curvilinearly between New Orleans and Minneapolis, running up through western Hudson Bay in Canada. If we were to theoretically travel either east or west from this point to encircle the Earth, we would come to a point of maximum declination between True North and Magnetic North during that journey. As we continue past that point, over the Atlantic Ocean and toward Europe, however, and approach the 0° line on the opposite side of the planet, the declination would decrease again until that line has been reached. That 0° line runs in Europe through eastern France up through the North Sea, just west of Denmark.

Forgoing the use of declination in the navigation process allows our compass to lead us far off course from our desired destination if we intend to head toward a specific direction or location on a map. The degree of deviation from that intended path only worsens with increasing distance. Imagine a 5-mile straight path on flat ground laid out in front of us. Instead of walking along that path, however, we decide to walk at a 2° angle from the starting point. The farther we walk along that angle from the original path, the farther off course we will have gone. After 5 miles, a deviation of about 900 feet will have been produced between our location and the original path's destination. The distance between the two end points in this example increases with higher degrees of declination and longer distances. The declination in the northeast and northwest corners of the continental US reaches to around 20°, so overlooking this correcting factor will lead us well off course!

See the following illustration of North America, with the grid of longitude and latitude lines laid over the continent. The vertical longitudinal lines converge on a common point north of Canada (the North Pole). The line that courses through the middle of North America identifies the 0° declination line, pointing to both

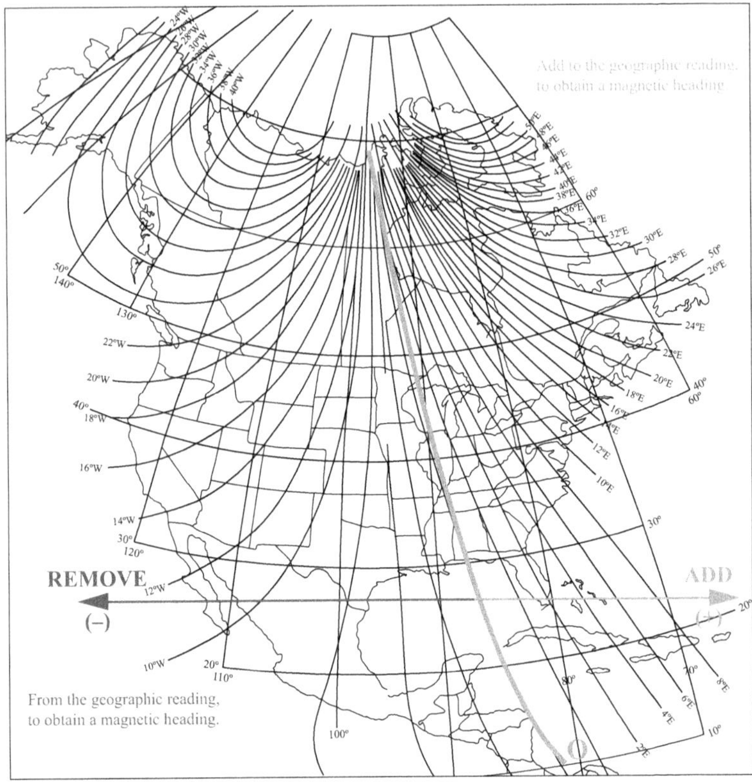

True North and Magnetic North. The curved lines on either side of this 0° line depict how the declination differs throughout the continent. At all points east and west of this line the declination determined for that spot allows us to translate the information between the compass and map.

Hopefully by now the basics of maps have been demystified for those who started with a rudimentary understanding. Using this fundamental information to then translate between what the compass reads and where we need to go on the map can be accomplished easily. We must first understand the basic functions of a compass, which comes next.

Dr. Rob's Notes

While the two-tree illustration does not reflect the 100 percent geomagnetic reality, the consideration of location difference between True North and Magnetic North and how that enters into our navigation plan becomes easy to conceptualize through this simpler example, while avoiding complex geophysics and mathematics.

To make matters more complex, the northern and southern magnetic poles remain in a slow migration over time, causing evolution in declination over the years. For over 100 years the northern magnetic pole has slowly edged away from northern Canada and toward Siberia. Outdated maps may not reflect accurate declination in a particular spot, due to this issue, with the rate of change occurring faster in locations closer to the North Pole.

The location and migratory pattern of the poles remain under constant watch by the US Geologic Survey (USGS), the US National Oceanic and Atmospheric Administration (NOAA), National Resources Canada (NRCan), the British Geological Survey (BGS), and the European Space Agency (ESA), to name a few.

The magnetic field map of the Earth reveals a convoluted pattern throughout most of the planet. Compasses will point to the local geomagnetic field, regardless of where we stand on the planet. The magnetic field through North America happens to flow more uniformly than on other continents though, making magnetic navigation more straightforward than elsewhere.

Using a Compass

Use of a compass completes the pair of tools necessary for a primary or backup analog navigation solution. Terrestrial and celestial cues provide a gross estimate of direction when lacking another source of information. Compasses provide a more precise indication of our direction of travel, and that of specific points in relation to our position. They provide accuracy of direction within a small margin of error.

Compasses rely on a steel "needle" (usually much wider than a needle) floating in a liquid or air-filled capsule with a central pivot point. The magnetizing process alters the needle to contain most of the "south" magnetic particles on one end and the "north" particles on the other. We were all taught in school that the "south" end of one magnet always attracts to the "north" end of another. Having a large magnetic field running through the center of the planet with its "north" particles exposed near the North Pole, Magnetic North serves as the ultimate point to which our compass will fixate, given no other strong magnetic field in the vicinity to confuse the needle. When enabling the compass to work properly, the red painted portion of the needle, composed mostly of "south" particles, points to Magnetic North every time we use it.

Multiple types of compasses exist. The two types used by most hikers, backpackers, and orienteers in scout troops, lensatic compasses and orienteering compasses, provide the same information but look and function slightly differently. Which one people use comes down to personal taste, comfort level, ease of use, weight/bulk, and prior experience (military, scouts, among others).

The first picture shows a lensatic compass, with an integrated folding cover to protect the compass from damage. The second picture is an orienteering compass, which features an extended clear base plate with an arrow etched at the end through the center and rulers on its sides.

The features of these two compasses are the following:

A. At least one straight edge

B. Rotating bezel

C. Indicator of direction of travel

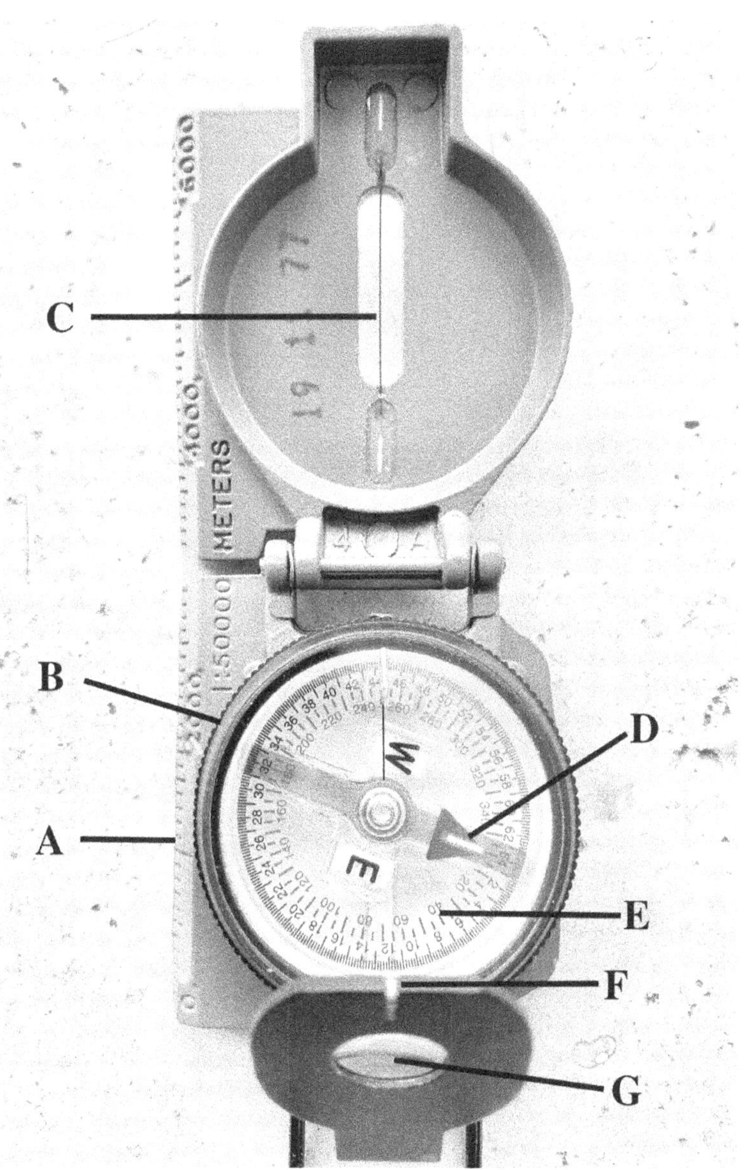

C
B
A
D
E
F
G
METERS
1:50000

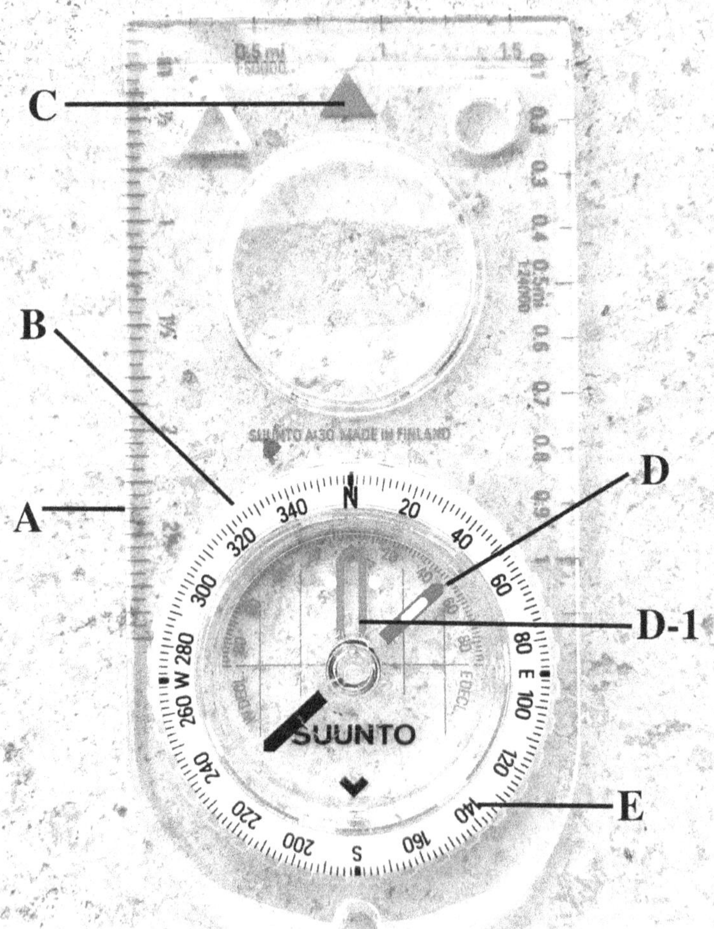

A
B
C
D
D-1
E
SUUNTO A-30 MADE IN FINLAND
SUUNTO

D. North-seeking portion of the needle, referred to as "the needle"
    D-1. Orienting arrow, which always points to "N" on the bezel of an orienteering compass

E. Degree indicator

F. Sighting notch (lensatic compass only)

G. Lens (lensatic compass only)

The lensatic compass carries as a bulkier and heavier item than the orienteering compass but preserves the compass from incidental hard trauma. Our military chooses this type of compass for this very reason. This particular lensatic compass, the M-1950 made by Cammenga, has been distributed to and relied on by countless military personnel for decades. The lens and sighting notch, unique to the lensatic compass, provide much more accurate readings of distant navigation targets than others that do not feature them. Backpackers, otherwise notorious for scrutinizing every ounce carried on trail, favor the orienteering compass over its heavier counterpart. This orienteering compass is made by Suunto, a top-tier manufacturer of analog and digital navigating instruments.

Compasses and their north-orienting needles work uninhibited when horizontal, either on the ground or in our hands. The lensatic compass must be used in the open position (see picture above with lens portion in a rear or in a slightly forward position), as the lens in the full forward and closed position locks the needle in place.

The ring of numbers on both compasses indicates the 360 degrees of the circle, and these will be utilized in the skills that follow. The lensatic compass displays these numbers in red, while its black numbers represent the circle as measured in milliradians (6,400 of them in a circle), used more in military applications than in civilian land navigation. These will be ignored here.

Which compass should you choose between these two types? That comes down to personal taste and what the activity and specific demands call for. Many own and utilize both types.

Taking a Bearing

Taking a bearing with a compass enables us to complete other skills. This basic skill identifies the direction another object/destination lies in relation to our position. Among the 360 degrees that surrounds us, a bearing leads us to one specific point in that circle. Determining that direction does not rely on declination, so accounting for True vs Magnetic North is not necessary for taking and following a simple bearing to an object in the distance. This simple numerical value, between 0° and 359°, leads us to a specific spot in the distance if we travel along a straight line and we've made the correct measurement to begin with.

The 360 degrees of the circle that surrounds us remain fixed in relation to the cardinal directions. The beginning of the circle, denoted 0°, identifies north. The degrees of the circle run in a clockwise direction. As we move through that circle, with the cardinal directions sitting 90° from one another, a bearing of 90° represents east, 180° indicates south, and 270° identifies west on the compass dial. Taking a look at the bezel of the orienteering compass pictured above, we can see the numbers with the cardinal directions inserted among them.

The next illustration depicts the degrees of the virtual circle that surrounds us existing in a fixed position. The figure of the person appears to be traveling in a western direction, and therefore heads toward a bearing of 270°. If that person were to then turn to their left and keep going, they will head in a southern direction, at a bearing of 180°. Whichever direction we face and travel toward has an assigned bearing, according to the numbers on the fixed 360° circle that surrounds us.

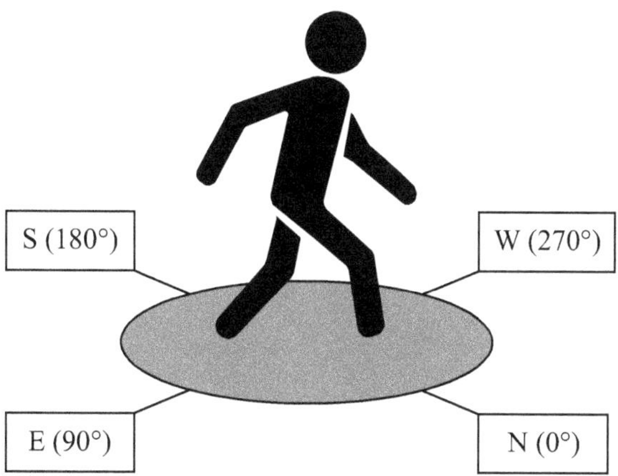

The method for taking a bearing differs slightly between the two types of compasses featured in this chapter. Using an orienteering compass to measure a bearing:

- Hold the compass horizontally with the nondominant hand with the direction of travel line/arrow pointing outward. Keep the rear of the compass in contact with the lower chest/upper abdomen and the elbow tight to the body. Let's call this "the bearing position."
- While holding the compass as above, we point our body toward the distant object.
- Using the dominant hand, rotate the bezel of the compass (next page, the picture on the left, white arrow) to where the orienting arrow (red outlined arrow on the compass, but shows as dark gray in the picture) lines up underneath the needle (below picture on the right).
- The number on the bezel lying along the direction of travel line (310°) identifies the bearing.

See the following pictures.

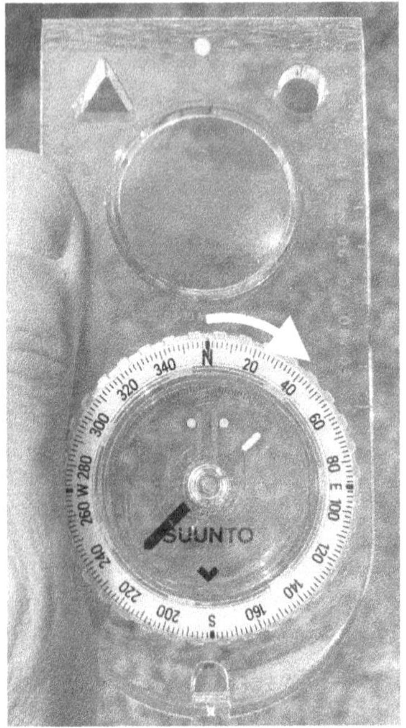

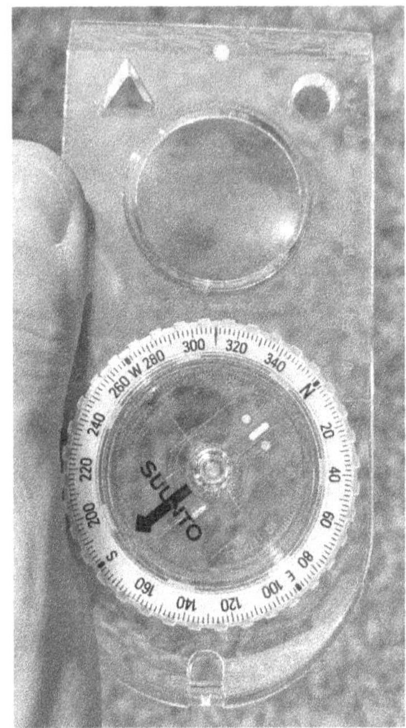

Using the lensatic compass to measure a bearing can be accomplished using two methods. The first method mimics that for the orienteering compass.

Method 1 (see the following pictures):

- Hold the lensatic compass with the dominant hand, placing the thumb through the ring, and support the compass with the thumb and index finger underneath.
- Pull the elbow tight to the body and keep the compass around the lower chest/upper abdomen, maintaining the bearing position.
- Point your body toward the object or desired direction in the distance.
- The magnetic needle on this type of compass sits on a disc, containing all the degrees of the circle on it (the innermost numbers), rotating the bearing number accordingly as we

adjust our position. Looking down at the compass (both pictures below), the innermost number that aligns with the direction of travel line (50°) indicates the bearing.

- With the other hand we rotate the bezel (picture below, curved arrow) so that the bezel marker (straight white arrow) aligns with the needle to allow for reference when following that bearing. The picture on the next page shows how this should appear when done.

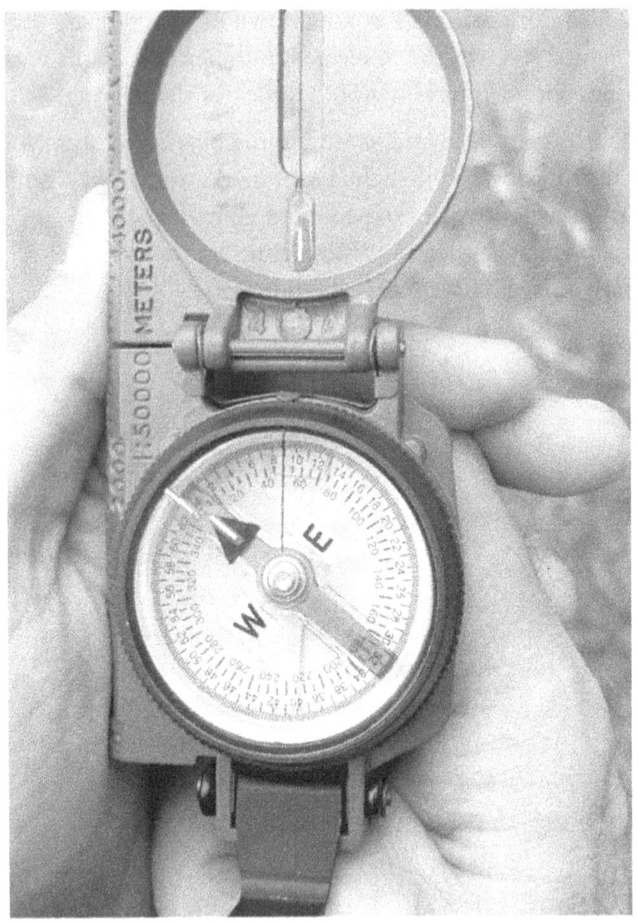

The second method for taking a bearing with a lensatic compass involves a few more steps but provides a more accurate bearing.

Method 2:

- While holding the compass with our dominant hand, just as with the first method, we lift the folding portion of the compass up to a 90° position and place the lens forward about 30° from the perpendicular position (but not forward enough to lock the compass needle from rotating).

- Raise the compass up to the dominant side cheek (see the following pictures).
- Visualize the desired destination in the distance while lining up the sighting wire (from the upright folding portion of the compass) and the sighting notch above the lens in the visual field.
- Looking down through the lens in the same position without moving ourselves or the compass, the visible innermost number (46°) tells us the bearing.
- Lower the compass to the bearing position and rotate the bezel marker to line up with Magnetic North, as described in Method 1.

Reference the bearing along the route while holding the compass in the bearing position with the needle lined up with the now-adjusted bezel marker. When done correctly the direction of travel line points toward the correct direction.

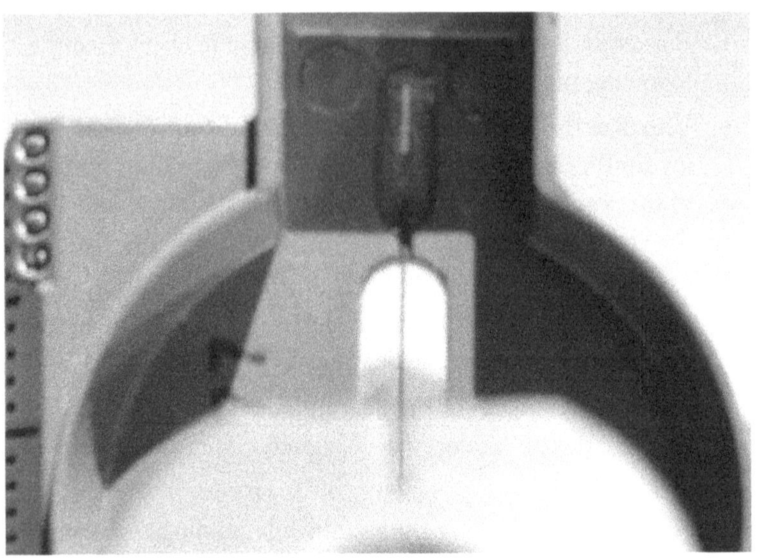
6000

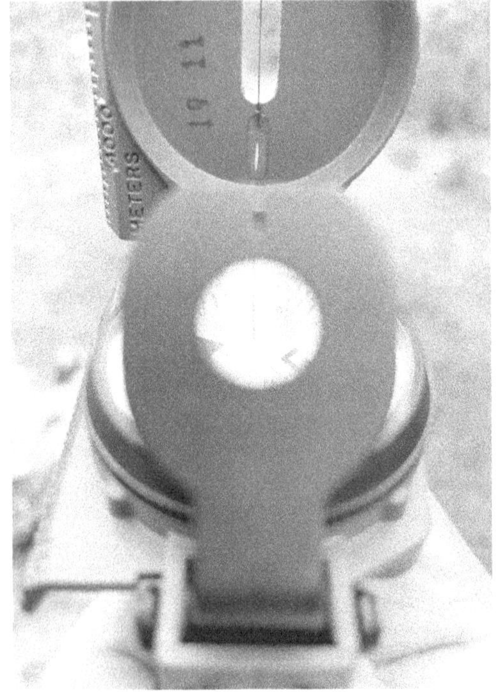
METERS

Adjusting for Declination

Adjusting for declination represents a second essential skill to effectively use a compass and map. This skill facilitates other useful skills, but it is not used for taking a bearing. Translating Magnetic North to True North enables us to pull our compass out and quickly reference our map to find our location and where we need to go. This helps us to become familiar with the terrain and our direction of travel, while decreasing the chances of becoming lost. The first step requires looking at the map to find the printed determination of declination for that region. Finding this sometimes takes a careful look at the map and the legend.

Declination requires adjustment only once, which remains constant as long as we stay in the same area. Using the example of hiking in western North Carolina, we look on the map for the indicator of declination. See the following picture.

The black star at the top of the outer circle identifies True North. The inner circle represents how the compass should read in relation to True North, with a line running through its axis (labeled "magnetic"), topped with a small arrowhead and canted off to the left of the True North line. The two white arrows point

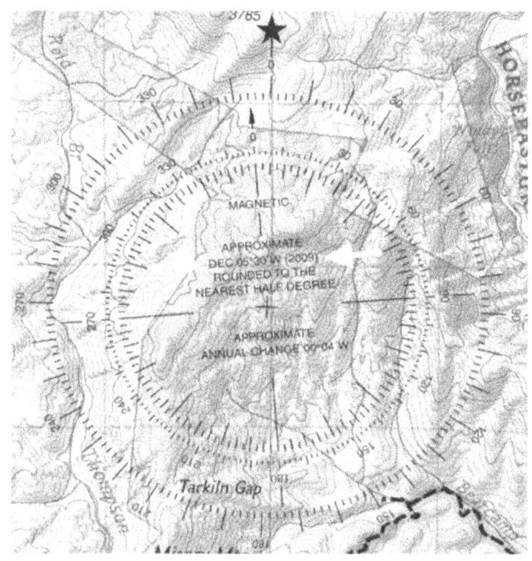

COPYRIGHT NATIONAL GEOGRAPHIC PARTNERS, LLC TRAILS ILLUSTRATED MAP, PISGAH RANGER DISTRICT, PISGAH NATIONAL FOREST / #780

For the Navigation Geeks in the Crowd

Reading through the declination designation in the previous picture, we also see the drift rate of Magnetic North, indicated as "approximate annual change 00° 04' W." This reads as "0 degrees and 4 minutes west." In angular measure, 60 "minutes" make up one degree. The declination of 05° 30' W therefore represents 5.5° W for practical use. This declination was determined in 2009, though. Over the 15 years between then and now (2024) the declination has changed 1° west (drift of 4' west per yr x 15 yrs = 60'), making the actual declination around 6.5° as of the writing of this book. We can use older maps as long as we adjust the declination when a significant span of time has lapsed since its publication. The pictures pertaining to this example therefore use the compass as close to 6.5° as possible.

to the declination, recorded at 5° 30' west of True North. As long as we remain in this area the point on our compass where the needle determines north will remain the same.

Whenever referencing True North in this area then, the compass needle should always point to 6.5° off to the left (west) of the Direction of Travel line (see above text box for why this value has changed from the preceding paragraph).

Adjusting a Lensatic Compass for declination:

- First rotate the bezel until the marker sits 6° to the left of the direction of travel line. The bezel of this compass rotates in clicks, at 3° per click. Adjusting this marker to exactly 6.5° cannot be done, so we adjust it to as close to the value as we can. The bezel should be rotated by two clicks to the left for this example.
- Hold the compass in the bearing position.

- Rotate your body and the compass as a unit until the needle sits to the immediate left of the bezel marker, adding an approximate 0.5° to complete the full 6.5° of declination adjustment.

The direction of travel line now points toward True North. See the next picture.

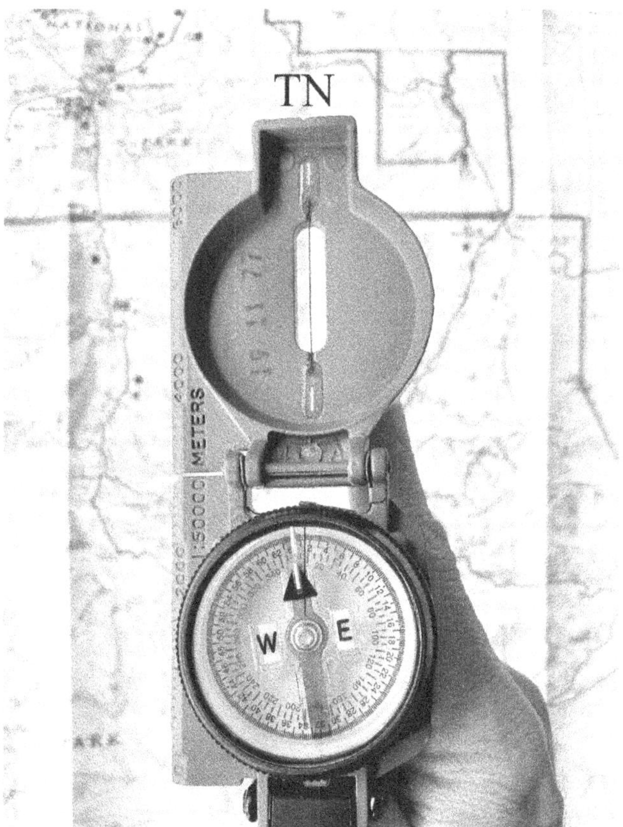

The needle rests just left of the 6° mark, to approximate the 6.5° declination adjustment. In this position the direction of travel line leads us directly to True North ("TN").

Adjusting for declination with an orienteering compass follows these steps:

- Rotate the smooth moving bezel (no clicks like as the lensatic compass) to the left of the direction of travel line to read 6.5° west. Each hashmark on the bezel represents 2°, so the bezel should be rotated until the direction of travel line sits just beyond three hashmarks to approximate the desired declination in this example.
- Hold the compass in the bearing position.
- Rotate the body and compass as a unit until the needle aligns with "N" on the bezel, inside the framed orienting arrow.

The direction of travel line now aligns with True North.

Picture 1 reveals the needle aligning with the "N" on the bezel and the direction of travel line. The curved arrow indicates the direction we need to rotate the bezel to account for magnetic declination in this area.

Picture 2 reveals the bezel has been rotated about 6.5° to the left of the direction of travel line. Since the orienting arrow moves with rotation of the bezel, always pointing to "N," we use this as the target for the last step.

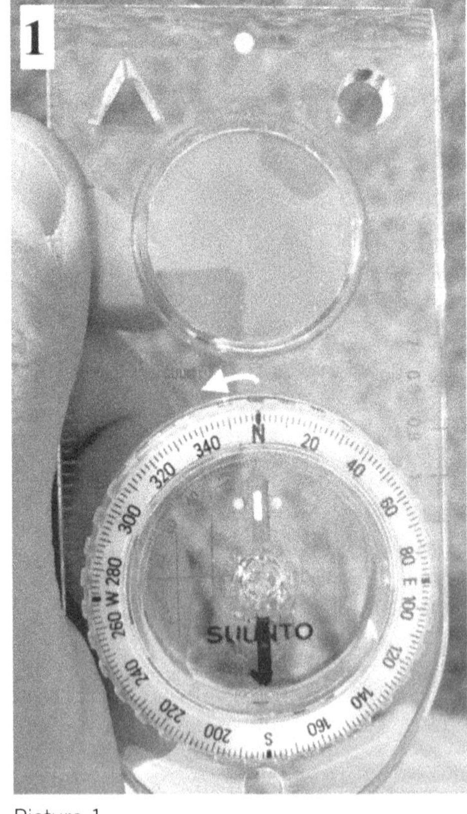

Picture 1

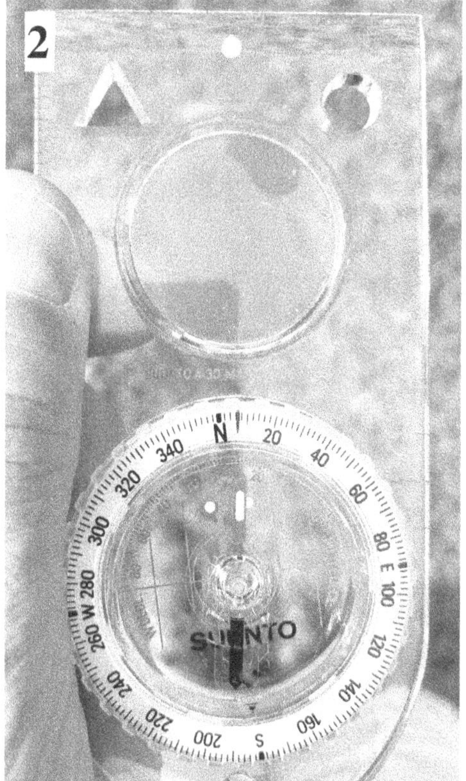

Picture 2

Picture 3 demonstrates the last step in the process, involving rotation of our body and compass as a unit until the needle falls inside the orienting arrow and points to Magnetic North ("MN"). In this position the direction of travel line points toward True North ("TN").

These skills take practice to use confidently on a trail. We can accomplish this by learning the declination of our local area and that of our usual hiking spots, if they differ from the home location. Practice taking a bearing in the backyard or local park and understand the simplicity of this essential. Adjust the compass for local declination and that of future hikes.

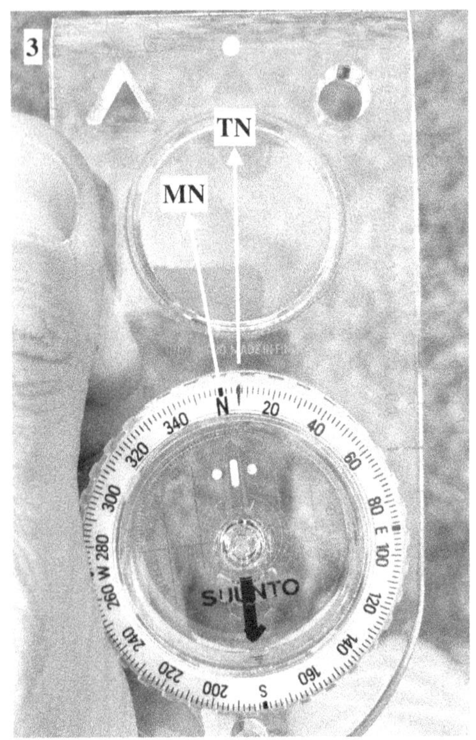

Picture 3

TRAILS ILLUSTRATED MAP, SAWTOOTH NATIONAL RECREATION AREA / #870

The last example reviewed adjustment for declination in the eastern US. Let's practice an example in central Idaho. In the western half of the continent Magnetic North (MN) sits off to the east (right) of True North (TN). The printed designation on the map (see picture below) indicates Magnetic North to the east (right) of True North at 13° in this location. To point the direction of travel line to True North, rotate the bezel marker to the right to match the declination and rotate the compass until the needle matches it. Now that the bezel marker lines up with Magnetic North, the direction of travel line through the center of the compass aligns with True North.

Now that we know exactly where True North lies in the 360 degrees that surround us, determining the direction we need to follow, whether that be north, south, east, west, or any point between these, becomes very easy to determine.

Advanced Declination Lesson

Much emphasis has been placed on finding True North in this chapter, but when hiking we follow all directions. What if we need to use our compass to direct ourselves toward west as it translates to the map? We know that 360 degrees of a virtual circle always surround us. The point at which both 0 and 360° lie on that virtual compass always denotes north (pointing toward the North Pole). We also know that where Magnetic North and True North sit in relation to one another varies throughout most of the Earth. Magnetic declination simply tells us how far off from the "True" cardinal grid-based directions and their assigned degrees of the circle the magnetic compass will point.

In the above example we looked at the portion of a map from Idaho, with a declination of 13° to the right (east) of True North. When we adjust our bezel mark so that the direction of travel line points toward True North, the compass bearing does not read 0° or 360° at that line, it reads 347° for True North. Making this adjustment, the declination **subtracted** 13° from 360° to derive the bearing of True North. **All of the cardinal directions feel this effect.**

If we want to travel in a true westerly direction in this same area of Idaho, we then place our compass in the bearing position and rotate our bodies until the direction of travel line reads a bearing of 257° (13° subtracted from 270°) and head off in that direction. For this specific area, with this declination, this bearing represents True West (TW). At that bearing point, the ordinary 270° mark of geographical west becomes aligned with the bezel marker, as adjusted for declination of this area, as did 0° when we determined True North (see picture below). When desiring to travel in any given cardinal direction we use the same methodology.

At all points on the continent east of the 0° declination line the same number of declination degrees become **added** to the assigned north, east, south, and west points when reading the magnetic compass bearing.

Going back to the previous example of hiking in western North Carolina, with a declination of 6.5° west (left) of True North, the bearing for True North reads 6.5° at the direction of travel line (see next picture), and not 0°. The declination adjusted bearings for east, south, and west then become 96.5°, 186.5°, and 276.5°, respectively.

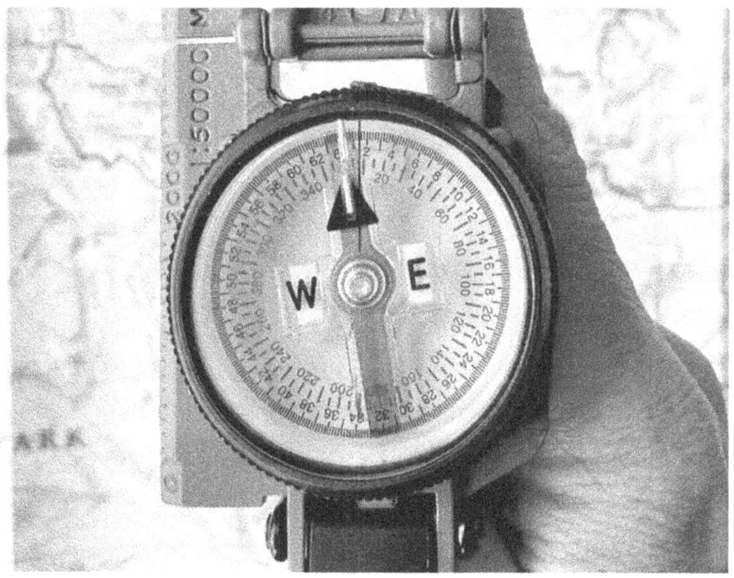

Orienteering compasses adjust differently when wanting to head in a True West (or other cardinal) direction than do lensatic compasses but follow a simple method. Review the picture on the next page.

When traveling in a westerly direction in the same area of North Carolina, but adjusted for declination, then the bezel of the orienteering compass becomes rotated to read the desired adjusted bearing (276.5°, as explained in the preceding paragraph) at the direction of travel line. Holding the compass in the "take a bearing position" we rotate our body and compass as a unit until the needle settles inside the borders of the orienting arrow.

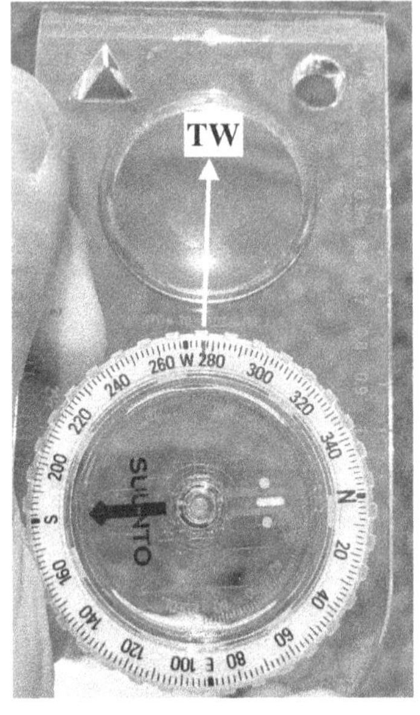

When done correctly the direction of travel line points to magnetically corrected True West ("TW"). We use the same methodology when desiring to travel in any given cardinal direction, corrected for declination. The greater the declination, the greater the importance for adjustment, as this significantly impacts the correctness of travel. This becomes extraordinarily important when our safe return to home becomes jeopardized.

These simple skills amount to building blocks toward other skills, much like needing to learn the letters of the alphabet and how they sound before we can begin to read. Taking these skills to the next level should clarify how they help us avoid getting lost and finding our way back when we do. The following intermediate skills require correcting for declination and taking a bearing, building the foundation for establishing our navigational independence. Read on!

Orienting Our Map to the Terrain

Orienting our map to the terrain increases the skill level, which aligns the longitudinal lines of the map between True North and South. We can then visualize objects, trails, and features in our surroundings, knowing exactly which direction it takes to get there. This becomes very useful for associating terrestrial cues with their placement on the map.

We also use this in the effort to find or confirm our location in the middle of nowhere, should the need arise. The following explains two easy methods for orienting our map to the terrain. While similar in the end, specific circumstances may call for one over the other.

Method 1: On the Go Method. This skill proves useful while on our feet midhike and resembles the same method as adjusting for declination. We first adjust the bezel of our compass to compensate for the declination of the area as described above. For this example, we'll use the 6.5° west (left) declination for the southwest area of North Carolina. The bezel marker position on the compass in picture 1 should look familiar and correct by now.

- Using a folded section of the map and representative of the specific area of the location, we lay the compass on the map with the side straight edge of the compass aligned with any of the longitudinal lines on the map (black arrow). In picture 1 on the following page the magnetic needle sits off to the right but needs to line up with the bezel marker to complete this skill.
- We then rotate our body with map and compass in hand as a unit (see white curved arrows in picture 1) to align the needle with the bezel marker (picture 2).

We now have the compass oriented to True North, and the map oriented to the terrain!

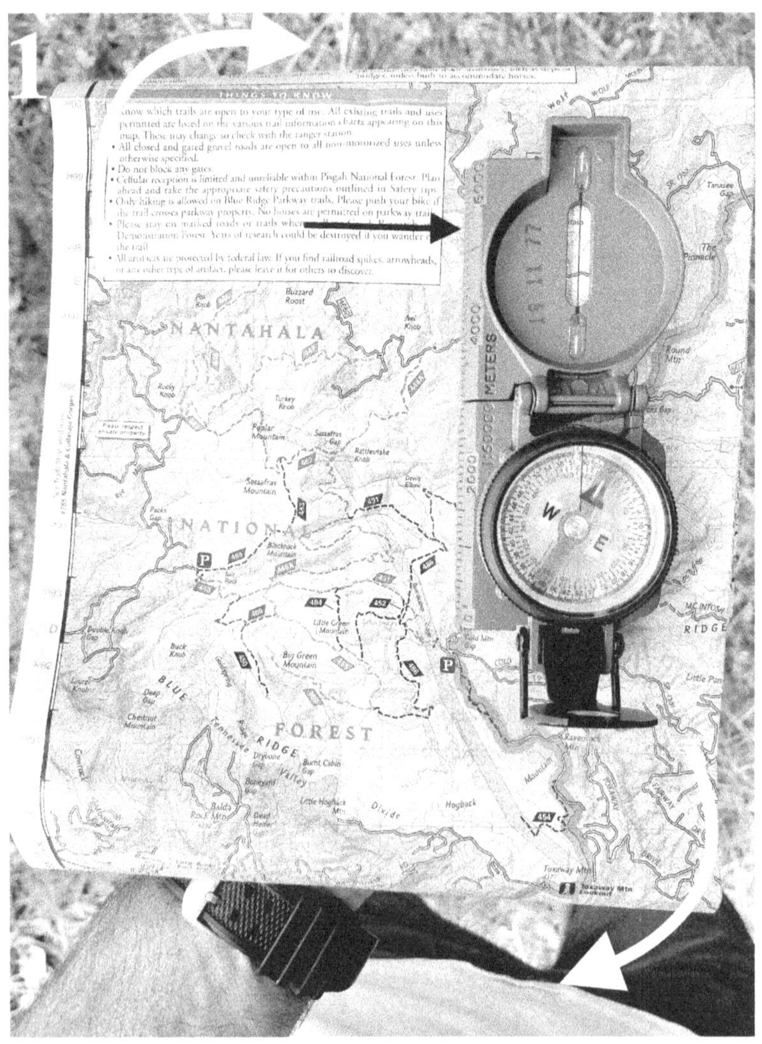

Rotate the body with map and compass as a unit. COPYRIGHT NATIONAL GEOGRAPHIC PARTNERS, LLC
TRAILS ILLUSTRATED MAP, PISGAH RANGER DISTRICT, PISGAH NATIONAL FOREST / #780

The map and compass after rotating them to align the needle with the bezel marker. The map is now oriented to the terrain and the direction of travel line points to True North. COPYRIGHT NATIONAL GEOGRAPHIC PARTNERS, LLC TRAILS ILLUSTRATED MAP, PISGAH RANGER DISTRICT, PISGAH NATIONAL FOREST / #780

Method 2: Pre-Hike/Trailhead Planning or Group Method. The first step involves laying our map out on the ground or other flat, nonmetallic surface. This provides a broader view of the surrounding area on the map and makes it easier for multiple people to see. For this example, we continue to use the declination of 6.5° to the west (left) of True North, as in western North Carolina, while using the map of this area. We take out our compass and lay it on the map with the straight edge along any longitudinal line on that map (black arrow, picture 1).

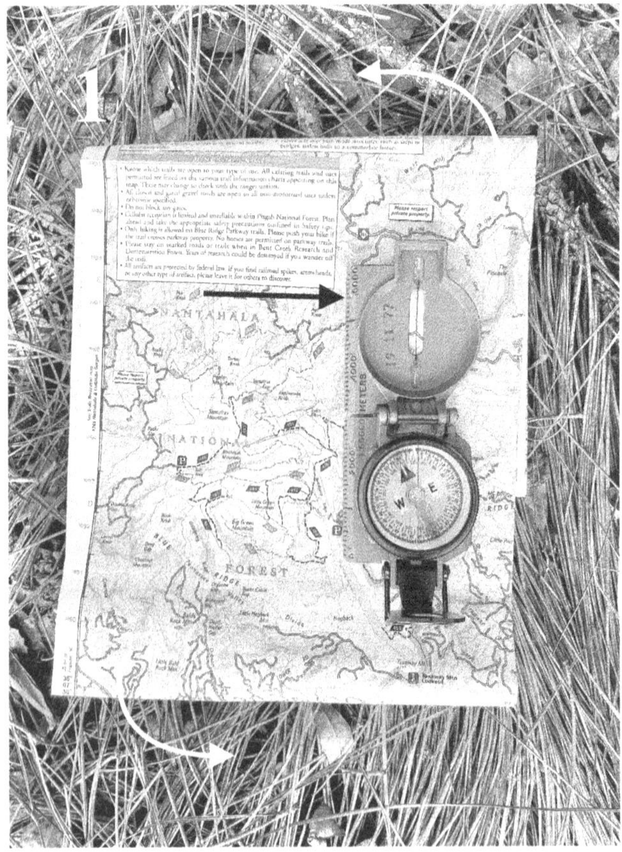

COPYRIGHT NATIONAL GEOGRAPHIC PARTNERS, LLC
TRAILS ILLUSTRATED MAP, PISGAH RANGER DISTRICT, PISGAH NATIONAL FOREST / #780

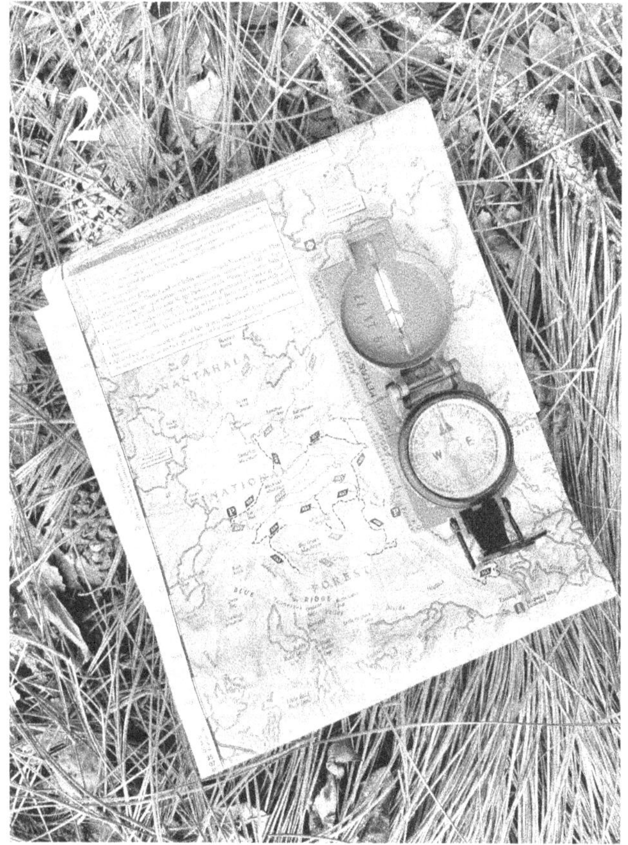

COPYRIGHT NATIONAL GEOGRAPHIC PARTNERS, LLC
TRAILS ILLUSTRATED MAP, PISGAH RANGER DISTRICT, PISGAH NATIONAL FOREST / #780

When using a lensatic compass rotate the bezel to match the declination of 6.5° west. In picture 1 the needle sits off to the left of the bezel marker. It needs to match the position of the bezel marker to complete this skill. With the straight edge of the compass still lined up with a longitudinal line on the map (black arrow in picture 1), simply rotate the map and compass together on the flat surface (picture 1, white curved arrows) until the needle lines up with the bezel marker (see picture 2 above). We have just oriented the map to the terrain!

When using an orienteering compass to orient the map to the terrain, using the same 6.5° west (left) declination, perform the following:

- Place the map (or folded section of the map) on the ground or other flat surface and place the compass on it, lining up the straight edge of the compass with one of the longitudinal lines of the map (black arrow in picture 1 below).

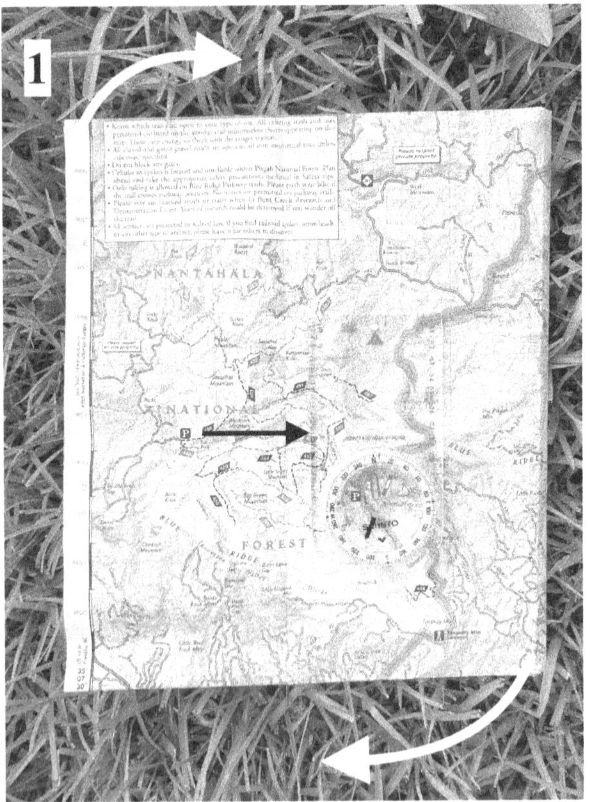

Rotate the map, with the compass in place, until the magnetic needle falls within the orienting arrow's outline.
COPYRIGHT NATIONAL GEOGRAPHIC PARTNERS, LLC
TRAILS ILLUSTRATED MAP, PISGAH RANGER DISTRICT, PISGAH NATIONAL FOREST / #780

- Rotate the bezel to the left of the direction of travel line slightly more than three hashmarks (2° per hashmark), placing the "N" on the bezel about 6.5° off to the left.
- With the compass's side straight edge still aligned with a longitudinal line on the map, simply rotate the map on the flat surface (see picture 1 below, white curved arrows) until the magnetic needle lines up within the borders of the orienting arrow (see picture 2 below).

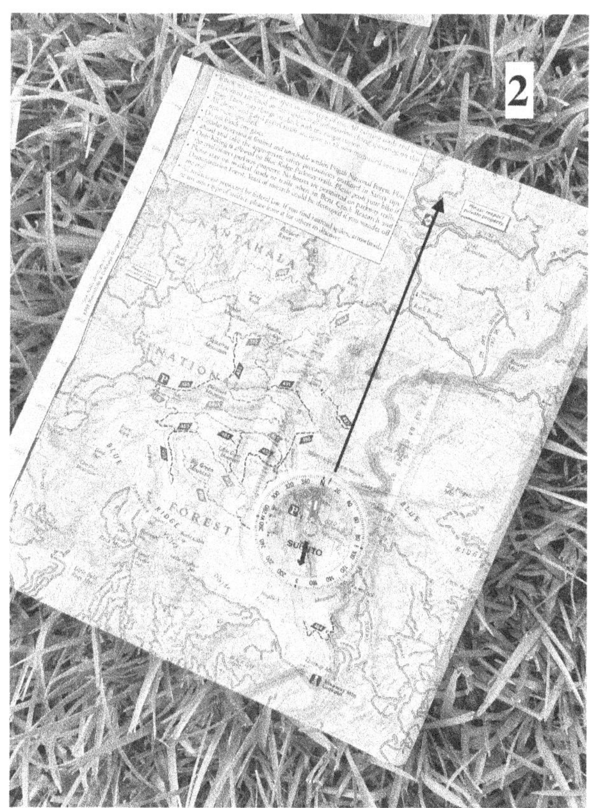

Now that the orienting arrow and the magnetic needle align, the map has been oriented to the surroundings and the direction of travel indicator on the compass points to True North. COPYRIGHT NATIONAL GEOGRAPHIC PARTNERS, LLC TRAILS ILLUSTRATED MAP, PISGAH RANGER DISTRICT, PISGAH NATIONAL FOREST / #780

The map has been oriented to the terrain. Easy!

Now that the map has been oriented to the terrain, we extrapolate beyond the direction of travel indicator (see picture 2 above, long black arrow) to determine True North. We can now look around us and match visible landmarks on the ground with their placement on the map, and the direction of travel to reach them. Desired destinations on the map also become associated with a direction we can follow to arrive there.

Basic Navigation Strategies

Basic navigation strategies help assure that we remain on our intended path and provide indicators of if or when we have wandered off the route. These strategies represent simple tools and tricks taught in the military and used by professional explorers. As amateur hikers and backpackers most of us will follow an established trail when venturing out into the wilderness. Experienced backpackers who seek to blaze their own trail through a particular area usually map out a general route ahead of time and follow it as a framework for reference. Regardless of which type of route we take, we should know the general course ahead of time.

1. Study the map well in advance. Know the distance (in miles or kilometers) of the intended route. Using our average hiking speed, or that of the group, we can figure out how long the entire hike will take. Use this timing factor to plan when the hike should begin and end, assuring daylight will not escape us until after the hike has been completed. This timing factor informs us of the latest time of day to begin that hike. Nightfall may otherwise occur before we complete the hike and impede our ability to get back to the trailhead, especially when hike prep did not anticipate the lack of daylight.
2. For out-and-back hikes know the one-way distance and general anticipated hiking time as an indicator of how long it takes

to arrive to the turnaround point. When having gone well beyond that time, we may have passed the turnaround point.

3. In studying the map ahead of time, look for important trail features. These may include right angles or hairpin turns and forks in the trail. Knowing which path to follow and which not to (always assume these forks will be poorly marked) ahead of time aids us in the effort to stay on the intended route. Seeing these features in the moment brings an element of familiarity to an otherwise unfamiliar trail, reassures us that we're on the correct route, and becomes a reference point to know our exact location along that trail. Becoming familiar with trail features beyond the intended path can indicate to us that we have wandered off course.
4. Look for permanent land-based features along the route on the map as well. A stream may run parallel to the trail or cross it perpendicularly at some point. A lake, rock features, an overlook point, and other permanent elements (water tower or power lines in the distance) also provide reassurance of our location when seeing these on the ground.
5. Periodically referencing the map on the trail when seeing unique trail and terrestrial features from our pre-hike map study helps maintain our sense of route progress and whereabouts. Knowing our location becomes important for expecting what lies ahead if and when we have to figure out the route back to safety, or if we ever have to call for rescue. Providing a near-exact position to dispatchers speeds up the time until help arrives.

The following example illustrates the above points. We intend to hike in western North Carolina and transition between three trails. From studying the map ahead of time, we can identify several features on the trails beforehand. Regularly referencing the

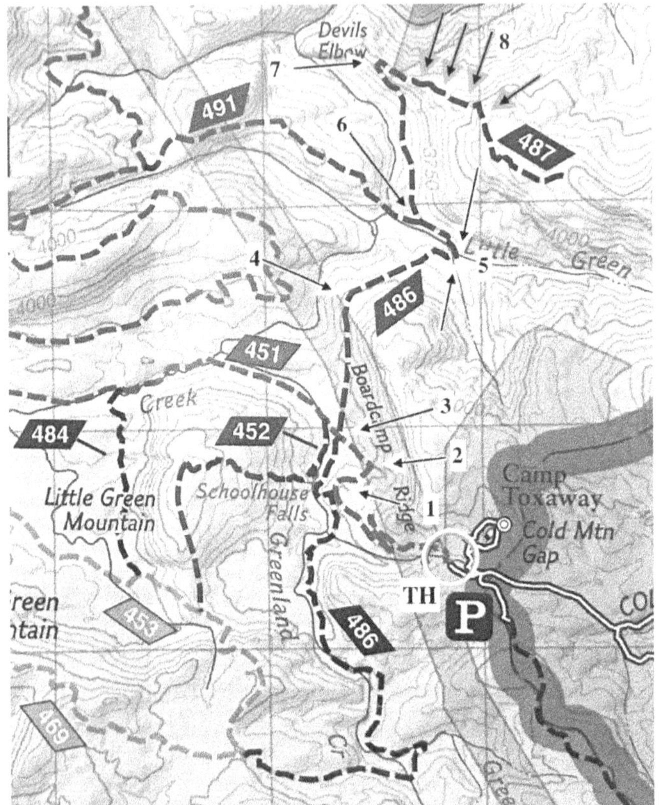

COPYRIGHT NATIONAL GEOGRAPHIC PARTNERS, LLC
TRAILS ILLUSTRATED MAP, PISGAH RANGER DISTRICT, PISGAH NATIONAL FOREST / #780

map along our hiking route allows us to anticipate and identify these features. They assure us we remain on the correct path and signal where changes in the path need to happen (see the above map). We intend to take trail 451, to trail 486 headed north, to trail 487, to a summit.

Starting from the parking lot (circle, labeled "TH") we begin on trail 451. This trail will remain straight for a short while, then takes a half-moon right turn (arrow "1"), followed by a 90° left turn (arrow "2"). After these turns, we can see that trail 486 crosses perpendicularly (light gray arrow, "3"). At that point, we need to make a right onto trail 486 and head north. Expecting this trail to cross after those turns in trail 451 helps make this transition much easier. Trail 486 then follows a straight path, but then it contours right (light arrow, "4") around the base of a small mountain and heads straight again. Up ahead we can expect a hairpin turn ("5") in the trail (two light arrows pointing at one another) at the same point where Little Green Creek crosses the trail. Referencing the map in real time here shows us our exact location and what lies ahead. After this turn we can see a fork in the trail (arrow "6"), where trail 487 begins and heads toward the summit. At that point we should know to bear right onto that trail. Another hairpin turn to the right (arrow pointing to Devil's Elbow, "7") appears on trail 487, after which we should expect a steep hike (four arrows, "8") along a ridge up to the summit.

Returning from the summit to the parking lot, we need to reverse course and expect the same features on the trail to identify our position and what to expect next. Reviewing these features before the hike heightens our sense of familiarity in real time.

Dr. Rob's Trail Habit

While traversing the trails I regularly pull out my map and hold it horizontally to view my location on the map in relation to what I'm seeing on the ground. I habitually rotate the map with the turns of the trail, so the next segment becomes laid out straight in front of me on the paper. Upcoming left and right turns on the trail appear as left and right turns on the map in my visual field. As I pass these turns and specific features in real time I pull the map out again. Having referenced it frequently along the way, it takes little time to figure out what position I previously held the map and where I am. I acknowledge what I just passed and know what lies ahead until the next time I need to look at it.

This fosters an awareness of what to expect, instead of accidentally making wrong turns, getting lost, and figuring it out in the moment. This mimics studying for an exam. If we prepare well, we will perform well. When we walk in dry without preparation, expect that failure may very well be the outcome.

Becoming familiar with features that lie beyond our intended route tell us we have gone too far or went off course. Encountering an unexpected lake, for instance, will bring a sense that we may be on the wrong route. If this happens, then stop and go back to the map. If we had referenced the map along the way and used trail features to acknowledge our whereabouts along the expected path, then we should be able to figure out where we had wandered off course. We can also gain a sense of which direction we need to follow to get back to the intended trail.

Finding Our Location on a Map

Finding our location on a map takes much less effort than most would think but requires the hiker to perform the above skills. Essential steps include taking a bearing and matching visible terrain features to our oriented map. When having to call upon this skill, we're either unsure if we are lost or we have become convinced of it. This will be stressful and disconcerting, prone to producing panic. Staying calm, focusing, and remembering our skills gives us the best chance for finding our way back to where we need to be. This book focuses on preparation. When having to perform these skills in the survival scenario, we prepare for this moment by having routinely practiced these skills to shift the momentum of the situation in our favor.

This skill needs to be used in two potential scenarios:

Scenario 1. We are 100 percent convinced we are on the trail that we intended to be on. After a bio break off-trail or having stopped at a lookout point, we come back to the trail and become confused. Looking one way and then the other, we don't know which way to go to resume the hike. Having learned and practiced the above skills, we can do the following with ease.

Look at the trail on the map. Note any map features that correspond to those we passed along the way to the current location. Look around and see terrain features in the surroundings. Anything look familiar? If this does not help, then locate the starting point at the trailhead and the furthest point we intended to go on the map. Which general direction does that path follow? Let's say it's a simple out-and-back trail flowing east-west. Our compass should then direct us toward the endpoint of the trail, or the trailhead, whichever we had been heading toward.

Still unsure?

1. Use the compass to orient the map to the terrain on the ground.
2. Identify the trail on the map. Use this as your approximate location.
3. How long has the hike lasted so far? Calculate the distance traveled on the trail based on average hiking speed and time spent hiking. This alone may pinpoint our location.
4. Look out for mountain peaks or other permanent structures in the surroundings. Seek higher ground if not able to see anything. Identify a target, such as a town in the distance, a lake, a river with a unique feature, or a hilltop or mountain peak.
5. Take a bearing to that most identifiable feature. Remember the bearing number.
6. Identify that same far-off terrain feature on the map.
7. Using the side straight edge of your compass, place the forward corner of the straight edge on the map-matched feature.

8. While keeping the map in place, pivot the compass from that one point until the bearing on the compass reads the same number as the above bearing reading to the terrain feature.

9. With a pencil or pen in hand, draw a line along that straight edge until it intersects with the trail you're standing on. If you don't have anything to write with, crease the map along the straight edge.

10. The point where the bearing line intersects with the trail identifies your location.

Using a simple example to illustrate this point, let's say we find ourselves on Signal Mountain in Grand Teton National Park, but while on the trail we're not quite sure where we are and where to head back to our origin. Looking out from a high point we can see the Tetons in the distance. Grand Teton, the tallest of them, sticks out as our best target. The bearing from this point reads 225°. As this point sits between 180° and 270°, Grand Teton sits southwest from our location.

After orienting the map to the terrain, using the local declination, we identify the target (black arrow pointing down to the circle) and our approximate location (gray arrow pointing upward to the black circle). See picture 1.

COPYRIGHT NATIONAL GEOGRAPHIC PARTNERS, LLC
TRAILS ILLUSTRATED MAP, GRAND TETON NATIONAL PARK / #202

See the following pictures. As in steps 7 and 8 above, we place the far corner of the compass's straight edge on the target (black arrow, bottom left of picture 2 on the next page) and pivot the compass (curved arrow, picture 2) until the bearing reads 225° (light arrows in picture 3).

Drawing a straight line with a pencil from the target, along the 225° bearing from the target (see picture 4), we extend that line until it reaches our approximate location.

Where that line hits the trail (picture 5, arrow pointing up on the right) pinpoints our location.

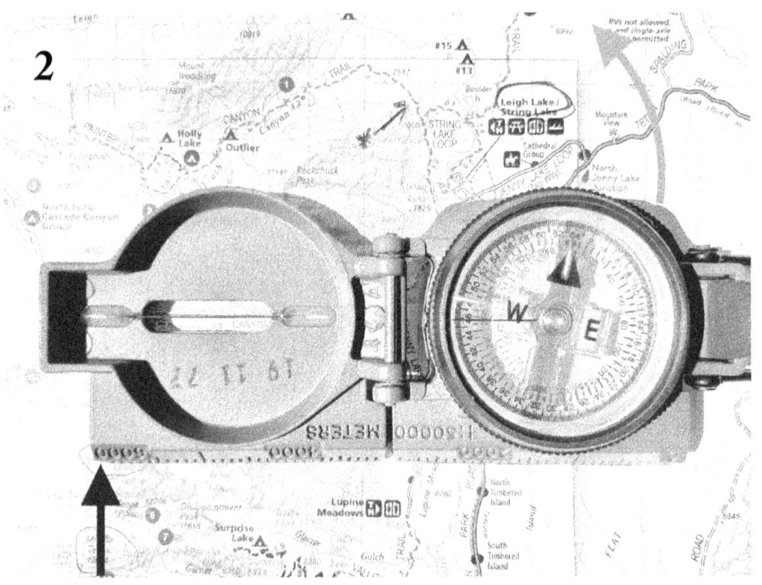
2
Leigh Lake / String Lake
STRING LAKE LOOP
Cathedral Group
North Jenny Lake Junction
Holly Lake
Outlier
Lupine Meadows
Surprise Lake
W
E
1:50000 METERS

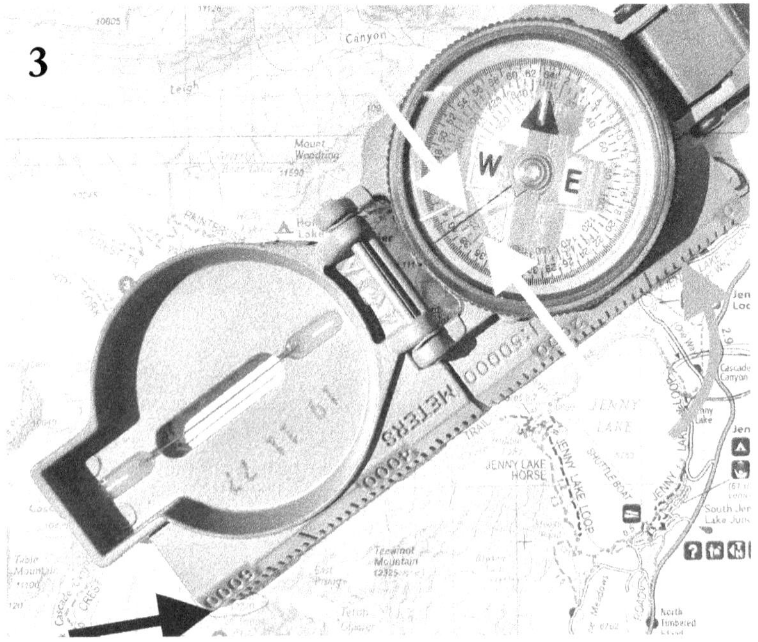
3
Canyon
Mount Woodring
W
E
1:50000 METERS
JENNY LAKE
JENNY LAKE HORSE
JENNY LAKE LOOP
SHUTTLE BOAT
Teewinot Mountain
Cascade Canyon
South Jenny Lake Junc
North Timbered

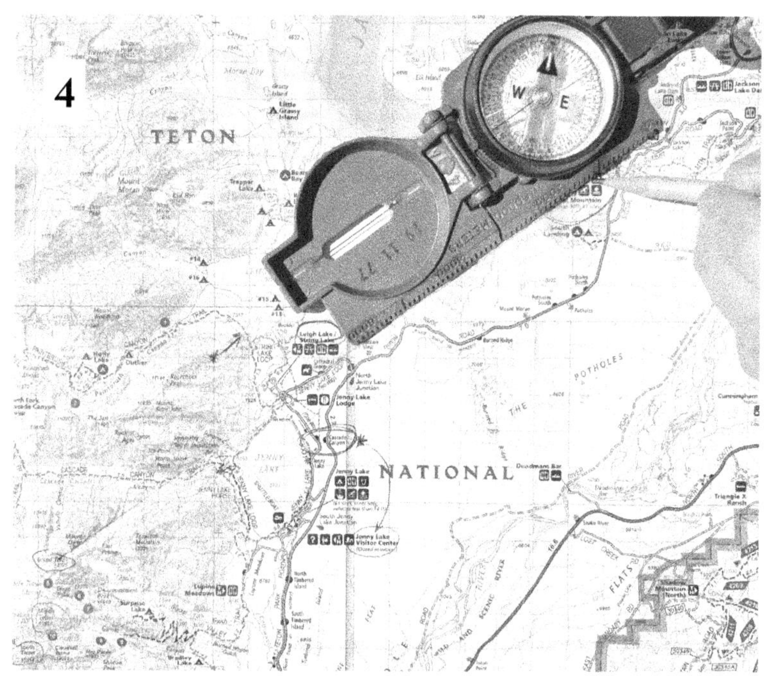

TRAILS ILLUSTRATED MAP, GRAND TETON NATIONAL PARK / #202

TRAILS ILLUSTRATED MAP, GRAND TETON NATIONAL PARK / #202

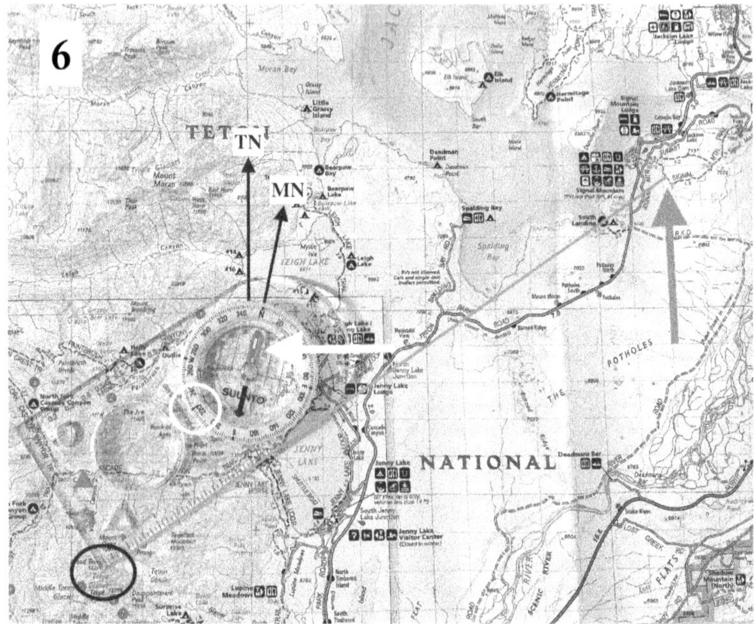

COPYRIGHT NATIONAL GEOGRAPHIC PARTNERS, LLC
TRAILS ILLUSTRATED MAP, GRAND TETON NATIONAL PARK / #202

Using an orienteering compass for this skill follows very similar steps, but the bezel of this type of compass functions slightly differently than the lensatic compass bezel. Refer to picture 6.

- Orient the map to the terrain.
- Rotate the bezel of the compass until the bearing of 225° lines up with the direction of travel line (white circle).
- Place the far corner of either straight edge of that compass on the target (black circle) and pivot the compass on that point until the compass needle lines up within the borders of the orienting arrow (white arrow).
- Draw a line along the straight edge of the compass and extend it to the area of our approximate location. Where it intersects with the trail (gray arrow pointing up, upper right in picture 6) indicates our position.

Notice that the vertical, longitudinal lines of the map still line up with True North ("TN"), while the compass needle points to Magnetic North ("MN") off to the right at an angle appropriate to the declination of this area (11° E).

Knowing our location (thick, gray arrow pointing up in picture 6) allows us to then determine which direction we need to follow to get back to the trailhead, to safety, or back on track to our objective. Determine where that destination lies in relation to the current position. While on the trail there are only two ways we can go. Choose the direction that leads there.

The number of individuals at this vista point and the nearby parking lot actually makes becoming lost on this part Signal Mountain difficult. The visibility from here to terrestrial landmarks otherwise makes demonstration of this skill much easier to understand.

Scenario 2. We believe we may be on the wrong trail or convinced we have wandered off trail and have become lost. Finding our position in this situation follows very similar steps as compared to the above but requires taking a bearing from two separate visible land features to triangulate our location. See the following steps and illustrations.

1. Adjust the bezel of the compass to reflect the magnetic declination of the area.
2. Orient the map to the terrain on the ground.
3. Locate the general region of the hiking location on the map. Use this as your approximate location.
4. Look for terrestrial landmarks in the distance. Get to higher ground if unable to do so from this position. Identify a town, a lake, a river, a hilltop, or a mountain peak. Note which direction these sit in relation to this vantage point (North? South? East? West?).

5. Choose two of these landmarks as targets, approximately 45 to 120° apart, and take a bearing to **both** terrain features.
6. Find and identify the distant terrain features on the map. When using an orienteering compass adjust the bezel to reflect the bearing of one of the specific terrain features.
7. Place the corner of the compass's edge on the map-matched feature.
8. While keeping the map in place, pivot the compass from that one point
    a. until the bearing on the compass reads the same as the above bearing reading to the terrain feature (lensatic compasses).
    b. until the needle lines up within the orienting arrow outline (orienteering compasses).
9. Draw or crease a line on the map along the compass's straight edge at the first bearing point toward your target area. Don't have something to write with? Use something from the environment to otherwise indicate a straight line.
10. Repeat steps 6 through 9 for the second terrain feature. Draw or crease a line along this second bearing.
11. Where the two lines bisect pinpoints our location.

The following example finds us in western North Carolina, hiking on Big Green Mountain. Here the rolling peaks appear similar to one another, making these more difficult to discern than the unmistakable granite skyscrapers in the west. This requires a sharp eye for far-off visible features. In this scenario we have become lost off-trail.

After orienting the map to the terrain, we locate the general area where we have been hiking (white circle, picture 7). From here we can see a taller peak (Cold Mountain, black circle) and the near corner of a lake (Lake Toxaway, black arrow) in the distance (both seen in picture 7).

Taking a bearing to each of the targets, we determine a reading of 110° to the north end of the lake and 78° to the peak of Cold Mountain.

Rotate the bezel to read 110° at the direction of travel line (white circle in picture 8). Using steps 7 through 9 above, we place the far corner of the compass's straight edge on the first target (near end of Lake Toxaway). While keeping the map in place, pivot the compass on the map from that point of the lake until the needle settles inside the borders of the orienting arrow (black arrow in picture 8).

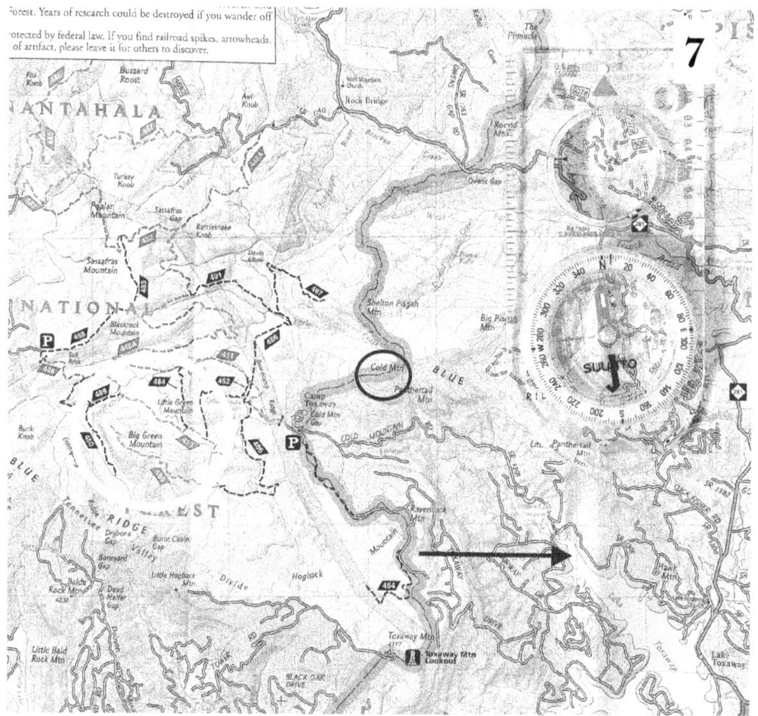

COPYRIGHT NATIONAL GEOGRAPHIC PARTNERS, LLC

TRAILS ILLUSTRATED MAP, PISGAH RANGER DISTRICT, PISGAH NATIONAL FOREST / #780

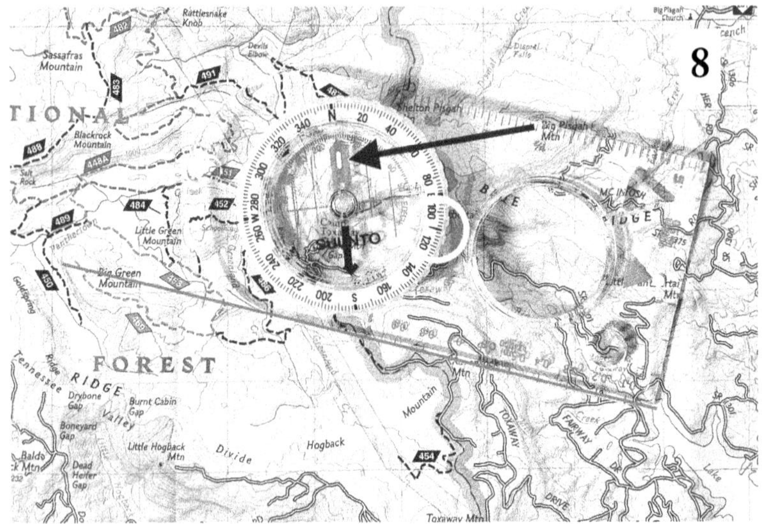

COPYRIGHT NATIONAL GEOGRAPHIC PARTNERS, LLC
TRAILS ILLUSTRATED MAP, PISGAH RANGER DISTRICT, PISGAH NATIONAL FOREST / #780

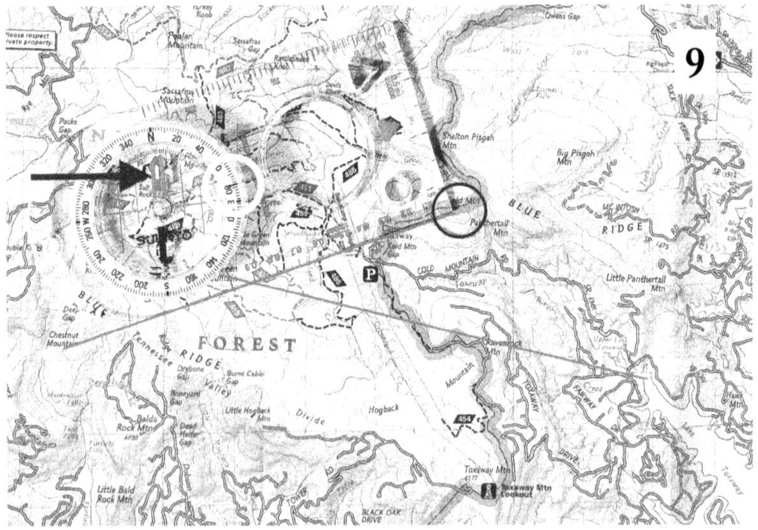

COPYRIGHT NATIONAL GEOGRAPHIC PARTNERS, LLC
TRAILS ILLUSTRATED MAP, PISGAH RANGER DISTRICT, PISGAH NATIONAL FOREST / #780

Don't have a pencil to draw a line from there? No problem. We can use a leaf of pine straw or other thin object from the surrounding environment to use as a straight line.

Repeat the same methodology for target 2 (Cold Mountain, black circle in picture 9), with the bearing of 78° at the direction of travel line (white circle) and pivoted until the needle falls within the outline of the orienting arrow (black arrow).

Where the two lines cross pinpoints our location (vertical arrow in picture 10)! This location sits between two trails (both with gray dotted lines on the map), which we can then follow back to safety. From this current spot we can use our compass to either hike in a northern direction and downhill to trail 453, or to hike south and uphill to trail 469. Following either of these trails

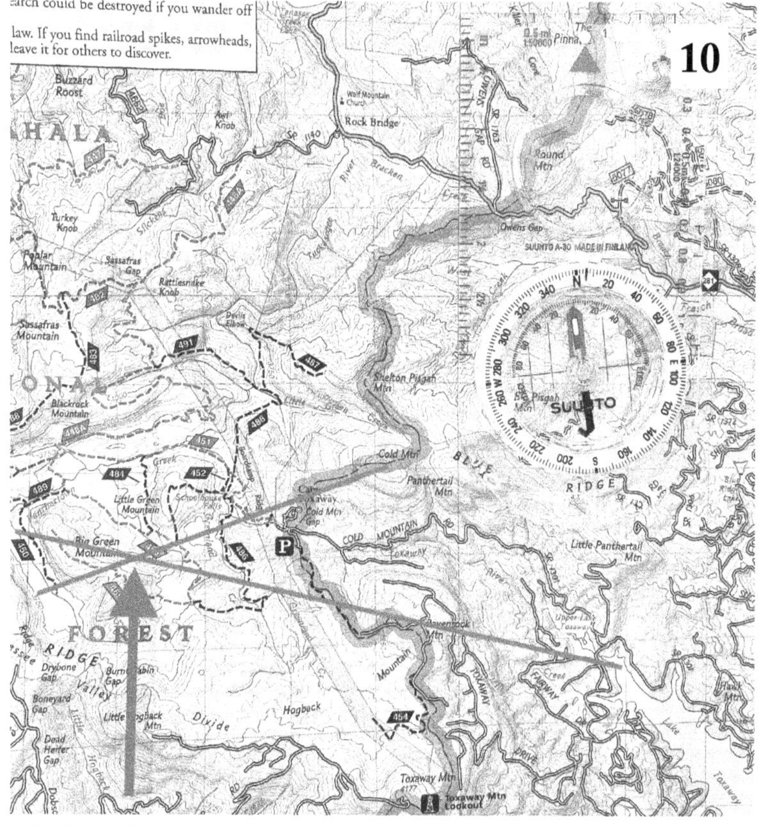

COPYRIGHT NATIONAL GEOGRAPHIC PARTNERS, LLC

TRAILS ILLUSTRATED MAP, PISGAH RANGER DISTRICT, PISGAH NATIONAL FOREST / #780

in an eastern direction connects us to trail 486, which leads to the parking lot "P," as indicated on the map.

Finding Our Way Back

Finding our way back represents the ultimate goal of having acquired and mastered the above skills. Learning them empowers the hiker by placing their safe return to home in their own hands and controlling the outcome. This frees us from the reliance on others and the chance to embrace reliance on oneself. Hiking embodies much more than just walking from one point to another. Most places we adventure pose an intrinsic threat to our safety and prove mercilessly unforgiving when ensnared in its pitfalls. Executing these skills places us at an advantage over the perils, but this requires forethought, situational awareness, desire of mastery, and appreciation for the accomplishment of having learned something truly special.

Once we locate ourselves on the map we can utilize our skills to reach the trailhead or a nearby point of safety. We need to seek out a reasonably close location with likelihood that we will be able to find others to help us. The closest safety point may be a nearby town, a major roadway, or a trail that we had wandered away from.

1. Having found our location on the map, look on the map and target the best safety point in the area.
2. Limitations between our location and that safety point may exist, such as steep drop-offs, rivers, or other features that look difficult to traverse. Pick the point of safety that appears most probable to reach. Know that a longer but less difficult path to safety may prove the better bet here.
3. Decide on the best target and determine the direction to it. If visible, take a bearing using the compass. When not visible, determine the bearing from the map itself to that location, using the same methodology we used to find our location.

4. Follow that bearing. Do not deviate from this direction or objective, as shifting directions and changing objectives lead to wandering aimlessly and spending much more time in the wilderness than desired.

5. Using the compass and map together, periodically confirm the intended direction and utilize map/terrestrial features along that route to judge progress.

In this example we have become lost in Denali National Park. See picture 11.

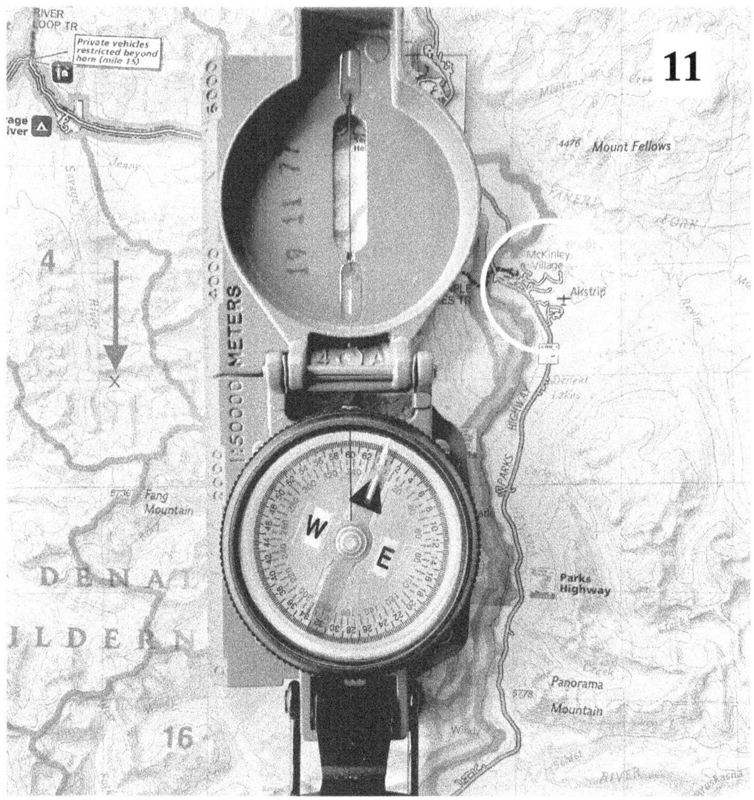

TRAILS ILLUSTRATED MAP, DENALI NATIONAL PARK AND PRESERVE / #222

We have oriented the map to the terrain, using the declination of 21° in this area, and have found our location (down arrow pointing to "X") using triangulation between two visible landmarks. We look at the map to find the nearest safety points:

1. The highway (to the right of the compass), which we will encounter if we head in any easterly direction
2. The access road to the north of our location
3. McKinley Village

Choosing the village (circled on the map) provides a higher probability of finding people to assist us. Heading to the access road may not help us find anyone who can help us. We can either head to the highway and walk north until reaching the village, or head straight to it.

Deciding to head straight to McKinley Village, we then reverse the preceding skill to find the bearing that gets us to that village.

Using a lensatic compass (see picture 12):

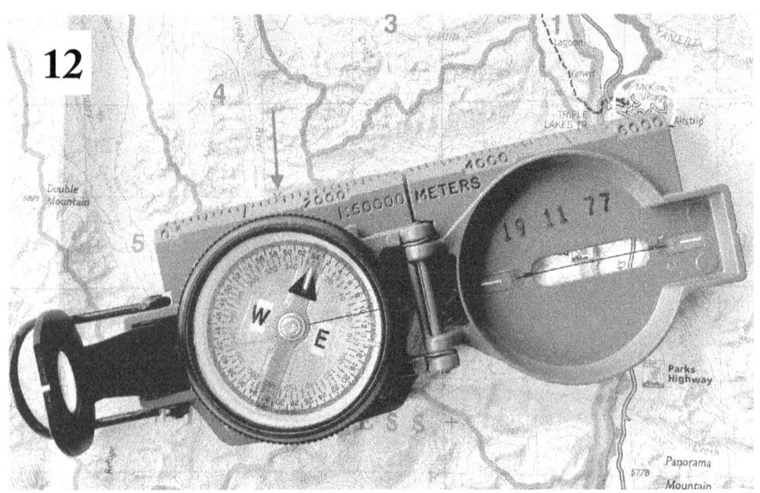

1. Place the corner of the compass's straight edge on the location of McKinley Village (circle) and line it up with the current location (down arrow).
2. Read the bearing on the compass at the direction of travel line (60°).

Using an orienteering compass (see pictures 13 and 14):

1. Place the corner of the compass's straight edge on the location of McKinley Village (circled) and line it up with the current location (down arrow).
2. Rotate the bezel (curved white arrow, picture 13) until the orienting arrow lines up with the magnetic needle.
3. Read the bearing of 60° at the direction of travel line (white circle in picture 14).

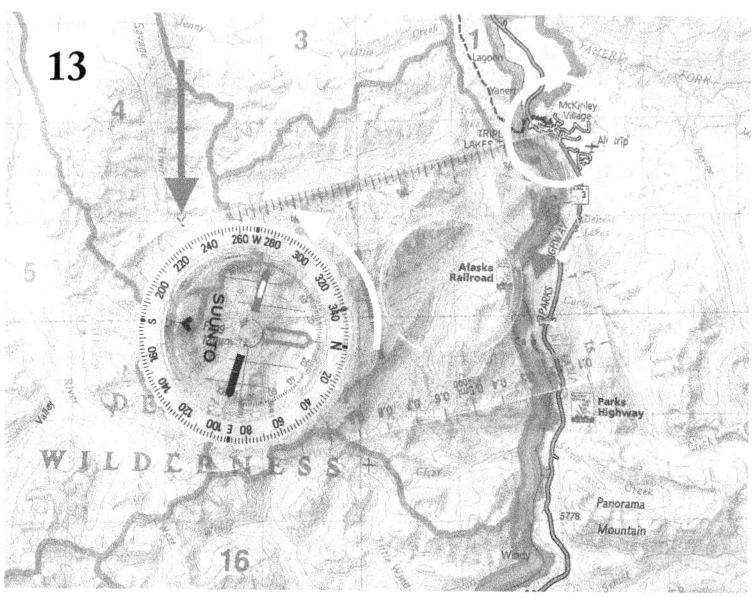

COPYRIGHT NATIONAL GEOGRAPHIC PARTNERS, LLC
TRAILS ILLUSTRATED MAP, DENALI NATIONAL PARK AND PRESERVE / #222

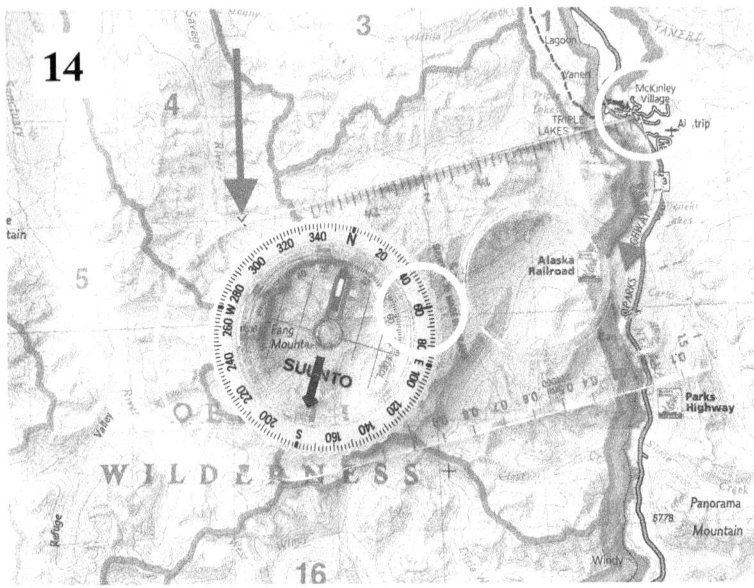

We cannot expect to walk in a straight line across this challenging terrain, making the expectation of following the exact bearing of 60° unrealistic. Anticipate having to traverse the wilderness at bearings off by 5 to 10° to the north and to the south, considering the number of potential obstacles in our way. Staying mindful of this and adjusting course whenever the landscape allows maintains us on track to arrive at the target destination.

Land navigation represents one the most important field skills we can learn. Most who approach the subject with interest can become proficient in these basics. The competency erodes over time without practice, however. The concepts may stay but the techniques do not and therefore must be routinely practiced. We should perform compass skills on every hike to maintain proficiency, which can also be utilized in our back yard for that matter. While sitting down for a midhike snack pull out the map and compass to orient the map to the terrain, match visible ter-

Dr. Rob's Suggestion

Before venturing out on any day hike or backpacking trip, study the map ahead of time and identify the nearest safety point to the anticipated location. This may be a road, railway, local airport, or nearby town with the highest potential for encountering others who can help us and the least number of visible obstacles on the map to arrive there. Know the general direction that safety point sits in, relative to the hiking location. Navigating to this safety point will be our fallback plan when we have become lost and all else fails to get us back to the trail or trailhead.

restrial features to the map, or take a bearing. The more we use a map and compass, the more we understand them. Our mastery of these skills, and the subsequent navigational independence, brings a liberating sense of security for wherever we roam.

Bottom Line

Becoming lost while hiking happens often, and likely much more frequently than has been reported. Some find their way, while others cannot. Knowing the most common reasons this happens can prepare us to defy the odds. Some have an innate talent for finding direction, while others work hard to get by and yet others struggle, but this has everything to do with how we have been wired and nothing to do with intellect or motivation. Those who have less ability need to acknowledge this and take steps to mitigate their risk, such as taking a friend who navigates well. We can all learn to become better at finding our way, though. Practicing determining direction forms new connections in the brain, making finding our way easier to accomplish.

- Memorize and understand how the cardinal directions relate to one another, for those who lack the familiarity.
- Using natural cues and landmarks to regularly practice guidance, even in our off-trail lives, forms new brain connections to improve our abilities in the backcountry.
- Realize that different regions and trails have various markings meant to keep us on the correct route, as the trail may not appear distinct from the rest of the woods. Understanding the less intuitive markers reduces the chances of getting lost during confusion in real time.
- Use a navigating tool, whether it be a paper map or an electronic means that does not rely on cell service to work, and with a backup battery power supply. Know how to use both and study the intended trail ahead of time, becoming familiar with direction and turns, terrestrial cues, and other landmarks to look for along the way.
- Understand that the sun provides a great source for directional guidance, a skill that can be practiced in our everyday lives to further develop an instinctive talent for determining the cardinal directions.
- The night sky offers some guidance when navigating at night becomes necessary. Look up in the sky and practice finding Polaris to determine north and Orion's Sword to determine south. Find Venus and become familiar with when it is visible in the eastern and western skies. Find Sirius to confirm a southern direction. Observe the positions of the moon, especially in the spring and fall, and when full, to provide us with directional guidance.

References

Hewitt, T. "Hikers Rescued After Getting Lost in Little Cottonwood Canyon." Utah Public Radio, October 25, 2021.

Iaria, G., N. Bogod, et al. "Developmental Topographical Disorientation: Case One." *Neuropsychologia.* 47, no. 1(January 2009): 30–40.

Iaria, G., and F. Burles. "Developmental Topographical Disorientation." *Trends in Cognitive Sciences* 20, no. 10 (October 2016): 720–722. doi: 10.1016/j.tics.2016.07.004. Epub 2016 Jul 21. PMID: 27450709.

Vargas, R. A. "Hiker Rescued After Wandering Lost in Texas Park for More than a Week." *Guardian*, November 11, 2023.

Weisberg, S. M., and N. S. Newcombe. "Cognitive Maps: Some People Make Them, Some People Struggle." *Current Directions in Psychological Science* 27, no. 4 (2018): 220–226. doi:10.1177/0963721417744521

Index

About the Author

Dr. Rob Scanlon is Board Certified in Pulmonary Medicine and Critical Care (ICU medicine) and actively in practice for over twenty years. He began his journey as a hiker/backpacker in 2002 to reduce the stress of work life. Throughout his clinical career he has followed his passion for patient education in his own field to improve outcomes and longevity for his patients with underlying lung disease.

He joined the Wilderness Medical Society (WMS) in 2018 through his love for the outdoors and medicine and to pursue his growing desire to impact the staggering rate of hiker death and

rescue. Along with attending conferences, he has been accepted as a fellowship candidate of the WMS.

Seeing where education can impact the hiking community, he draws the parallel between empowering patients to prevent complications of disease and the hiker's potential to prevent the complications of exploring the unforgiving great outdoors by an increased knowledge base, core skill set, and better preparation.

His passion for education as the means for preservation of life has fueled his effort to bring this knowledge in book form to the vast hiking community. He has pursued this project to fill the void between the books that encourage people to hike and those that depict how to survive in the wilderness. His purpose is to minimize hiker death and rescue by addressing the common perils of adventure. This book embodies his mantra: "Preparation Is the Ultimate Survival Skill."

www.ingramcontent.com/pod-product-compliance
Lightning Source LLC
Jackson TN
JSHW071500061025
92151JS00020B/267
9781493090129